EYEWITNESS TO A GENOCIDE

EYEWITNESS
TO A
GENOCIDE

The United Nations
and Rwanda

MICHAEL BARNETT

CORNELL UNIVERSITY PRESS Ithaca and London

First published 2002 by Cornell University Press
First printing, Cornell Paperback, 2003

Printed in the United States of America

Library of Congress Cataloging-in-Publication Data
Barnett, Michael N., 1960–
    Eyewitness to a genocide : the United Nations and Rwanda / Michael Barnett.
        p. cm.
    Includes bibliographical references and index.
    ISBN-13: 978-0-8014-3883-7 (cloth : alk. paper)
    ISBN-10: 0-8014-3883-7 (cloth : alk. paper)
    ISBN-13: 978-0-8014-8867-2 (pbk. : alk. paper)
    ISBN-10: 0-8014-8867-2 (pbk. : alk. paper)
    1. Genocide—Rwanda.   2. United Nations—Rwanda.   3.
Rwanda—History—Civil War, 1994—Atrocities.   4. Rwanda—Ethnic
relations.   I. Title.
    DT450.435 .B38 2002
    967.57104—dc21
                        2001005561

Cornell University Press strives to use environmentally responsible suppliers and materials to the fullest extent possible in the publishing of its books. Such materials include vegetable-based, low-VOC inks and acid-free papers that are recycled, totally chlorine-free, or partly composed of nonwood fibers. For further information, visit our website at www.cornellpress.cornell.edu.

Cloth printing   10   9   8   7   6   5   4   3   2
Paperback printing   10   9   8   7   6

For Maya and Hannah

Contents

PREFACE   ix

INTRODUCTION: DEPRAVED INDIFFERENCE?   I

I **IT WAS A VERY GOOD YEAR**   22

2 **RWANDA THROUGH ROSE-COLORED GLASSES**   49

3 **"IF THIS IS AN EASY OPERATION . . ."**   74

4 **THE FOG OF GENOCIDE**   97

5 **DIPLOMATIC GAMES**   I30

6 **THE HUNT FOR MORAL RESPONSIBILITY** I53

BRIEF CHRONOLOGY OF RWANDAN CONFLICT   I83

SELECTED CHRONOLOGY OF UNITED NATIONS' SECURITY AGENDA   I89

ACKNOWLEDGMENTS   I93

NOTES   I97

INDEX   209

Preface

Rwanda lives inside of me. Sometimes I find this lingering obsession bewildering, almost as unexplainable as the genocide itself. I have never set foot on Rwandan soil. My first sustained images of Rwanda were pictures of the genocide, the same pictures that assaulted millions of people around the world and came to define much of what they know about the country. At the time of the genocide, however, I knew more than the average viewer because I was a political officer at the U.S. Mission to the United Nations.

A fellowship from the Council on Foreign Relations had funded a year's leave from academia and placement in government service. I arrived in New York late in the summer of 1993 and was assigned to follow various aspects of the UN operation in Somalia. By early January 1994 my duties had diminished as the United States was preparing to withdraw from Somalia. At that time my superiors asked me to work on various African operations, including the one in Rwanda. I knew very little about the country but quickly came to understand that the peace agreement that was supposed to effect the transition from civil war to multiethnic democracy—the Arusha Accords—was at risk. In early April the civil war returned with a vengeance, an outcome many had fearfully predicted, and left thousands upon thousands of Rwandans dead.

I vividly recall sitting at my desk, reading the morning cables. They detailed the gruesome nature of the violence, a murder campaign that seemed to have no limit, and reported bodies lining the streets and mutilated corpses piled high in churches and schools. But I honestly cannot say that my horror then fed into demands that the UN do something. In fact, I opposed intervention. The UN recently had demonstrated in Somalia and Bosnia that it was not fit to get involved in civil wars. The peacekeepers on the ground in Rwanda were in mortal danger—ten already had died under brutal circumstances. There were no troops ready to march into this paroxysm. The combination of the maelstrom on the ground and the UN's weaknesses made it quite likely that the UN would meet only "failure" in Rwanda. Not only would the UN receive no thanks for trying, but also it would suffer fresh and increasingly harmful recriminations from Washington and elsewhere.

My views were hardly idiosyncratic. Others were arguing that peacekeeping was appropriate only when there was a peace to keep. They too held that the reality of the situation dictated that the UN withdraw its peacekeepers. Some in the Security Council argued for intervention, but I distinctly remember sitting there and wondering how long before they too would succumb to the inevitable. Two weeks into what most were defining as a "civil war," the council unanimously voted to withdraw all but a few hundred peacekeepers from Rwanda.

After that vote it rapidly became clear that Rwanda was no run-of-the-mill ethnic conflict. Any moral imperative I felt was now smothered by a creeping cynicism born from the realization that the UN preferred talk to action. The council now was attempting to assemble, piece by piece, an intervention force. At the time I looked upon this effort as all theater and public relations. There was an anxiety at the UN, but it seemed to originate less from genuine urgency and more from a desire to play the role expected of it. The UN had slim hopes of fielding a rescue party, but going through the motions would certainly take the edge off the criticism. At this point the U.S. government was alone in publicly denying that the killing in Rwanda constituted a genocide and was virtually isolated in opposing intervention. Watching politics played at its cynical finest in the midst of a genocide left me feeling relieved that I could leave the "real world" and return to academia.

For the next year I occasionally wrote and lectured on UN peacekeeping and Rwanda. I emphasized that while the UN's decision might seem heartless to those on the outside, to many on the inside it was proper and correct—and the *only* available choice given the reality on the ground, what member states were willing to do, the rules of peacekeeping, and the all-too-clear limits of the UN. Rwanda was beyond those limits.

I can pinpoint the exact moment when I began to reconsider the moral metric that I had been using to justify the UN's actions. I was watching a news program commemorating the first anniversary of the beginning of the genocide. Dreadful, searing images radiated from the television screen as the commentator's voice provided the jarring counterpoint—that the UN had done nothing. I instinctively launched into my frustrated "you don't get it" recitation. But I caught myself in mid thought, interrupted by a private, emotional dissent. Why had there been so little debate on the feasibility and desirability of an intervention? I certainly understood the "reality" of the situation. I remained doubtful that intervention would have halted the genocide, as some were beginning to argue at the time. Yet I was unnerved by the recognition that almost all of the UN's anxious concern was self-absorbed. There was remarkably little space for the Rwandans. How could it have been even faintly principled to ignore such crimes against humanity?

I began to examine the UN's actions from any number of angles, but I found a disturbing familiarity in writings that consider how a bureaucratic culture shapes individuals—how they come to see and act on the world. My year in New York had given me a dose of reality, as my colleagues liked to remind me teasingly, but after the fact I became increasingly aware of how the bureaucratic culture had a distinctive way of constructing that reality. The culture within the UN generated an understanding of the organization's unique contribution to world politics. It produced rules that signaled when peacekeeping was "the right tool for the job." It contained orienting concepts such as neutrality, impartiality, and consent, which governed how peacekeepers were supposed to operate in the field. It shaped how the UN came to know countries like Rwanda that were attempting to move from civil war to civil society. In brief, those working at the UN approached Rwanda not as individuals but rather as members of bureaucracies. They occupied roles that organizationally situated and defined their knowledge, and informed what they cared about, what behavior they considered appropriate and inappropriate, how they distinguished acceptable from unacceptable consequences, and how they determined right from wrong. Something about the culture at the UN could make nonintervention not merely pragmatic but also legitimate and proper—even in the face of crimes against humanity.

Employing different moral benchmarks to generate alternative understandings of the UN's involvement in Rwanda has profound implications for assessing the UN's responsibility for the genocide. For those who construct a UN that had uninterrupted sight lines into the present and the future, and had the singular duty to aid when civilians began to die at breathtaking speed, the UN bears much responsibility. For those who construct a UN that was relatively ignorant of events on the ground until it was too late, and was so constrained that effective action became nearly unthink-

able, what occurred was not irresponsibility but instead a series of honest
mistakes and tough choices with horrendous consequences. For a time I
placed myself in the latter camp and was troubled (and occasionally incensed) by those in the former. I began to re-examine my position, however, after I learned that various high-ranking officials probably were not as
ignorant as they let on. I began to consider the extent to which the constraints were self-imposed, and came to consider how those who assumed
roles that gave them authority over Rwanda allowed alternative commitments to trump their obligations to the Rwandans. Under these circumstances the UN might very well bear some moral responsibility.

This ethical history of the UN's intervention in Rwanda reconstructs the
moral universe at the UN that helped to legitimate its decision to stand
aside while crimes were committed against humanity, *and* aims to isolate
those at the UN who might bear moral responsibility. It requires recognizing the consanguinity between the normative and the empirical. I realize
that such a position will offend those who hold that ethics are absolute.
Moral philosophers have been largely concerned with abstract duties and
ideal norms that are thought to have universal application. Yet it is the existence of many moralities that, I want to argue, helps to define the UN's actions and demands our attention. I realize, as well, that my insistence on
the necessary and intimate relationship between the normative and the empirical will rankle those who insist that normative questions are part of the
humanistic enterprise and separate from empirically grounded explanations
that are central to our explanations for events. Yet our attention is drawn to
the subject of genocide because it rips a hole in what we believe is possible.
Utilitarian theories of genocide or of its bystanders rarely satisfy. My personal introduction to Rwanda and my subsequent scholarly undertakings
have made me both highly appreciative of the constraints on the UN's actions and acutely aware of the need to go beyond surface appearances to
shed light on the event and its meanings. The policymaking and scholarly
sides have fed into an enduring concern: to understand the ethical field that
made it possible for decent and responsible individuals to stand aside from
such suffering.

I am well aware that Rwanda touches an emotional core. I will always see
Rwanda from an ever-changing subjective standpoint. My first images of
the Rwandan genocide are now situated alongside those of a UN so consumed by fears of its own mortality that it had little evident compassion for
those on the ground. When I now think of "Rwanda," I imagine not the
country but the UN. I think of diplomats and UN officials hurriedly
milling in and out of Security Council meetings. They are reciting their
talking points and proclaiming, in the UN's locution, that they "remain ac-

tively seized of the matter." And they deliver only rhetoric in the hope that rhetoric represents its own consolation. The Rwanda that now dwells inside me is not a geographical territory. Rather, it is a metaphysical space—a space that changes with time and experience but ultimately is defined by a profound sense of loss.

MICHAEL BARNETT

Madison, Wisconsin

EYEWITNESS TO A GENOCIDE

Introduction:
Depraved Indifference?

Very little about the Rwandan genocide is comprehensible. A Hutu elite came to believe that Hutu salvation necessitated Tutsi extermination. The Hutus enacted their conspiracy with startling efficiency. In one hundred days, between April 6 and July 19, 1994, they murdered roughly eight hundred thousand individuals. For the statistically inclined, that works out to 333⅓ deaths per hour, 5½ deaths per minute. The rate of murder was even greater during the first four weeks, when most of the deaths occurred. The Rwandan genocide, therefore, has the macabre distinction of exceeding the rate of killing attained during the Holocaust. And unlike the Nazis, who used modern industrial technology to accomplish the most primitive of ends, the perpetrators of the Rwandan genocide employed primarily low-tech and physically demanding instruments of death that required an intimacy with their victims. The genocide was executed with a brutality and sadism that defy imagination. Eyewitnesses were in denial. They believed that the high-pitched screams they were hearing were wind gusts, that the packs of dogs at the roadside were feeding on animal remains and not dismembered corpses, that the smells enveloping them emanated from spoiled food and not decomposing bodies. One is reminded of Primo Levi's observation about the Holocaust: "Things whose existence is not morally comprehensible cannot exist."[1]

Almost as inexplicable is the reaction of the international community. What sets the Rwandan genocide apart from all other genocides is that the international community could have intervened at relatively low cost before the effects were fully realized. A genocide convention enjoined states to do something. There were twenty-five hundred United Nations peacekeepers on the ground, and indeed, soon after the killing began, the UN's force commander, Canadian General Roméo Dallaire, pleaded for a well-equipped battalion to stop the slaughter. Yet the UN immediately ordered its forces not to protect civilians. And on April 21, it ordered that all but 270 troops be withdrawn.

The fact of willful indifference continues to amaze. The Rwandan genocide is not only about the evil that is possible. It is also about the complacency exhibited by those who have the responsibility to confront that evil.

The UN's languid response to the Rwandan genocide has produced countless studies, reports, and commissions that attempted to piece together what happened and, ultimately, to determine whom to blame for the cowardly act of abandonment. Many of the early investigations effected a diplomatic version of racial profiling and used circumstantial evidence to create a simplistic story that indicted the usual suspect—the United States. The suspicions were not unjustified.

The United States used its considerable power in the Security Council to help muzzle the call for intervention and later obstructed those who wanted to intervene. While everyone else at the UN put on their best funereal faces, not the United States. It responded to the subsequent barrage of criticism by swerving from one justification to another. At the time of the genocide U.S. officials argued aggressively that there was no basis for intervention because there was no peace to keep in a country in the midst of a civil war. Later President Bill Clinton insisted that he was unaware of the genocide and would have acted had he known. It was quickly shown that the United States was not nearly as dull-witted as it pretended to be. At other times the United States objected to the insinuation that it should provide troops for every humanitarian emergency. And, it was frequently added, the United States was only behaving like other states: sure, it did not care enough to send troops, but no state did. American behavior was excusable because everyone behaved badly.

A subsequent wave of investigations revealed a more complex story, shifting the drama away from the United States and toward the Security Council and the Secretariat.[2] In the council, isolated voices had appealed for troops, but their words were drowned out by the clamor for withdrawal and they, too, eventually favored scaling back the UN's involvement. The council's reasons were many, including the simple fact that there were no troops available for intervention. Immediately after the council had voted to reduce the United Nations Assistance Mission for Rwanda (UNAMIR) to a shadow of its former self, the genocide became clearly discernible. But the council's duplicitous reaction was to refuse to call the events by their proper name—*genocide*—for fear of being compelled to act. Once genocide became publicly undeniable in early May, the UN quickly jerry-built a proposal for intervention. One glaring problem, however: the requisite troops could not be located. The council was noisy with passionate speeches on behalf of dying Rwandans but fell quickly silent when the Secretariat asked for volunteers. This collective silence from the UN from start to finish can be attributed to a "lack of political will."[3] Sometimes this platitude is code used to single out particular, powerful states. In this instance, however, practically the entire council can be credited for "failing" Rwanda.

Various studies widened the circle of blame to include the very UN officials who presented themselves as enthusiasts for intervention. Secretary-General Boutros Boutros-Ghali insisted that he had begged the Security Council to intervene in Rwanda. "More than 200,000 people have been killed, and the international community is still discussing what ought to be done. I have tried. I was in contact with the different Heads of State, and I begged them to send troops."[4] Try as he might, he was frustrated, left aghast by the West's unwillingness to stop the killings.[5] Officials from the Department of Peacekeeping Operations (DPKO) claimed that they had done everything they could based on the sketchy information they were receiving from the field, insinuating that UNAMIR's Force Commander Dallaire was not up to the job.[6] Few observers probed the Secretariat's self-presentation as the lonely conscience of the international community. Why did its assertions go unquestioned? An unspoken presumption holds that because UN staff are representatives of the international community, they will be tireless advocates for the weak and vigorous champions for humanitarian intervention.

Sometime thereafter, however, the Secretariat's own failings became known. Cables from UNAMIR to DPKO in the months before the genocide had warned of mass ethnic killings and pleaded for permission to undertake military operations. The Secretariat had failed to inform the Security Council of this sobering news and instead ordered the peacekeepers to remain "impartial." UN officials also had distinguished themselves at the outbreak of the crisis by virtue of their disappearing act. Boutros-Ghali was positively anemic. Even more incredible was the news that the Secretariat had failed to pass along Dallaire's detailed accounts of ethnic cleansing and repeated requests for reinforcements. Instead, Boutros-Ghali's office reported "chaos" on the ground, emphasized the enormous threat to peacekeepers, and apologized for its inability to present contingency plans. These reports depicted international civil servants who were timid, indecisive, and deceitful.

The inescapable conclusion from these accounts is that the UN responded to the genocide with willful ignorance and indifference. States allowed an almighty realpolitik to smother their faint humanitarianism—a depressingly familiar story that reinforces the time-worn view that cold-hearted strategic calculations always trump noble ideals. Member states did not have a monopoly on duplicity and moral shallowness, for UN staff also knew what was transpiring on the ground yet still favored detachment until it was too late. Confronted by the greatest of all moral imperatives, the UN had delivered a whimper of a response. Inquiries into this international indifference have seemingly exhumed an entire system that is rotten and, to paraphrase the philosopher G. W. F. Hegel, run by "men without chests."[7]

These autopsies, however, do not go far enough. They presuppose that exposing the failure to respond to the genocide disinters a UN body that was spiritless. Doing so omits a central feature of the UN's response that makes its behavior simultaneously more understandable and more disturbing: At the time and with knowledge about the crimes against humanity, many in the Security Council and in the Secretariat concluded that withdrawal was ethical and proper. Few believed that they were acting in a guileful, heartless, or callous manner. All were disturbed that they were failing to raise an army to halt the slaughter. And although most were ashen-faced by a departure that they understood looked cowardly to the international public, many still reasoned that their decision was not merely pragmatic but also, on its own terms and in its own way, the right thing to do. Many contemporary accounts insinuate that only an amoral UN could have responded to the killings in the way that it did. My personal reflections and subsequent inquiries lead me to conclude that the UN's actions were guided by situated responsibilities and grounded in ethical considerations.

THIS book is an ethical history of the UN's indifference to genocide. In it I identify the various commitments those at the UN felt during this period; I try to understand how they adjudicated between broad moral imperatives and the situational constraints to derive what they considered to be ethical and proper behavior; and, after all is said and done, I want to recover individual and moral responsibility. The story of Rwanda is quickly becoming received, predictably so, as a sorrowful parable about how humanity responds to crimes against humanity and genocide. To speak of Rwanda is to summon images of individuals and institutions who cared little or not at all, whose responsibilities were easily consumed by self-interests, and who medicated themselves with hollow expressions of concern. I aim to disturb this future of the Rwandan genocide. I want to replace the secure conclusion that unethical behavior begat indifference with the discomfiting possibility that for many in New York the moral compass pointed away from and not toward Rwanda.

To do so necessitates the reconstruction of the moral universe at the UN at this particular moment. Anyone who has ever worked in an organization recognizes that its inhabitants use a discourse and reason through rules that are molded by a common history. While this discourse and these rules are usually intelligible to those who are outside the organization, for those inside the organization these rules and discourse can have such power that they mold their identities and ways of knowing and thinking about the world. The UN is no different in this regard. It too contains a discourse and formal and informal rules that shape what individuals care about and the practices they view as appropriate, desirable, and ethical in their own right.

The centrality and distinctiveness of this moral universe have often been overlooked, and for a simple reason: the authors of many of the more popular accounts have allowed the genocide to govern their reading of the past. Historical hindsight (and a good dose of indignation) can induce even the most conscientious investigators to impose their own moral demands on the central decision makers, leading them to conclude that the very failure to act by logical necessity demonstrates an absence of ethical scruples.

Many inquiries have projected a false morality that derives from a false methodology. The methodological error is to impose one's own moral sensibilities, commitments, and categories on a radically different moment. When moral sensibilities are driven by knowledge of an outcome that was not known to those whose actions are considered, the consequence is a radically ahistorical reading of the past. Nietzsche raised a similar point in the *Genealogy of Morals*. He assaulted various English historians for imposing their own commitments on an earlier time. Instead, he insisted on the adoption of a "historical sense" that forgoes prejudicial understandings of what is "good" in order to reconstruct the moral architecture of the historical period under scrutiny. While I do not subscribe to the moral relativism often associated with the strong version of this argument, I do insist that in historical inquiry we should attempt to understand how the participants themselves looked forward upon objects or events that we now observe in the rearview mirror. I intend to develop what the historian R. G. Collingwood called an "empathetic reconstruction." By reconstructing the moral universe in New York in 1993 and 1994, I hope to contribute to the understanding of the ethics of nonintervention.

The UN is a multidimensional, not a unidimensional, ethical space. Underlying any indictment of the UN is the presumption that it had a moral responsibility to stop the genocide, a duty to aid and protect the innocents. We instinctively believe that genocide and crimes against humanity trump all other moral claims and obligations—other commitments, loyalties, and obligations must melt in their presence. But before we accept this moral fundamentalism, we must recognize that the UN, like all institutions, assumes at any single moment a multitude of responsibilities and obligations. Those at the UN could surely relate to the philosopher's claim that "our everyday and raw experience is of a conflict between moral requirements at every stage of almost anyone's life."[8]

Institutions must constantly choose among various responsibilities, responsibilities that have immediate consequences for various constituencies. Fulfilling one set of responsibilities may lead to the neglect of another. It is in this way that the act of indifference can have an ethical basis. The UN had responsibilities not only to Rwandans but also to UN personnel who were at risk in the field and to the integrity of an institution that might be severely damaged by another Somalia-like failure in the field. To authorize intervention required the UN to decide that its responsibility to the Rwandans overrode its other commitments. It had to be willing to accept the many consequences of a failed intervention on the grounds that there was no greater moral imperative than to stop the killings (killings that were breathtaking in number but until late April were not yet known as genocide). At the end of the day we might conclude that their choices were not only regrettable but also morally reprehensible, that the UN's responsibility to act in Rwanda should have transcended other commitments. But at the least we have to recognize that, for the UN, Rwanda was situated on a deceptively uneven and crowded moral plane.

The significance I attach to the moral universe at the UN leads me to construct a narrative that gives prominence to the "cultural landscape": the discourse and the informal and formal rules that shaped the goals of the organization, the acceptable and unacceptable means to achieve those goals, and the meaning of ethical action at concrete moments. I want to consider how individuals offered different interpretations of these rules at different historical moments, and to recognize that they had some degree of autonomy that allowed them to appropriate rules and discourse for ulterior ends. This approach, in many ways, reverses the tack taken by prior accounts. To overstate matters: many of them tend to build an explanation for the UN's failure to act from the ground up, beginning with the interests of the most powerful states in the Security Council that presumably shaped the council's decisions and then introducing other actors and values as needed along the way. This perspective generates important insights that must be included in any record of the UN's involvement. But it tends to undervalue how the broader culture in which these actors were embedded significantly shaped their outlook on the world.

My decision to give prominence to the UN's culture crystallized after I reflected on my personal experiences and listened carefully to the accounts and testimonies of various participants. The UN was not a totalizing institution that transformed fairly independent-minded diplomats and international civil servants into bloodless bureaucrats, but it did profoundly influence how they looked at and acted upon the world. Government officials and UN staff came to know Rwanda as members of bureaucracies; the bureaucratic culture situated and defined their knowledge, informed their goals and desires, shaped what constituted appropriate and inappropriate behavior, distinguished acceptable from unacceptable consequences, and helped to determine right from wrong. Bureaucracy is not only a structure; it is also a process. Bureaucracies are orienting machines. They have the capacity to channel action and to transform individual into collective conscience. The existing stock of knowledge, the understanding of what constitutes proper means and ends, and the symbolic significance of events were organizationally situated.[9]

The bureaucracy is not merely a place for the congregation of already established ethical stands; it is an incubator of ethical claims. On such matters I have found the insights of Max Weber and Hannah Arendt quite evocative. Both had tragic images of the future. They saw danger in the very icons of modernity and progress and worried that modernity could not be reconciled with humanity. Both worried that an increasingly bureaucratized world would be an increasingly dehumanized world. Through different channels, both arrived at the conclusion that bureaucracy could generate a world that defined ethical action in ways that run roughshod over individuals.

Weber had much to say about bureaucracies, seeing in them the same double-edged sword that he believed existed in most modern institutions. He believed that bureaucracy was a powerful force for spreading liberal and rational values. Bureaucracy, after all, used expertise and merit to dole out social power—far preferable to family ties and social status, the criteria of earlier European politics. Modern bureaucracies provide rational, technical, and objective criteria to select means and organize action.

But Weber also saw that a bureaucratic world contained risks. It produced increasingly powerful and autonomous bureaucrats who could be spiritless, driven only by impersonal rules and procedures, and with little regard for the people they were expected to serve. Weber famously warned that those who allow themselves to be guided by rules will soon find that those rules have defined their identities and commitments. Because individuals are expected to execute rules and obey orders even if they depart from their private convictions, civil servants are built to be of "low moral standing." The very institution that individuals create to help them realize their ends can become disconnected from its original purpose and lead to a world where rules become ends in themselves. The possible disconnect between the acts executed by a bureaucracy and the community in whose name it acts is one of Weber's most chilling visions of modern life.

Outsiders may observe a cultural separation between the bureaucracy and the community, but bureaucrats may develop a system of thought that allows them to maintain a connection—even while acknowledging, and occasionally dispensing, acts that depart from the ideals of the community.[10] Bureaucrats can see themselves not only as bloodless drones but also as servants of the broader community and its transcendental ideals. The organization in which they are embedded is not merely a machine but a representative of the community; it purveys and protects its values. The rules that guide their decisions may be stated in the language of efficiency and appropriateness, but they also are subtly connected to wider values and aspirations. Yet staff often enforce rules that seemingly run roughshod over the very individuals they are supposed to serve, and are forced to deliver disappointments and to commit the occasional sin. This breach between rule-governed actions and community values might be expected to cause severe dissonance or ethical contradictions for public officials. But because they continue to connect these rules to abstract moral principles, they are able to ignore their occasional sins and exonerate themselves. As representatives of the common good, bureaucrats can remain comfortably indifferent to the individual, and the existence of universal principles cannot be undone by what they witness or dispense.

It is impossible to put the words *bureaucracies* and *evil* together in the same sentence without evoking Hannah Arendt's controversial phrase "banality of evil."[11] She famously argued that the Nazi bureaucratic machine that engineered the Holocaust transformed "normal" and "respectable" people like Adolf Eichmann into purveyors of evil. Although nearly every aspect of her argument has generated considerable criticism, the concept's power and insight continue to provoke because it continues to illuminate.

Her argument can be restated briefly.[12] Bureaucratic institutions can dehumanize individuals. The socialization into the bureaucracy and the denouement of dehumanization occur through a variety of mechanisms, but the result is that bureaucrats become mere functionaries. They see themselves as "cogs in an administrative machinery" so expansive that it is virtually impossible for any individual to understand the mechanics and purpose of the larger machine. This is why Arendt suggested that the political form of bureaucracy is best understood as the "the Rule of nobody." Bureaucrats suspend personal judgment and begin to treat rules as a source of divine guidance. They do not see themselves as being in charge or having any real autonomy: the psychological effect is to relieve them of responsibility for their actions, allowing them to act unreflexively. Dehumanization elides into an identification with the bureaucracy, a loyalty fastened once bureaucrats believe that the goals and values of the institution are superior to those once privately held. At this moment there occurs a Nietzschean "transvaluation of values," and actions one might formerly have judged morally wrong become activities that one finds merely difficult to bear.

The banality of evil now materializes. A bureaucratic mentality, not religion or ideology, encourages ordinary individuals to tolerate and perpetrate evil deeds. Bureaucratic duty and virtue are now found in having to suffer the existence of immoral acts. Because bureaucrats no longer see themselves as actors but rather as being acted upon, they relieve themselves of concern for what they see and the implications of their actions. It is only a small step from finding virtue in the dutiful tolerance of such acts in the name of the bureaucracy to participating in them. Indeed, the loyalty and legitimacy conferred on the bureaucracy now generate a definition of virtue that encourages the bureaucrat to go beyond the call of bureaucratic duty. The evil committed is evil committed by institutions and not by individuals. Although each step of Arendt's argument has sparked controversy, it is on this claim regarding the distribution of responsibility that she has been most thoroughly criticized.

Arendt derived extreme arguments from an extreme case, and Weber's ideal types are intended to embellish in order to isolate the bureaucracy's defining characteristics. I nevertheless find that these two theorists capture elements of my own experiences and provide conceptual cairns for understanding how the UN came to see its actions as ethical. The international community contains transcendental values. Progress, human rights, development—such values are accorded a Kantian quality and viewed as the constitutional fabric of the international community. These values transcend the nation-states that formally comprise the international system. The UN is more than an instrument of member states. It is also the concrete expression of the hopes and ideals of the international community. UN staff often talk about the UN as if it were a church, suggesting that they are guardians of a religion whose tenets are transcendental.[13] Even doubting states observe the High Holidays.

New York, as headquarters is referred to by UN hands, developed peacekeeping rules that limited who would qualify for relief and assistance; developed a system of thought that helped them to maintain a faith in the val-

ues of the international community, even while acting in ways that potentially violated those values; and developed a sense of powerlessness that
could lead them to deny their capacity for action. After sobering experiences in the field and a more realistic appraisal of the foundations of peacekeeping, New York developed a more precise and restricted set of rules to
determine when peacekeeping was appropriate and how peacekeepers
should operate in the field. Peacekeeping was appropriate when there was a
"peace to keep"; peacekeepers should follow the principles of neutrality,
impartiality, and consent. The reason for these rules was the recognition
that the misapplication of peacekeeping was leading both to costly failures
in the field and to fatal damage to the institution. But another consequence
of these rules was the reduced likelihood that peacekeepers would be deployed during moments of mass human suffering. Those at the UN, member states and staff alike, were overwhelmed by the sheer number of worthy
cases. They used the peacekeeping rules to discriminate between those who
could and those who could not be helped. Virtue could be found in helping those who could not help themselves because such action could help
maintain the health of the UN.

A malnourished and overused UN was highly dependent on the whims
of the volatile Great Powers. In response, UN staff began to deny their
own responsibility and capacity to act. Time and again, UN officials used
words like *servants* and *subordinates*, self-effacing descriptions that they delivered sarcastically but which betrayed their feelings of vulnerability. The
tremulous times at the UN and the constant reminder by powerful patrons
not to cross any red lines encouraged UN staff to adopt a "pragmatic" and
highly cautious approach to world events. The development of more discriminating rules of peacekeeping, of a system of thought that found virtue
in detachment, and of a growing sense of powerlessness meant that UN
staff could find some redemption, even moral solace, in the decision not to
intervene.

The value of taking seriously the culture at the UN can become a vice if
that culture is presumed to have an integrity that washes over individuals in
identical ways and eliminates the space for private judgments and interests.
Weber produced an X-ray of bureaucratic life, one in which the soul is
omitted and only the skeleton remains. His bureaucrats cannot be much
more than obedient, rule-following supplicants. Arendt envisioned an om-
nipotent institution that so thoroughly socialized individuals that they lost
the capacity for independent judgment. Her bureaucrats easily lost their
private morality in a bureaucratic world. Such diagnoses are clearly unsuit-
able to the UN (and to most bureaucratic contexts). The moral universe of
UN staffers might contain a north star that inhabitants could use to guide

their actions, but they disagree over the route to follow and even the reasons for their sojourn. I attempt to sidestep these pitfalls by immediately introducing a few salient observations.

The UN oftentimes was forced to choose among competing obligations. To adjudicate between commitments, they frequently appealed to rules connected to different languages that featured appropriateness and the transcendental. Some rules won over others because they appeared less risky in an environment defined by immediate danger and overbearing uncertainty. Member states and UN staff attempted to adapt their moral concerns, trying out various relationships between the rules of peacekeeping and their practical ethics, struggling as best they could knowing what little they did about the situation. For many, their decisions about Rwanda were hard fought and not easily won, as Arendt and Weber suggest.

The UN, like most bureaucracies and organizations, is differentiated and hierarchically arranged. It is a collection of semiautonomous and overlapping parts, of which three are most important. Central is the Security Council, composed of five permanent, veto-wielding powers and ten nonpermanent members. Those with the greatest power wield the greatest influence, and the United States has the greatest influence of all. But the council is not a simple aggregation of fifteen separate interests; it is more than the sum of its parts. The council also has a semblance of solidarity, presents itself as a representative of the international community, and contains collective norms that keep in line even the most independent-minded. The second part is the Secretariat, the permanent administration of the United Nations. The lead figures are the Executive Office of the Secretary-General and the Department of Peacekeeping Operations; their views are not identical. Last is the field operation, such as UNAMIR, made up of troops lent by member states. States contribute troops for diverse reasons, including monetary compensation, a desire to curry favor with powerful states, and a sense of obligation to the UN and, in this case, to Rwanda. Power formally and usually flowed from the Security Council to the Secretariat to UNAMIR. But as in most organizations, practice typically departs from the formal organizational chart: different parts hold different degrees of influence at different moments.

As a collection of related units and subunits, the UN contains subcultures that have distinct interpretations of how the rules and standards of appropriateness can and should be applied. Hardly synchronized in their movements or thoughts, the Secretariat, the council, and the field can have very different ideas about what is appropriate, how they should prioritize their commitments and responsibilities, and what constitutes an acceptable level of risk. These three UN elements disagree among themselves over the meaning of neutrality, impartiality, and consent—disagreements that have their roots in rival interpretations of recent history and present circumstances.

Finally, some states and UN staff judge their primordial interests as far more compelling than transnational commitments or obligations to others, in this case the Rwandans. Not everyone at the UN desperately sought a way to balance their desire to help the Rwandans with their other obligations and responsibilities. This was not "Sophie's choice" played on an international stage. In some cases, the lack of concern for Rwandans was arrestingly callous, with an easy willingness to sacrifice the victims when they became inconvenient. The French have the distinction of calling the killers their friends and allies. The American role was less intimate but clearly insensitive. During this period the United States was ready to make examples of delinquent operations, notwithstanding the severe consequences for those on the ground. It publicly held that this position was justified given the UN's scarce resources, and privately confessed it was motivated by a desire to avoid a domestic headache. Also on the roll call of shame should be the vast majority of governments that held perfunctory conversations before politely declining to contribute troops to an intervention. UN staff also acted in ways that suggest that they believed the organization's interests (and perhaps their own careers) would be better served by remaining distant. Any account of the genocide must preserve the abundance of politically expedient and strategically calculated indiscretions.

THIS ethical history of the UN's involvement in Rwanda examines the dynamic relationship between the UN's culture and the mixture of reasons that motivated UN staff and key member states on the Security Council. The UN's buildup to indifference had a history, just as surely as the actual genocide did. Its response to the genocide was not a radical break with the past; rather, the detached nature of its involvement was evident in nearly every single compromising step it took, beginning with the decision to authorize UNAMIR in October 1993 and continuing through the end of the genocide in July 1994. A series of steps, both strategic and expedient, principled and protective, contributed to its negligence.

Chapter 1 provides the global backdrop for the UN's growing visibility and its accompanying anxieties. With the demise of the Cold War, the international community turned to the UN to further its aspirations for peace and security. Blue helmets were the icons of the moment, the symbols of deliverers of a more peaceful world. By mid-1993, however, there was growing concern that the UN's promise was being undermined by the weight of its own ambitions, by high-profile disasters in the field, and by the failure to identify the conditions under which the UN might be effective. And then came the American deaths in Somalia on October 3, 1993. This proved to be a dramatic turning point for the operation and the organization, with the failed operation possibly taking the organization with it. What would later be dubbed the "shadow of Somalia" cast a pall across the UN.

Those who lived through these times experienced a daily anxiety. They were loyal to an organization that was coming under direct assault from powerful and unforgiving states that were ready to use failures in the field as evidence of the UN's permanent shortcomings. To limit demands on the UN and ensure that peacekeepers were deployed only under the proper conditions, the Security Council and the Secretariat reunited around a traditional interpretation of the rules of peacekeeping: peacekeepers should remain neutral and impartial, and operate with the explicit consent of the parties. These rules restricted the UN's scope of caring and operation; it was prepared to assist when it had the consent of the parties and there was stability on the ground, but it would shy away from humanitarian disasters. The UN's new traditionalism would ensure that the UN was "effective when selective." A more effective peacekeeping regimen would shore up the institution's sagging fortunes, and a healthier institution would help foster and protect the values of the international community.

The UN's relationship to Rwanda bore the genetic imprint of the moment, the subject of chapter 2. The Security Council was unenthusiastic about establishing its eighteenth operation in five years, especially two days after American Rangers had been killed in Somalia. But reservations were partially overcome by the promise that Rwanda would be an "easy" operation. This label was fastened to Rwanda for two related reasons. Few knew much about Rwandan history; those making the decisions at the UN were experts in peacekeeping operations, not in the particulars of Rwanda. But most knew that the parties to the conflict had signed the Arusha Accords, which gave the surface appearance of fulfilling all the conditions required for a potentially successful transition from a civil war to a multiethnic democracy. The UN was ready to capitalize on this apparently easy operation to demonstrate, once again, its distinctive contribution to international peace and security. The organization was desperately looking for good news to show an increasingly doubting world, and by helping the Rwandans, the UN would help itself.

The operation quickly foundered. Chapter 3 opens with the secretary-general's first report on UNAMIR. There was little good news to deliver. The security situation was showing signs of deterioration, and the cornerstone of the agreement, the broad-based transitional government, was now several months overdue. According to most at headquarters, these developments were related: only immediate establishment of the transitional government would arrest the deteriorating security situation. The dangers became more apparent in late December 1993 and the first weeks of 1994 when there appeared various "warning signs," most famously the January 11 communiqué from Force Commander Roméo Dallaire that warned of threats to civilians and peacekeepers. The UN's DPKO and Boutros-Ghali responded by instructing UNAMIR to abide by the rules of neutrality, impartiality, and consent. Departure from these rules, they warned, was ill-advised for a threadbare operation and was eerily reminiscent of Somalia. The only appropriate way to resolve the security situation was to establish the transitional government.

By the time the operation came up for renewal at the end of March 1994, a growing sentiment, led principally by the United States, held that because the Rwandan government was not honoring its responsibilities to the Arusha Accords, the UN should threaten to walk away. It was argued that such a threat would bluff the parties into following through on their agreements. If the transitional government was not established in the near future, the UN should consider closing down the peacekeeping operation. This threat might be the only leverage available, and the UN could live with the reputation of being tough on delinquent operations if it had to follow through. As UN officials and the Security Council struggled to manage an increasingly troubled operation, they had one eye on the present of Rwanda and the other on the future of the UN.

The operation disintegrated on April 6, 1994. Chapter 4 explores the critical fifteen days between April 6 and the Security Council's decision to reduce UNAMIR to 270 peacekeepers on April 21. Several factors influenced the council's decision. Standing rules instructed them to employ peacekeepers only when there was a workable cease-fire and stability on the ground. They could not locate reinforcements for a peacekeeping force that was coming apart at the seams, had already lost ten soldiers, and could barely protect itself. They were operating under the influence of uncertainty and organizationally scripted descriptions of the violence as a civil war with unfortunate civilian killings, not a prelude to genocide. The council's debate gave priority to the threat to the peacekeepers and the future of the UN. What was at stake was bigger than Rwanda. There was a virtue in learning to say no in these trying times, particularly if such responses were connected to a broader purpose.

The Security Council was not alone in balking at intervention. So, too, did the Secretariat. There is considerable controversy over why it failed to provide the moral language and logistical blueprint for intervention—language and plans that Dallaire had made available to headquarters but

Boutros-Ghali never communicated to the council. In my judgment the evidence points to one of two possible explanations. One is that the Secretariat was operating under a culturally and crisis-induced haze that caused it to mishandle and misinterpret the information coming from the field. In short, these were honest mistakes that had horrific consequences. An alternative possibility is that UN staff heard Dallaire loud and clear but estimated that the council would not authorize what was undoubtedly a very risky intervention—and if it did authorize intervention, failure might be not merely troubling for but lethal to the organization. I lay out two scenarios, but my cautious conclusion is that Boutros-Ghali and his staff knew what they were doing. Regardless of the reasons for their silence, the effect was to discredit the cause of intervention and to reinforce those in favor of withdrawal. Passionate pleas from Boutros-Ghali would have been necessary if nonpermanent members in the council who advocated intervention were to overcome the objections of the powerful. No such words were ever delivered.

The council's April 21 vote ushered in a new phase of the debate. Chapter 5 narrates how the genocide's increasingly undeniable presence sharpened the pressure on the council to do something besides, in the constantly uttered phrase of the council, "remain actively seized of the matter." Several members of the council urged the body to call genocide by its proper name, only to find that their views were unwelcome. By early May the council became more inclined to authorize intervention, if only to keep up appearances. And at this time Boutros-Ghali finally stopped referring to the killing in Rwanda as a civil war and publicly called it a genocide. Through mid-May the council debated what should be the shape of a possible intervention. The United States, however, impeded intervention on the grounds that there still did not exist a workable plan. It finally consented to an intervention but only after attaching several riders which further retarded a rescue party that was already moving at a glacial pace. After authorizing an intervention, the UN slid back into a tragicomedy where diplomatic negotiations took the place of concerted action. The Rwandan Patriotic Front (RPF) was the only force that had a chance to stop the genocide; the council refused to recognize this truth because doing so would lend diplomatic support to one of the two combatants, thereby departing from its sacrosanct position of neutrality. The genocide finally ended on July 19 with an RPF victory. Roughly eight hundred thousand people had been slaughtered and another two million fled to neighboring countries.

INVESTIGATORS have struggled to understand how an institution shaped by the Genocide Convention, one that had peacekeepers on the ground from start to finish, could stand by and do nothing. Their searches involve a desire to know not only how this was possible but also who was to blame. As they attempt to draw back the Oz-like curtain of the "United Nations," a curtain that concealed the individuals who contributed to the decision not to intervene, they discovered a highly complicated story of individuals who knew too little and too much, of individuals who leaned on well-established precedents as they acted meekly in response to possible threats, and of a UN that functioned effortlessly to coordinate the desire of states and UN staff to remain uninvolved. Blame seemed so widely distributed that it proved nearly impossible to recover.

My ethical history has been motivated by twin aspirations: to reconstruct the moral reasons that guided the actions of the UN, and to isolate who, if anyone at the UN, bears moral responsibility for the genocide. I know there is a delicate balance between the two goals that can be easily upset. Those who begin their investigations with a desire to assign blame sometimes allow their search for justice to color their writing of history. I detect a rush to judgment regarding what the UN knew or could have known about the genocide; the January 11 cable was a warning that was impossible to miss, and the killings in April erased any doubts about the nature of the crimes.[14] By not fully incorporating the role of background forces, however, these inquiries paint for us individuals who appear to know more than they really did and to possess more choices than they actually had.

The danger inherent in empathetic reconstructions is that they can easily induce a fatalistic view of history. The gravitational pull of history and culture is so powerful that, it seems, individuals could hardly have acted otherwise. Under circumstances of limited knowledge and formidable constraints, it becomes unfair to hold the UN morally responsible. Few inquiries have gone this far.[15] Yet many participants' accounts stress these forces in their explanations. Indeed, my own initial response to the UN's critics certainly leaned heavily in this direction. I defended the UN on the grounds that it had no reasonable choice and no real knowledge of the genocide until it was too late. Those in New York, in short, made understandable, though highly regrettable, decisions. I have since backed away from this fatalistic view of the UN's actions as a consequence of new information regarding what individuals knew or should have known and the possible factors that informed their decisions.

Chapter 6 completes this ethical history by considering the UN's moral responsibility for the Rwandan genocide. In what way might the UN have been responsible for the genocide? The answer depends on the meaning one gives to this multisided concept. Its meanings can include occupying a role that has specific duties or obligations; acting conscientiously; or causing the outcome. Past inquiries relied on different meanings, and the predictable consequence was to leave unclear how and why the UN might have been responsible.

I have found it useful to draw on the philosophical debate on moral responsibility. Philosophers have long been engaged in hand-to-hand combat over the exact meaning of moral responsibility, and that struggle shows no signs of ending any time soon. Yet they generally accept that individuals can be held morally responsible if their actions or omissions are causally effective and they have no valid excuses for their behavior. This loose consensus is hardened when dealing with omissions, the central issue in this instance of nonintervention. Transported from the philosophical to the worldly plane, the claim is that the UN is morally responsible if its actions or omissions are causally linked to the genocide and it does not have a compelling excuse for its behavior. Three central features of this view—the relationship between moral and causal responsibility, the standing of omissions, and the nature of excuses—proved invaluable in helping me to assess when, how, and why the UN might bear moral responsibility.

Moral responsibility is contingent on causal responsibility.[16] It is unfair to hold someone morally responsible for an outcome over which he or she had no control. This does not mean, however, that causal responsibility begets moral responsibility. Oftentimes actors cannot be held morally responsible because there was no reason why they should have expected that their actions would contribute to the event. All actions have unintended consequences, but actors are not necessarily morally responsible for them all. The October 1993 coup d'état in neighboring Burundi is frequently cited as providing the *genocidaires,* the perpetrators of the genocide, with the last bit of evidence they needed to convince them that the Tutsis were a mortal threat. Yet no one can reasonably hold the Burundi military responsible for the Rwandan genocide. There is little doubt that the internationally brokered Arusha Accords contained components that the extremists viewed as a political death sentence; while these international participants might have acted in ways that had unintended consequences, they certainly did not design the accords for this purpose, nor did they have reason to believe that the accords might contribute to genocide. Moral responsibility presupposes causal responsibility, but causal responsibility does not logically imply moral responsibility.

I am just as concerned with omissions as commissions because the road not taken might have led to a different outcome. Simply stated, the failure to prevent harm can be tantamount to contributing to harm.[17] Demonstrating a causal link between actions and outcomes can be difficult enough when dealing with sweeping historical forces and a rare event such as genocide. But how can it be convincingly argued that an isolated action here or there might have altered all that came after, and so erased the genocide? To sustain the claim that an omission had such a status requires the construction of a counterfactual world in which a possible action is logically connected to a chain of events that would have caused the perpetrators to abandon their crusade.

Many participants and observers have worked in this counterfactual universe. I and others scrutinize the Secretariat's refusal to allow Force Commander Dallaire to seize arms caches weeks before the killings started, the failure of Boutros-Ghali to pass on critical information from the field to the Security Council for much of April, and the council's failure to authorize an intervention during those first few weeks. Investigators visualize alternative actions, building imagined worlds in which actions not taken resurrect hundreds of thousands of dead. If this world can be sustained, then it becomes reasonable to assign some causal responsibility to the UN, bringing us one step closer to finding it morally responsible.

Many of these counterfactual worlds contain two noteworthy features. One is the existence of a moral division of labor. Many parties were on the sidelines, but typically it is only the UN and the Great Powers who are asked to account for their behavior. This special treatment comes partly from their proximity to the genocide and the philosophical injunction that those who can act ought to act. Yet this moral division of labor presumes that the Secretariat and the Security Council accepted roles that included obligations to Rwanda. Acts of omission typically are not viewed as malfeasance unless the actor has assumed some sort of responsibility. Good Samaritan laws are difficult to sustain, but police officers have an obligation to assist citizens in distress.

When we trace whose omissions mattered, the list of suspects shrinks to a chosen few. And, those chosen few had a "duty to aid." This controversial injunction is more frequently thrown around than it is examined.[18] It insists that individuals have a duty to assist those they can, that *can* implies *ought*. Even the utilitarian theories of Peter Singer can provide a reasoned basis for believing that member states and the UN should relieve suffering where and when they can.[19] But such injunctions overlook the sheer number of claims on the UN's attention at any one moment. Pushed to the extreme, the UN's responsibilities are endless given the amount of suffering in the world. Because the UN and other bodies cannot aid everyone, they must develop rules that tell them who they should care about and when they should care. They have to be selective samaritans.

All such rules and restraints are supposed to vanish, however, in the face of crimes against humanity and genocide. At such moments moral distance should be horizonless, even the most selective of samaritans should stop to help, and even at some risk to bodily harm. It is the fact of genocide that triggers our moral attention and offends our sense of responsibility. Stated cynically, if the killings had left only two hundred thousand dead, then we would be less outraged by the absence of a response. I do not recall much outcry during much of April, when there were thousands upon thousands of dead in Rwanda. It was only after the killing in Rwanda was labeled a "genocide" that it received international attention and there were demands that something be done. The duty to relieve suffering may be barely audible at lower numbers, but it becomes a deafening imperative in the face of undeniable genocide. The UN's apologetic language, as we will see, betrayed the fact that it knew that it was behaving badly.

Even if it can be shown that the UN's actions or omissions contributed to the genocide, the UN might have a valid excuse, some extenuating circumstances that interfered with its ability to act. Such excuses typically revolve around claims of ignorance and duress: its actions were appropriate given what it knew or could have known at the time; or it was unable to act properly because of pressures that could not be defied. Many decisionmakers have claimed ignorance, insisting that the situation was highly uncertain. Others, notably those in the Secretariat, have cited pressures and the constraints imposed by the Security Council. A striking feature of the form and content of these excuses is that they tend to implicate the "UN." Many of the participants have argued that their position in the bureaucracy gave them a partial view of Rwanda, and therefore, they were not fully informed. Others have insisted that they were immobilized by constraints imposed on them by others. The UN becomes either a veil of ignorance or a bureaucratic restraint.

Their excuses point to a troubling truth: the larger and more complex the organization, the more difficult it is to recover individual responsibility. A nearly bottomless history of small decisions amassed to make a particular outcome almost inevitable. Many individuals in different parts of the organization were involved along the way. Individuals made decisions under the influence of historical dynamics, an organizational culture, and uncertainty. The sum total of these considerations makes it nearly impossible to disentangle the individual from the organization. Organizations, not individuals, become blameworthy. After all, individuals can be assigned responsibility only if they act freely, but these organizational, structural, and historical forces obliterate personal agency. I intend to resist this structural seduction. I maintain a belief in individual responsibility by assessing what was and what could have been known (and by whom) in relationship to the actions that were and might reasonably have been taken.

My view is that the UN bears some moral responsibility for the genocide. Its moral responsibility derives from its actions in April 1994, not during the period leading up to the genocide. There is little doubt that the Secretariat mishandled the January 11 cable and other warning signs from the field. I find wholly credible its claim that it could not predict the genocide or envision anything but a return to civil war. The council labored under the same false impressions. Earlier and more aggressive UN actions might have deterred the extremists, as Dallaire predicted, but I hold that the Secretariat's actions, though shortsighted and lamentable, were not morally culpable.

The ignorance excuse, however, becomes literally incredible as events proceed from the first forewarning of a humanitarian nightmare in early January to its full-throttled execution in late April. At this point the Secretariat, and especially Secretary-General Boutros-Ghali, bears some moral responsibility. Boutros-Ghali possessed information that illuminated the nature of the crimes. He had an obligation to transmit that information to the Security Council but failed to do so. Had he presented that information in a compelling way, he might have convinced the council to authorize an intervention. Had an intervention occurred, it is possible that the genocidaires would have called off their master plan. Instead, he failed to do what he could and acted in ways that he had good reason to know would frustrate the cause of intervention. The claim that the Secretariat's behavior is excusable because of duress is untenable at best and dangerous at worst. Given the extraordinary nature of the situation, it had an obligation to act. The sorts of consequences that make a duress argument reasonable do not apply here. Fear of unforgiving, powerful states is not sufficient.

With the exception of those who argued for intervention, namely, Nigeria, New Zealand, and the Czech Republic, members of the council bear some moral responsibility. They did not come to recognize the genocide for what it was until after April 21, but at that point the council had an obligation to try to assemble an intervention force. Yet many dillydallied and clearly preferred buck-passing and endless Security Council sessions to concerted action. The behavior of the United States during this period is simply unconscionable. It continued to deny in public that there was a genocide and then actively obstructed the only half-decent intervention plan available because it feared any intervention, by necessity, would include American participation. It was not obligated to provide the lead troops for any rescue mission, but I believe that it was duty-bound to make it easier for those who might. Diversionary tropes such as the "UN" and the "international community" must not be allowed to conceal the simple fact that individuals were aware of crimes being committed and were in positions of responsibility—but chose not to act.

I frequently detect a hint of satisfaction in the accounts that manage to excavate moral and individual responsibility from the historical debris. Perhaps it is because of the unspoken belief that changing the people will change the outcome. "No Hitler, no Holocaust." If only a few individuals had resolved that it was unconscionable to be a bystander, then perhaps thousands would have been saved. I suppose there is some solace in recovering a history in which altering an isolated event transforms all that follows. But personalizing the story in this way can obscure how these were not isolated individuals operating on their own but rather were people situated in an organizational and historical context that profoundly shaped how they looked upon the world, what they believed they could do, and what they wanted to do. The UN staff and diplomats in New York, in the main, were highly decent, hard-working, and honorable individuals who believed that they were acting properly when they decided not to try to put an end to genocide. It is this history that stays with me.

I

It Was a Very Good Year

The atmosphere at the UN during the early 1990s was positively triumphant. The sheer exhilaration of the moment can be fully appreciated by knowing what the organization had endured in the previous years. The 1980s had represented a low-water mark for the UN. It had made an impressive and active contribution to the remarkably peaceful decolonization process of the 1960s, but since then had been sidelined and maligned. Decolonization changed the character and the agenda of the General Assembly, bringing to numerical majority the emerging Third World. However, the more anti-American the UN became, the more the United States treated it as a misbehaving adolescent not deserving of any responsibility. In 1975 the General Assembly passed the infamous resolution equating Zionism with racism, which made even some of its closest friends worry that the UN was making bad choices for the wrong reasons. Soon thereafter, two U.S. representatives to the UN, Daniel Patrick Moynihan and Jeane Kirkpatrick, became household names because of their willingness to publicly ridicule the organization. The UN also had to endure a secretary-general, Kurt Waldheim, accused of being a Nazi war criminal. The Security Council, never a model deliberative body, became hopelessly gridlocked by an increasingly confrontational U.S.-Soviet rivalry. The years during the presidency of Ronald Reagan unleashed a string of indignities, as his unilateral approach made it clear from beginning to end that he had little patience for multilateral organizations that were at best talk shops and at worst potential usurpers of American power if given the chance. "Morning in America" meant "twilight for the United Nations."

The UN's fortunes began to change with the thawing of the Cold War. After 1986 the United States and the Soviet Union began to work in concert to end various regional conflicts, including those in Africa and Central America, and to convince their war-weary clients that it was better to negotiate than to fight. They enlisted the UN in their conflict-resolving efforts, viewing it as a credible intermediary because of its perceived impartiality. UN diplomats shuttled to some of the world's toughest spots, but unlike in years past when they had to wait outside in the hallways, they were now admitted into the negotiating sanctums. Certainly the Soviet-American détente and willingness to turn off the arms pipeline created the conditions for conflict resolution, but the UN also distinguished itself and received its just due.

Aiding the resuscitation of the UN was Mikhail Gorbachev, the Soviet premier who was now stressing simultaneously the importance of international cooperation and the centrality of the UN. His reasons for singing the UN's praises were many, but a prime consideration was that by strengthening this international body where the Soviets had a permanent seat and veto power, he might help buffer the Soviet Union's declining power and prestige. The change in American administrations also produced a more sympathetic ear. Unlike the Reagan administration that was scornful of the United Nations, President George H. W. Bush, a former U.S. ambassador to the UN, made clear at the outset of his term that he was a cautious multilateralist and held a more charitable view of the world body.

These important changes in the world, and their resulting effects on the UN, could not prepare the organization for the global attention that would come its way. The rapid-fire and relatively nonviolent revolutions in Eastern Europe, the in-the-blink-of-an-eye end to the Cold War, and the peaceful implosion of the Soviet Union introduced an almost ethereal quality to world politics. The Cassandras were silenced. The UN was a prime beneficiary of these changes.

To begin with, when the Cold War was over the Soviets and the Americans signaled their readiness to redistribute the security load as they tended to long-ignored domestic ills. World politics abhors a security vacuum, and almost by default the UN became a prime candidate to help organize international peace and security. Moreover, the defining conflicts of the period favored the UN. Ethnonationalist conflicts were erupting in places that had little strategic relevance to the Great Powers, but the humanitarian consequences of these conflicts were impossible to ignore. The UN provided the ready answer for states that wanted to do something but not too much. Or, as less charitably put by former UN official Sir Brian Urquhart, the UN proved to be a useful dumping ground. Furthermore, policymakers were now openly talking about dismantling militaries and building institutions to promote a stable peace. The UN's commitment to security through peaceful means and multilateral institutions represented a perfect fit for the security moment. Finally, even when the UN sanctioned force, as it did with the Gulf War, many took it as a sign of progress; after all, such operations represented not the familiar imperial imposition but rather collective security as it was originally envisioned.

The UN became the darling of the international community. The early 1990s produced a steady stream of glowing testimonials to the long-suffering but never-more-needed-than-now UN. Independent commissions, study groups, newspaper editorials, and news weeklies rediscovered the UN. Leading dailies routinely stressed how the UN was capable of assisting in the peaceful resolution of disputes and should be given the chance by the Great Powers. The Commission on Global Governance observed that the end of the Cold War and cascading globalization were creating new opportunities and problems in their wake, that the obvious solution to these problems was greater global management, and that the UN was the right steering mechanism to confront these challenges. In his 1992 address to the General Assembly, a post–Gulf War euphoric President Bush gave an impassioned speech in favor of the UN, praised its contributions to peacekeeping, pledged the United States' support to peacekeeping efforts, and advised the American military to take a more active role in logistics, communications, and training.

These psalms of promise imagined a UN that personified the central values of the international community, defended and spread those values, and was a central instrument in the management of international peace and security. This represented a radical reappraisal of the UN's role in global politics. For most of its life, the UN was instructed to protect the interests of states, which almost invariably revolved around the promotion of state security and the preservation of state sovereignty. None of this was very surprising. After all, notwithstanding the pretense to represent all of humanity, the UN is an intergovernmental organization: only sovereign states can be formal members, only sovereign states can sit in the General Assembly and on the Security Council, and only sovereign states can give formal instructions to the Secretariat. The predictable result was that while states might have a nominal interest in promoting the values of the international community, they have a far greater interest in protecting and promoting their individual security and sovereignty.

And when states did speak of the life-giving values of the international community, the vast majority conveniently defined those values in a way that furthered their security and protected their sovereignty (oftentimes to the detriment of their citizens). For decades the subject of human rights was virtually taboo in the UN, seen as an ideological whip of the West and representing a violation of the principle of noninterference—that is, unless human rights was defined as full and complete independence for colonized and recently decolonized states. Equality referred less to the rule of law and protections for all citizens than it did to sovereign equality between states. Questions of democracy were treated as an illegitimate intrusion into domestic affairs, an insidious and unwelcome attempt to impose Western standards. This was a state's world.

But as states ascended from the bomb shelter that was the Cold War, they rediscovered and reswore their commitment to these foundational values. The peaceful end to the Cold War seemed nearly miraculous after a decade filled with nuclear clocks and apocalyptic arms races, and states were now filing into the UN to give their benedictions and recite the values that bound them as a single community. Human rights, liberalism, peaceful settlement of disputes, freedom, progress, development—these and other values were ritualistically recited in General Assembly addresses and populated UN documents. States insisted that while these values had always been present in the founding texts and the UN Charter, the Cold War had prevented them from fulfilling and honoring that initial vision. These values, they reminded themselves at every turn, were cosmopolitan and transcendental. States had rights, but so too did individuals and peoples. A "rights" discourse now bubbled to the surface. This development was remarkable and almost revolutionary given that in decades past states had vigorously and collectively railed against such claims because of the threat they potentially posed to their sovereign prerogatives.

The values of the international community were not only ends in themselves but also means to achieve genuine and stable international peace and security. During the Cold War international peace and security meant state security. "Threats to international peace and security," therefore, largely revolved around the projected and realized dangers posed by two opposing, militarized states. In an international system where peace was a chimera and war was either present or in preparation, the best that could be hoped for was international stability secured through a balance of power and sovereignty's mutual recognition of the right to exist. Not only was there no place for shared values in the management and diminution of international conflict, but also allowing values to hijack foreign policy could lead to ideologically minded campaigns and violations of the principle of noninterference, creating the conditions for instability and war. A mutually recognized balance of power, and not a mutually recognized community of values, was stability's best friend.

The end of the Cold War introduced a reconceptualization of the meaning of security and its accomplishment. Whereas during the Cold War security meant the security of states, there was now a willingness to consider "human" and "cosmopolitan" security, the security of individuals and peoples. This alteration in the concept of security was due to two related "discoveries." The state frequently was not the guardian it pretended to be but rather was the principal threat to its citizens. In theory the state was to provide security against foreign intruders, but in practice many societies had more to fear from their imposed protector than they did from other states. Also, domestic and civil wars seemed to be outstripping international wars in number and ferocity. Interstate war, though far from solved, paled in comparison to the growing number of ethnonational conflicts that were producing grim upheavals, crimes against humanity, and mass population movements. These conflicts would jar visions at any time but did so particularly now because of the presumption that a kinder, gentler world was to succeed the Cold War. Something had to be done.

These new security threats called for new security remedies. If domestic conflicts were a security threat and a potential source of regional instability, then these societies had to be reconstructed and redirected in ways that eliminated the roots of these conflicts. Domestic stability was essential for international stability. Stable states make for a stable international order. This was a revolution in strategic thought. The Cold War emphasis on balances of power and noninterference was steadily eclipsed by the belief that international security was best attained by creating regions that had shared values and by creating states that had domestic legitimacy and the rule of law. The strategic logic ran as follows: international order is premised on domestic order, domestic order is contingent on the state being viewed as legitimate by its society, states are most legitimate when they operate with the consent of their societies and honor the rule of law, and the principles of consent and the enshrinement of the rule of law are tantamount to democracy.

Because of the emergent belief that the domestic rule of law promotes the international rule of law, democracy was increasingly treated as a principle of international order and a cornerstone of international security. The diagnostic implication was that widening the circle of democracies automatically would widen the zone of peace. The prescriptive implication was that the international community should feel no shame in promoting and nurturing democratic norms. In contrast to the Cold War period when projects designed to cast states in certain molds were treated as destabilizing, now such projects were viewed as essential for promoting a genuinely stable peace.

The Secretariat lent support to this new security discourse. Boutros Boutros-Ghali, the new secretary-general, frequently stressed "human" security, arguing that the UN must be as concerned with the security of peoples and individuals as it is with the security of states. The clearest and boldest statement on such matters is *An Agenda for Peace*. The Security Council invited the secretary-general to outline his vision of the UN's future security role. As Boutros-Ghali recalled, he quickly capitalized on the opportunity to deliver a more ambitious, far-reaching, and forward-looking proposal than was expected.[1]

The heart of the document is a meditation on the changing nature of security and the UN as the midwife for a new international order. State security should not be allowed to overshadow individual security. Individuals' security and safety were more likely to be endangered by food scarcity, a crumbling economy, environmental degradation, and political instability than by an invading army. Indeed, the state was frequently not a source of protection but rather a source of harm. The combined effect of state-sponsored insecurity and a crumbling domestic environment was to suggest that domestic security overshadowed international security. The oft-made claim was that the location of most security crises occurred within states and not between them. The only way to fix this problem was to promote the rule of law, a point made in countless speeches and documents.

Enter the UN. The near consensus was that the best way to strengthen the values of the international community and the prospects for international peace and security was to strengthen its principal organ—the UN. The UN provided the legitimation forum. Only by enshrining these values in the international community's singular and universal organization would they obtain legitimacy, retain a magnetic appeal, and compel states to honor them. But the UN was expected to be more than a clearinghouse and debating parlor for these ideas. It also was entrusted with a new mission, to become a missionary. The UN would spread the word and convert nonbelievers. It was better suited for this globalizing project than states were because it was perceived to be neutral and because it had a legitimacy that came from its status as a global organization.

Boutros-Ghali and other high-ranking UN officials insisted that this work was an integral part of their job and not an interference in states' domestic affairs. In large measure most states agreed, though important dissenters like China, Egypt, and India objected on the grounds that these intrusions mocked the principle of noninterference. Locked into place was a growing view that expanding the values of the international community would deepen the prospects for international peace, and the UN represented the right applicator.

UN staff were thrilled with this sudden burst of attention, acclaim, and activity, which nearly healed the psychic and institutional wounds caused by decades of smear campaigns and humiliations. Secretary-General Javier Pérez de Cuéllar, who suffered through some of the worst of times only to savor the beginning of the best, captured the mood in his farewell address in late 1991:

> I need hardly recount all the areas in which operations of unprecedented versatility, nature or scope have been mounted during these [recent] years. You know them all, since you have served in them. You know what innovative ideas, what improvisation, what harnessing of resources, often at short notice, they have required. You know also their reward: how much human pain has been reduced and the waste of conflict averted by these operations. . . . For us, it has not only been an exciting period, but also one of greater responsibility. I know that most of us came to the United Nations because of a profound commitment—this was not to be "just another job," with whatever degree of prestige and material reward. We came to serve the United Nations through our conviction that there is no worthier form of service. We were prepared to accept sacrifices and hazards in pursuing the aims of the United Nations charter. . . . I am quite aware that over the years some of you have had a sense of frustration as you have felt your talents and idealism have not been fully utilized. There was, in addition, deep consternation and even bewilderment, as hostile and clamorous voices berated the United Nations and those who serve it. You bore these unjust attacks without flinching.[2]

A few months later the new secretary-general, Boutros-Ghali, spoke for the entire organization when he beamed that "[n]ever before has the United Nations been so popular with its member states. Never before have its services been requested with such frequency."[3]

The Secretariat bathed in the limelight and capitalized on every imaginable opportunity to reinforce the emerging conclusion that the Cold War provided an opening for both a more peaceful world and a rejuvenated UN whose purpose was to bring about that vision. The building was alive with activity and a new spirit, a sense that anything was possible and that everyone involved was part of a new global project. As Kofi Annan, who at the time was undersecretary general for peacekeeping, reflected on this period, "[W]e were all expectant. It was thrilling, and we saw possibilities of doing . . . what the organization was expected to do [in 1945]. So we were all excited."[4]

For once the UN was not merely a talk shop but a place of action. Whereas once the Security Council was a fairly moribund institution, now it had its hands full as it was becoming *the* forum to handle matters of international peace and security. During the Cold War it was not unusual for days to pass without a single session; now it was unusual if the Security

Council did not have both morning and afternoon sessions. The eruption of peacekeeping operations was the most visible indicator of this new activism. The Security Council established a total of thirteen operations between 1945 and 1988, and then authorized that same number in the next three years; in short, the UN had taken on as much in three and a half years as it had in the previous forty. With more operations there was an unprecedented number of peacekeepers. Whereas in 1978 there were only 9,700 peacekeepers, by 1994 there were over 73,000 peacekeepers in seventeen UN operations (with an additional 21,000 in the U.S.-led Haiti operation). The peacekeeping budget rose eightfold between 1988 and 1992 and then doubled in the next two years. This organizational expansion was breathtaking in its speed and scale.

Perhaps more impressive than the expanding numbers of peacekeepers were the expanding responsibilities and activities being entrusted to them. Many of the operations resembled the "classic" prototype—a lightly armed interpositioning force stationed on a border between two states to monitor a cease-fire or peace treaty. But an increasing number were situated in highly unstable environments, where a cease-fire was barely in place if at all, where governmental institutions were frayed and in need of repair, where there were roving armies that were not parties to the agreement, and where the UN was charged with multidimensional and complex tasks designed to heal deeply divided societies.

The real breakthrough in peacekeeping operations occurred with the Namibian operation in 1988. What was expected to be an already challenging monitoring operation burgeoned into an ambitious multidimensional exercise, with the UN unexpectedly playing a leading role in areas as wide-ranging as monitoring the disengagement of forces and the return of refugees. The El Salvador operation, which began in 1991, allowed the UN to display more acumen and skills in every step of the peace-building process, from the actual negotiations for the peace treaty to the running of the elections. The operation in Cambodia from 1992 to 1993 represented another developmental milestone, for the UN Transitional Authority in Cambodia became the governing body of the country as it executed an exceedingly complex, expensive, and dangerous transition process. Interventions in Bosnia, Somalia, and Haiti opened new chapters in the UN's enforcement operations. The UN's distinctive instrument for peace and security, peacekeeping, became part of most blueprints for the future world order and was deployed to more and more places in the world. Blue helmets were the iconography of the day.

But peacekeeping was not a value-neutral activity. In order to make sure that these failed states were healed, that the fallen from the international community were saved and redeemed, peacekeeping turned into a peace-building project to create stable, legitimate, and democratic states. The end of a peacekeeping operation was signaled by a "free and fair election." Holding and monitoring an election was not merely a technical activity but was viewed as the instillation of new norms and values. Many of these operations had a human rights module, and UN human rights monitors were expected not only to monitor and prevent the violation of human rights but also to teach political authorities the need to value and respect human rights principles, to honor democratic practices even when they believed they would not get caught if they failed to do so. Because in these conflict-ridden countries the public security apparatus was not a neutral enforcer of law and order but rather a repressive arm, the peace-building process included developing independent judiciaries and training new civilian police that would protect and not harm the community. These peacekeeping and peace-building operations were nothing short of nation-building by another name.

After its long period of inactivity, the UN was not prepared for the tasks assigned to it. Certainly the UN did not have the bureaucratic and administrative muscle to carry out everything it was asked to do. Although the UN is renowned for being overly bureaucratized, the Department of Peacekeeping Operations (DPKO) was shockingly malnourished. In October 1989 DPKO had a staff of only nine, six civilians and three military advisers, which was woefully insufficient, but managed to oversee eight thousand soldiers in five highly stable operations. Quite understandable given DPKO's skeletal staff, the post-1989 explosion pressed DPKO to the brink, forcing it to keep pace as best it could and to improvise wherever it could and whenever it must (which was nearly everywhere and always).

Member states were sympathetic to DPKO's plight and pleas for more staff, and by 1993 its personnel had expanded sixfold. But this still meant that there were only fifty civilians and military officers to oversee its two dozen operations and seventy thousand peacekeepers in conflict-ridden environments. Even though member states agreed that the situation was shameful and that DPKO's performance was nearly miraculous given its bureaucratic straits, a tight-fisted constituency refused to appropriate the funds for the badly needed personnel. DPKO demonstrated a remarkable ability to move quickly up a very steep learning curve, but the shortage of qualified staff meant that it was always struggling to keep pace with the excruciating workload.

Advance planning for future operations reflected the threadbare bureaucratic situation. Rare was the advance team that had more than a working knowledge of the conflict. The reconnaissance team sent by DPKO to

Croatia in late 1991 to determine the facts on the ground and the possibility of an operation consisted of "two men in a jeep," neither of whom was a Yugoslav expert.[5] If only Croatia were the odd exception and not the rule. No one thought that this was an ideal situation, but there was no point in clinging to ideals because there was no alternative. Assessment missions had to be run, and they could only be run with the available staff and expertise that could be mustered on short notice. While those undertaking these missions typically departed with real doubts about their capacity to assess the feasibility of an operation in places that they barely knew, they returned brimming with confident suggestions and recommendations. Being charged with the mission and spending even a short time in the field was all that was needed to transform any self-doubts into the assuredness expected of an expert.

The UN began to undertake substantial reforms to correct these obvious shortcomings. Modernizing the Secretariat for peacekeeping meant not only organizational expansion but also reorganization. Peacekeepers were performing new activities and confronting new situations, and the bureaucratic structure had to change with the times. Until 1993 there was no "situation room," with the very dire implication that if a field commander got into trouble over the weekend, there literally was no one to reach at the UN headquarters in New York. As UN Protection Force (UNPROFOR) Commander Lewis McKenzie once controversially exclaimed, "If you are a commander of a UN mission, don't get in trouble after five P.M. or on the weekend. There is no one in the UN to answer the phone!"[6] Soon after that statement was made, the UN created a situation room. Compared to the situation rooms in most states, it was almost comically outfitted: 1950s fake wood paneling, makeshift maps on the wall, an array of phones sitting on top of mismatched desks, and a few, scattered fax machines. It looked more like the accommodations for a public-access television station than it did the military nerve center for very tenuous peacekeeping operations. Still, this was a vast improvement over what had been.

In addition, the UN created new departments reflecting its new responsibilities. It was now overseeing humanitarian operations, so it created the Department of Humanitarian Affairs. It was now running elections and giving technical assistance throughout the world, so it created the Electoral Assistance Unit. And it was now using civilian police in greater numbers, so it created the Civilian Police Unit.

New organizational charts were constructed to organize these new units. The expansion of DPKO, the growing number of personnel, and the addition of new activities that blurred the distinction between political, peacekeeping, and humanitarian affairs necessitated the development of new hierarchies, divisions of responsibilities, and decision-making processes. Although it was possible to sit down with paper and pen and draw a coherent organizational chart, what was reproduced on paper bore little resemblance to practice, which itself was an ever-changing reality. And while these units might have been represented on the same piece of paper and as part of the same mission, coordination was haphazard at best and undermined by petty bureaucratic jealousies.

After having been relegated to the sidelines for so long, the UN conveyed the image of a weekend warrior showing its rust in the heat of battle. To be sure, member states were directly and indirectly responsible for a good portion of the UN's shortcomings in the field. They were incredibly cheap. The UN's always-troubling financial situation teetered at the point of bankruptcy in the early 1990s, and secretaries-general and independent commissions pleaded with member states to give the UN the resources it needed to carry out its increasingly heavy responsibilities. Until that fanciful day arrived, the UN indulged in creative accounting, juggling the books and transferring funds from one account to another to pay the next overdue bill. States were certainly troubled by this financial situation, but not as troubled as they were by the prospect of increasing their contributions to the UN.

Adding to the UN's woes, the council was approving one operation after another, appearing as if it had never met an operation it did not like. And many of these operations had practically unworkable mandates. Consider Bosnia. The secretary-general certainly did not seek to expand UNPROFOR to include Bosnia. In 1992 Boutros-Ghali begged the council not to dump this problem into the UN's lap; after all, if the muscular Great Powers could not fix Yugoslavia, then certainly a resource-strapped and army-less UN could hardly do any better. But the Security Council imposed the mandate on the UN and made one compromising decision after another. The result was a string of contradictory resolutions, around eighty in total by the end of UNPROFOR, that almost always pledged strong action but delivered little but false promises to the peacekeepers and the people on the ground. Although the UN certainly could not be blamed for the unraveling of Yugoslavia and the Bosnian conflict, once it had the mandate, it quickly became a scapegoat for the failures of member states, an outcome the Great Powers certainly enjoyed and probably wanted.

The initial stories of peacekeepers taking up positions in some of the world's hot spots were almost always coated in heroic language, but soon thereafter the soft-focus images began to become more ragged as the underside of peacekeeping became exposed. Although these forces might have been smartly outfitted, the fact was that they were composed of troops of varying qualities that were slapped together without any training. The media began to portray these operations as something between a well-oiled military machine and the Keystone Kops. Newspapers were running more and more critical stories about UN operations, many of which had a sensationalistic quality—peacekeepers frequenting brothels, beating up locals, smuggling exotic animals. Although member states were largely responsible for the conduct of their contingents in the field (the UN had no mechanism to either send back the unfit or discipline the offender), each story contributed to a growing sense that the UN was not fit to do the job.

Member states could not be blamed for all the failures in the field. The UN was overly bureaucratic and built to stay that way. Officials worried that the UN's possible contribution to security was being undone by a Rube Goldberg–like bureaucratic structure that could waylay the simplest to the most urgent request. The UN was organized around diplomatic time and had a bureaucracy that was almost pre-modern in form. It was used to making decisions based on shallow reports and in lengthy, time-consuming plenary sessions. Its own bureaucratic pace could not keep up with the demands of military operations. Rather than have the former adjust to the latter, however, the Secretariat would passively force essential features of military operations to adjust to its more leisurely style. Admiral Jonathan Howe, the secretary-general's special representative in Somalia, discovered to his horror in late December 1993 that a radio transmitter he had requested several months before, a transmitter that he deemed vital to countering the poisonous propaganda being spread by General Mohamed Farah Aideed, was still sitting on a bureaucrat's desk waiting for a signature. But this was the UN.

By mid-1993 these front-page failures and closed-door defects were amassing into an indictment of the UN as an institution and of its activities, or at least a reconsideration of its possible contribution to international peace and security for the foreseeable future. Not even the relatively successful elections in Cambodia in spring 1993 could dilute the growing censures and critiques. In his first address to the UN General Assembly, in September 1993, President Bill Clinton pledged his support to the UN but then proceeded to push hard for reform, to warn the Security Council that it would have to learn to say no to peacekeeping if the American people were going to say yes, and to propose some basic criteria that the Security Council employ as it considered whether or not to authorize an operation. Certainly many in the audience objected to the blatant hypocrisy; after all, this messenger just happened to be the most powerful member of the Security Council that was authorizing these operations. But they silently acknowledged the kernels of truth. Similar messages delivered by other heads-of-state were digested more easily because these messengers were not viewed as part of the problem. One Canadian official with an extensive peacekeeping background noted that the UN was now stretched so thin and its financial situation was so precarious that it could not provide the required military and political direction.[7] If the UN could not handle the many tasks or the new challenges, then perhaps the best thing for all concerned was to reduce the caseload and scale back the ambitions.

And then came Somalia. The background to this saga, which would come to dislodge the promise of the UN and bear down hard on Rwanda, can be told briefly. Ever since the late 1980s, there had been a bitter power struggle in Somalia. At the outset the contest was between the Ethiopian-funded Somali National Movement (SNM) and the Somali government of Siad Barre. The conflict took a violent turn in 1988 when the SNM launched a guerrilla war against Barre. An increasingly unpopular Barre began to retaliate severely and indiscriminately, and fairly soon after there emerged different clan-based militias vying for power. The greatest military threat, however, came from General Aideed, and by mid-1991 his forces overthrew the Siad Barre government. The result was a power vacuum and the devolution of political control to the local level. Aideed immediately claimed that he was the heir apparent in Somalia, a claim that did not sit well with his rivals. Any hope of a political breakthrough was quickly shattered by the reality of warfare between rival clans, whose sole accomplishments were the destruction of most urban centers, the collapse of all political institutions, a stagnating economy, at least twenty thousand civilian casualties, a million displaced people, and the specter of mass starvation. The scenes were gruesome and apocalyptic.

Into this Mad Max–like environment rushed various nongovernmental organizations, which attempted to alleviate the suffering and distribute food, and in, too, stepped the UN, which began to sound out the possibility of a negotiated settlement. From here on, a cycle developed where civil war led to more famine, which led to greater involvement by the Security Council, which had no visible impact on containing the civil war or halting the famine, which led to more Security Council involvement, and so on. The Security Council's first foray was Resolution 704, which passed on April 24, 1992. This resolution established the United Nations Operation in Somalia (UNOSOM) and called for the immediate dispatch of fifty unarmed military observers to monitor the tenuous cease-fire and the future deployment of five hundred observers for the same purpose. By mid-1992 the civil war was still raging, and there was a distinct possibility of widespread famine that placed at risk nearly one million children and another four and half million people. This dire humanitarian emergency spurred the

Security Council to pass Resolution 767 in July 1992, which called for an emergency airlift of food and medical supplies and five hundred peacekeepers to secure the ports, guard the food supplies, and protect the humanitarian aid workers. The United States contributed to the cause with Operation Provide Relief. Although the food was arriving, it was not getting to the people; militias began hijacking the food supplies, using the booty to bolster their political power and to purchase arms. In response, in August the Security Council increased the number of peacekeepers from five hundred to five thousand. Security Council resolutions alone could not stop the famine, however. By the fall of 1992 the two-year death toll had risen to five hundred thousand, and there were very grim predictions for the future. The humanitarian relief that was supposed to feed the hungry instead was being used by militias to fund their civil war, and there was little that the out-manned peacekeepers could do.

The three-way picture of starving Somalis, well-fed, khat-chewing youngsters in jeeps fitted with machine guns, and impotent peacekeepers was a horrific spectacle. The situation was clearly untenable. Discussions began in Washington and New York about a hammer-like operation that would defeat the militias and distribute the relief. The United States finally warmed to the idea of leading a humanitarian intervention by mid-November, and on December 3 the Security Council passed Resolution 794 requesting a "member state" to lead an international task force into Somalia for the purposes of humanitarian relief. This force was not to be a UN one but rather a UN-sanctioned operation. The following day President Bush announced to the American public that American forces would be used to feed the starving Somalis. The U.S.-led United Task Force (UNITAF) was born. Its relationship to UNOSOM was never made clear, though it was expected that UNITAF would hand over its responsibilities and duties to a reinforced UNOSOM II by mid-January (in fact, it was not until mid-March that the Security Council authored the transition resolution, and it was not until May 4 that the first peacekeeping troops were deployed; the United States left four thousand soldiers in UNOSOM II).

The initial made-for-television show in December 1992 of American forces landing on the beaches of Mogadishu to blinding camera lights settled down to the more mundane but essential task of distributing aid. Once this task was well under way, the UN and the United States contemplated how to erase the political roots of the humanitarian crisis, to make sure that, in the oft-heard phrase at the time, the international community was not laboring to feed Somalis one day so that they could starve the next. The key issues here were the need to create a workable political settlement and to disarm the militias. Fairly soon, rather ambitious plans amassed and the

UN became involved in a "nation-building" project, running reconciliation conferences, sponsoring rebuilding efforts, developing plans to transform the justice system, and on and on. The United States and Boutros-Ghali, however, had very different ideas about what role the American military should play in disarmament. Boutros-Ghali was adamant that the militias must be disarmed, if not voluntarily, then by force, and the U.S. military was perfect for the job. The Americans consistently rebuffed Boutros-Ghali's plans and stated publicly and privately that American forces would not be collecting weapons without the consent of the parties.

The UN's intervention did not sit well with Aideed, who believed that Boutros-Ghali had grand designs on Somalia and was intent on keeping him out of power. So, Aideed opposed the UN-sponsored peace process and then felt increasingly marginalized and angry as it continued without him. Aideed began to lash out at the UN with aggressive radio broadcasts and confrontational military maneuvers, and the UN gave little ground. The running tension exploded on June 5, 1993, when Aideed's forces ambushed and killed twenty-four Pakistani peacekeepers. Two days later, in a quickly called Sunday session, the Security Council, with the United States' firm support, hurriedly passed a resolution that called for "all necessary measures" to be used to apprehend and punish those responsible for the attacks. Aideed had now become Public Enemy Number One. UNOSOM trained its energies on capturing Aideed (and placed a bounty on his head).

Over the summer most news spilling out of Somalia concerned the mounting casualties on all sides, which was leading to a growing unease in Washington and elsewhere that UNOSOM was dangerously off track. Presciently, on September 20 Secretary of State Warren Christopher communicated the United States' disquiet to a visibly unmoved Boutros-Ghali. Five days later, Boutros-Ghali wrote to Christopher predicting that the mission would fail "unless we can disarm the clans and factions," essentially arguing that the problem was not too much force but too little of it. The same day that Boutros-Ghali wrote his letter to Christopher, an American helicopter was shot down, killing three Americans. Congress demanded to know what was happening, Democratic Senator Sam Nunn openly called for the American withdrawal from Somalia, and some in the administration were favoring Nunn's recommendation.

The tragic culmination of these developments occurred on October 3. In another attempt to capture several top leaders of the Somali National Alliance (SNA), U.S. forces stormed the Olympia Hotel. The beginning of the operation went relatively smoothly as the Rangers apprehended several ranking members, but events quickly soured when they tried to leave the area. They were immediately surrounded by an SNA counterattack, and hundreds of other Somalis jumped at the opportunity to fire on the much-resented Americans. By the end of the day two American helicopters had been shot down, eighteen American soldiers had been killed and seventy-eight wounded, and somewhere between five hundred and one thousand Somalis were either dead or wounded. This day also produced the defining images of the American presence: one dead American soldier being dragged through the streets of Mogadishu while throngs of Somalis cheered wildly and hurled insults and threats against the United States and the UN, and another soldier, visibly shaken and badly bruised, being held hostage by Aideed. For those Americans whose last memory was of U.S. soldiers delivering desperately needed food to grateful Somalis, this was a jolting change. As caustically remarked by Republican Senator Phil Gramm, "The people who are dragging around the bodies of Americans don't look very hungry to the people of Texas."[8]

The events of Mogadishu reverberated around the world and sent Washington into an apoplectic frenzy. The criticisms hurled at Clinton's foreign policy and the UN were many and coming from both sides of the aisle, though longtime Republican critics seemed to take almost perverse pleasure in the tragedy because of the opportunity it gave them to pounce on Clinton. This sort of crisis was expected from a president who had little experience or interest in foreign policy, who had entrusted the nation's foreign policy to holdovers from the Carter administration, and who was incapable of distinguishing vital from peripheral interests. None should be shocked, either, to discover that Clinton, who showed little sympathy for the military, would recklessly endanger American soldiers for idealist projects. The critics also drew a direct line between the failures of the Clinton administration and the Napoleon-like ambitions of the secretary-general. Either by default or by design, the critics argued, Clinton had essentially given the UN carte blanche over the deployment of American soldiers. In an editorial, the *New York Times* asked, "What happens to American credibility when the secretary of state spells out the ground rules and the U.N. Secretary-General ignores them?"

For many in Congress who were already sounding the increasingly popular, post–Cold War theme of unilateralism and isolationism, watching Americans die in Somalia for some misguided UN nation-building project only reinforced their firmly held views. From far and wide came solutions to these perceived omissions and excesses. They generally began with the immediate withdrawal of U.S. forces from Somalia and the prohibition of American personnel from serving in UN operations, continued with the demand for a reduction of U.S. support for a downsized UN, and ended with a hue and cry about the need for Congress to wrest control of U.S. foreign policy from an irresponsible and idealistic Clinton administration.

Clinton was unprepared for the political fallout, which came fast and furious. Unlike previous presidents who found their stature rise with an international crisis, a public opinion–sensitive Clinton, who was elected to take care of business at home, had to watch the public's disapproval of his handling of foreign policy rise from 32 percent to 52 percent and find that foreign policy was threatening his domestic agenda. Desperately wanting to stop the political hemorrhaging, he was caught in a political bind because the truth was no tourniquet. The truth was that the Rangers in Somalia had been under American command-and-control; that American officials had been increasingly uneasy about the violent turn associated with the "get Aideed" policy; that because they could not decide on the proper course of action, they allowed the present policy to drift toward the tragedy; and that at no time did Washington communicate to its forces to halt its hunt for Aideed. Careful observers of American policy toward Somalia knew this much at the time.

But for Clinton to state all this would have required him to take responsibility for the tragedy. He never seriously entertained that possibility. Yet neither could he completely deny any role without lending support to the claim that he had handed American policy toward Somalia and American troops over to Boutros-Ghali. At first he let his top foreign policy advisers do his talking for him. They marched up to Congress to explain American policy on Somalia, but were remarkably inarticulate in the face of a hostile crowd. The result was that the lions were further riled and more convinced than ever that Clinton's policy was confused and disjointed. There was now the very real possibility that Congress might pass a resolution demanding the immediate withdrawal of American forces from Somalia, and handing the young president a major foreign policy humiliation.

For the next two days the Clinton team debated several options, including a massive deployment to wipe out Aideed and an immediate withdrawal, but in the end decided to steer a middle course between retreat and continued involvement. On October 7 Clinton announced in a speech that he would send reinforcements of fifty-three hundred troops to Somalia, widen the search for a political solution, and withdraw all American forces by March 31, 1994. This policy was designed to give the UN time to find replacements, to signal that the UN was committed to a political solution and would abandon its confrontational line, and to ensure that American forces were as protected and quarantined as possible. The speech was memorable not only for the announced policy shift but also for the language used to justify that shift. With liberal use of the passive voice and a description of decisions that apparently were made by no one, Clinton managed to observe that the Somali operation had gone dangerously off course over the last several months but conveniently forgot that the United States was directly responsible for this "get Aideed" policy and that American forces were under U.S. command. The speech, in this crucial respect, was crafted carefully to deflect criticism from him and redirect it toward the UN. Indeed, statements like, "[T]hese [post–October 3] forces will be under U.S. Command," delivered in an accusatorial and angry tone, were calculated to leave the impression that the UN was responsible for the recent loss of American life.[9] The UN was a scapegoat.

Although Clinton hoped that this policy shift and these incriminating statements would soothe the critics, they did little of the sort. Those in Congress who believed that the UN was somehow connected to the American deaths now had indirect evidence, which only fueled the fire. Responding to the insults hurled by Congress at "dummies at the UN" and a Boutros-Ghali who was portrayed as intent on carrying out his personal vendetta against Aideed, Joe Sills, Boutros-Ghali's spokesperson, shot back: "This practice of insulting the competence of the UN is not to anyone's benefit. Name-calling and asking who's to blame is not going to help very much."[10] Those who believed that Clinton and his contradictory Somali policies were to blame were unconvinced by his vaguely worded denial.[11] Boutros-Ghali did not make Clinton's life any easier. When asked to respond to the criticisms being leveled by administration officials in Washington at the UN, he would respond with comments like, "If it helps the Americans solve their problems by blaming me, I'll be a scapegoat."[12] By the end of the crisis the three-way exchange of accusations between Clinton, Congress, and the UN had produced a highly noxious atmosphere.

It is virtually impossible to exaggerate the impact of Somalia on the UN. *Somalia* was no longer a place name but was now a moment and a warning. *Somalia* could have any number of meanings, and none of them were flattering. *Somalia* could be a code word for the hypocrisy of the Great Powers who are willing to make the UN the fall guy. *Somalia* could refer to what happens when good intentions are corrupted by unchecked ambitions, or "mission creep." *Somalia* could mean the need for the UN to get back to basics, to deploy peacekeepers only when there was a peace to keep and to decline the invitation to halt civil wars. What would later be dubbed the "shadow of Somalia" was omnipresent, casting a dark cloud across the headquarters, limiting the sight lines, and directing its future practices.

The political fireworks barely had begun to settle from Somalia when on October 11, officials in Washington and New York had to deal with yet another, highly visible reversal. This time the scene was closer to home, in Haiti. As part of the negotiated agreement to reinstall the democratically elected Jean-Bertrand Aristide and return the military to the barracks, a

UN technical team was to deploy to Haiti. But when the U.S.S. *Harlan County* approached the dock at Port-au-Prince, it was greeted by a motley group of armed individuals making threatening gestures at the vessel. Rather than force its way into port and risk a nautical version of Mogadishu, the *Harlan County* turned around. Visibly embarrassed by the spectacle of the American military being cowed by a rag-tag opposition, the Clinton administration defensively asserted that it was not in the peace enforcement business and that if the parties could not stick to their agreements, then the United States had no business being there. That was the painful lesson of Somalia, American officials claimed, and the United States was not going to make that mistake again. "We were not asked to come in there to make peace or to keep the peace," Clinton defensively remarked. But watching the mighty United States scamper in response to this almost comical display of force in its "own backyard" further angered the political Right and swelled domestic criticism of American foreign policy and multilateral operations.

Clinton's short-term response to Somalia and these other UN-associated setbacks quickly developed into a long-term strategy regarding how to continue to support UN operations in this more hostile environment. While claiming that it remained firmly committed to the view that the UN could further U.S. national interests, the Clinton administration cautioned that these more dangerous times demanded a more refined approach. The ambitious proposals and vitriolic statements that characterized the administration's policy during the first few months in office were ill-suited for the current climate and could engender even greater backlash against the UN. The administration's strategy was that the best way to preserve U.S. support for the UN was to halt the more far-reaching proposals to strengthen the UN; to demonstrate to a suspicious Congress that it too could be tough on the UN; and to limit the amount of energy the administration had to expend on Capitol Hill defending UN operations.

The administration downsized its vision of the future UN. Once Clinton had spoken approvingly of a standing army. Such statements were never to be repeated. Once U.S. Ambassador to the UN Madeleine Albright had spoken of assertive multilateralism and the need to inject more resources into the UN. Never again would she advocate such measures. Once the Clinton administration had proposed a host of reforms that were designed to expand the UN's scope and strength. Those plans were immediately shelved.

There was no greater sign of peacekeeping's changing fortunes than the debate over Policy Review Directive (PRD)-13, the United States' ongoing review of multilateral operations. In 1992 President Bush began an extensive internal review of U.S. support for peacekeeping, with the intention of creating a national and bureaucratic consensus for an expanded peacekeeping agenda. This review was still in process when Clinton entered office in January 1993, and his initial reaction was that Bush's lack of vision was as true for foreign policy as it was for domestic politics. Clinton wanted a more visionary and far-reaching plan. The review process sputtered and then stalled after the peacekeeping operation in Somalia collapsed. Months later a significantly more modest document emerged, one that closely resembled that initially drafted by the Bush administration (the final document, PDD-25, was signed in May 1994). The situation in Somalia caused Clinton to disassociate himself from any image of a more muscular UN.

The emerging private line during these increasingly troubled times was that the Clinton administration could best help the UN through a "tough love" strategy. Foreshadowing the triangulation policy that would become a hallmark of Clinton's political strategy, he claimed that he was an ally of Congress in its attempt to reform the UN and reduce its excesses, and an ally of the UN in its effort to convince an increasingly hostile Congress that the UN furthered international peace and security. This strategy began to emerge in small doses over the course of the summer of 1993 and in response to growing unease over UN operations. It was fully unveiled at Clinton's address to the UN General Assembly in late September. His message of "just say no" to peacekeeping was well received at home and in the press. And the events in Somalia gave Clinton no reason to break from this strategy. Clinton officials would justify this strategy in any number of ways: this was simply a bow to reality and the best that could be gotten given this Congress; one good friend, that is, the United States, has a responsibility to tell another good friend, that is, the UN, when it is in trouble; a more critical policy coupled with a more humble and reformed UN would save the institution from itself and its critics. These and other rationalizations could not conceal the fundamental fact that the administration had visibly shifted tone and policy toward the UN.

This tough love strategy would work only if the UN toed the line, which meant no more American casualties, no more operations that were either costly or unconnected to some conception of American national interests that could be sold to Congress, and a UN secretary-general who was more modest in ambitions, was more humble in presentation, and behaved more like a supplicant of the United States. An even more cost-conscious United States began to emerge, scrutinizing the bottom line on every peacekeeping operation and imagining how to cut even further already underfunded operations. Some American officials privately worried that this miserly approach would make it more difficult for the UN to carry out its mandated responsibilities. However, most concluded that Congress would not approve anything more, and asking it to do so would only give it another opportunity to place peacekeeping and the Clinton administration's foreign policy in its crosshairs. This was the new reality.

Not surprisingly, Washington's new approach was not well received at the UN. For UN officials, this tough love strategy appeared to be "blaming the victim." After all, this so-called good friend was highly responsible for its current plights in Somalia and Bosnia, and its "reform" largely revolved around cutting the budget and not giving the UN the resources it needed to carry out its nearly impossible tasks. No UN official was more indignant than a proud and supremely confident Boutros-Ghali. Annoyed that he was being asked to be the bag man for various "UN" failures that were properly blamed on member states, and dismissive of Washington's calculation that the best way to protect the UN was to keep it (and its secretary-general) far away from Congress, time and again he tried to convince leaders in Washington that they were hurting their own short- and long-term foreign policy interests. His didactic style, diplomacy as a private tutorial from the headmaster, increasingly irked Clinton officials, who did not appreciate being lectured that their foreign policy was short-sighted or hypocritical. The growing strains between the United States and the UN now had a personal dimension.

The UN-U.S. rivalry sometimes obscured how it was not one state bringing down the whole system but rather an entire system showing its shortcomings. States were handing the UN nearly impossible mandates, and too many of them, and then failing to provide the political and financial resources to carry them out.[13] States slowly were becoming engaged in a reform process that had identified areas of needed attention, including a fast track system for funding and deploying peacekeeping operations, clearer training procedures, greater attention to interoperability between forces, and on and on. But instead of action they delivered more meetings, an outcome that was not wholly unwelcome given that any reforms invariably imposed more costs and expectations on them. States also responded to failures in the field in a way that only compounded the UN's travails. Instead of identifying the many ways they contributed to the outcome, states tended to dump on and scapegoat the UN or overreacted to setbacks, in either case overlooking the UN's many peacekeeping successes. Alvaro de Soto, an adviser to Boutros-Ghali, once said that he would like to hang a sign above his desk that reads, "It's the member states, stupid."[14] Such quips might have been soothing, but they failed to recognize that a slowly moving and cumbersome Secretariat also bore some responsibility for these problems.

While there were strong differences of opinion over the root causes of the UN's recent failures, most officials in New York agreed that it was time to assess whether peacekeeping was unsafe at high speeds, what had become of peacekeeping, what had gone right, what had gone wrong, and why. As Albright liked to say at the time, everyone had to figure out when the UN was "effective when selected," which also meant being more selective.[15] The conversation in New York turned to three critical areas: enforcement, the meaning of neutrality and consent, and the conditions under which the Security Council would authorize an operation.

Enforcement was out. The Gulf War as well as the generally high spirits of the times led to an overly optimistic assessment of the utility and desirability of peace enforcement. The assessment failed to consider fully the dangers and complexities, including how to establish unified command-and-control, what the proper rules of engagement (ROEs) were, and whether there was solid political will and a sound resource base.[16] The shortcomings of Yugoslavia, Somalia, and Haiti introduced tremendous caution regarding the wisdom of Chapter VII operations that operated without the consent of the parties and introduced new concepts like "delegation" and "subcontracting." These new concepts strongly suggested that it would not be the UN but rather states and regional organizations acting under UN authorization that would do the enforcing.[17] Many in DPKO increasingly questioned whether enforcement was wise or what the UN was about. Even Boutros-Ghali tempered his initial zeal because of Somalia and Bosnia. Returning from a trip to Africa in October 1993, he said that his new message to African leaders was, "The United Nations cannot impose peace; the role of the United Nations is to maintain peace."[18] The UN was getting out of the war business.

The UN also repeated its vows of neutrality, impartiality, and consent. During the period of classic peacekeeping, when the consent of the parties was firm and the UN typically monitored an agreement that both parties desired, consent was automatic, neutrality was easily maintained, and impartiality was questioned only occasionally. The UN's foray into civil wars and humanitarian assistance, however, stretched its ability to maintain a neutral and impartial stance—and the very desirability of doing so. Consent could become a cowardly and dysfunctional shield that nearly transformed the UN into an unwitting accomplice to human rights violations and war crimes. The alternative was, if need be, to enforce the mandate without the parties' consent. Doing so, however, could sacrifice the UN's impartiality and embroil it in a military adventure that it neither wanted nor was capable of fighting. And if the UN departed from neutrality and became another combatant, then it might sacrifice its special standing in global politics, becoming just like a state but without the resources, and forfeiting its authority and influence.

With little experience in such matters and little time to carry out a lengthy debate, UN officials married pragmatism to established modalities to guide them through turbulent times and tricky predicaments in the field. Controversy followed. The archetypical debate was waged between Boutros-Ghali's view of how to implement the Somalian mandate and UNPROFOR General Michael Rose's view regarding how to implement the UNPROFOR mandate.

Boutros-Ghali insisted that the principle of consent was of little value in a country where there was no effective government, where warlords controlled the streets, obstructed the delivery of food, refused to participate in the process of national reconciliation, and fired upon UN forces carrying out their mandate. Insisting on consent was a futile exercise in this environment and gave armed extremists veto power over the future.

General Rose, and many others in Bosnia, held tightly to the principle of consent. The moment that the UN was no longer viewed as impartial and neutral, then it would compromise its very standing and ability to carry out central parts of the mandate. The principles of neutrality and consent in these war-ridden circumstances could leave the UN in the dangerous position of having to either bear witness to violations of the mandate and human rights abuses or be near-accomplices to them.

By late fall of 1993 UN officials largely agreed that the dangers of "Somalia" were greater than the dangers of "Bosnia," and therefore retreated to a more traditional view of consent and impartiality. Somalia was the transformative event, giving birth to a so-called "Mogadishu line," the dangerous tipping point where peacekeeping became peace enforcement and the UN found itself in over its head. Because peacekeepers could never be certain how close they were to the line, they ultimately kept at a safe distance. Reflecting on the experience of Somalia, DPKO head Kofi Annan said that "in these situations the impartiality of the force and the principle of consent of the parties are crucial. If you are perceived to be fair, you do not run the danger of being engaged. If you are seen as taking on initiatives that could change the military balance on the ground and favor one group or another, the troops who see themselves as disadvantaged might decide you've taken sides and declare war on you."[19] A blue-ribbon commission composed of longtime UN hands and mandated to investigate the deaths of the UN peacekeepers in Somalia urged the UN to return to its traditional principles of consent, neutrality, and impartiality. The former head of the Department of Humanitarian Affairs, Jan Eliason, spoke for many when he warned in late 1993 that the UN must "adhere strictly to the guiding principles of humanity, neutrality, and impartiality. Once those principles are compromised, our legitimacy and utility are at risk."[20] "Impartiality is the oxygen of peacekeeping," reflected DPKO official Sashi Tharoor.[21] And now an oxygen-starved UN was about to breathe a little easier.

The UN embarked on a search to devise a more rational and methodical set of criteria to determine whether or not to authorize a peacekeeping operation. Peacekeeping was not an elixir. It worked under highly limited circumstances and for limited objectives. An undiscriminating Security Council had established too many operations in inappropriate places, resulting in the corruption of peacekeeping. By mid-1993 it became determined to establish some collectively legitimated criteria to control its own trigger-happy tendencies. In many respects, the council was engaged in an act of self-binding. Recognizing that its own lack of self-control was potentially exploiting a scarce resource into near extinction, it attempted to save peacekeeping from itself by devising a set of rationalized criteria that could become the focal points for its discussions and ensure that it selected peacekeeping when it was the "right tool for the job."

In a meeting with Boutros-Ghali in September 1993, representatives of the five permanent members of the Security Council demanded a more careful review of peacekeeping operations, to ensure that demands did not exceed capabilities and that new commitments would be made only after "fundamental questions" were resolved, including the precise nature of the operation's objectives and its material and political foundations.[22] In his General Assembly address in September 1993, President Clinton explicitly referred to various criteria that were part of his administration's own review process. There was grudging but growing acceptance that some criteria were required, and Clinton's provided a good starting point.

The October 1993 events in Somalia kicked into high gear the Security Council's discussion, and by the end of the year it had largely agreed on the following criteria for authorizing peacekeeping operations: (1) when there is a genuine threat to peace and security, (2) when regional or subregional organizations can assist in resolving the situation, (3) when a cease-fire exists and the parties have committed themselves to a peace process, (4) when a clear political goal exists and is present in the mandate, (5) when a precise mandate can be formulated, and (6) when the safety of UN personnel can be reasonably assured.[23] There was no delusion that these criteria had completely and magically rationalized and depoliticized the decision-making process, but there was general agreement that they represented a marked improvement.

The Secretariat largely welcomed these developments. Although many UN staff feared that these rules might be applied to arrest rather than assist peacekeeping, not an unreasonable fear given that a more openly critical United States was leading the campaign to construct a standardized test, most were equally worried that the UN was about to perish from excessive use. DPKO chief Kofi Annan, for instance, said that "nobody would disagree with . . . the U.S. . . . when they say there should be some guidelines for the council to determine when they take on a crisis and when they do not—provided it's applied in a flexible and practical manner."[24] On another occasion, Annan summarized the lessons he had learned from recent experiences: "Peacekeeping works when you have a clear mandate, a will on the part of the people to make peace. The inspiration for acceptable and viable peace can only spring from the leaders and the people in the country."[25] Eliason vehemently argued for the establishment of firmer guidelines on the deployment of peacekeepers, particularly in situations of internal conflict and the use of force.[26] Boutros-Ghali "used to say that the UN, like a good doctor, could not say No when asked to intervene. He has now amended this. It will intervene, but only when the patient takes its advice."[27]

An end to enforcement, a reunion with traditional peacekeeping rules, and the articulation of a more restrictive set of conditions for peacekeeping significantly contracted the UN's aperture. The United States' "effective when selected" vision meant that the UN would be selected a lot less and only for situations that resembled classic peacekeeping. UN staff were increasingly of the view that the organization should "discreetly withdraw to its traditional, impartial role of tending sleepy, cease-fire lines in international conflicts."[28] In late 1993 de Soto said that the year's string of tragic events had caused many to rethink the activism championed by Boutros-Ghali, to call *An Agenda for Peace* "premature," and to confess that "we only realized all the ramifications of getting involved in internal conflicts fairly late in the game."[29] The overall drift was toward a UN much less likely to intervene in moments of domestic turmoil, even if that turmoil included a humanitarian crisis. These crises are by-products of wars, wars are defined by instability, and a modicum of stability is a precondition for effective peacekeeping. The UN could only be effective when there was a "peace to keep."

Moreover, whereas once the Security Council and the Secretariat routinely noted that it had a responsibility to help those who could not help themselves, they were now suggesting that they could only help those who were willing to help themselves. As Annan later wrote, "One can ask whether it is ethically sound for the international community to expend resources and political will coaxing recalcitrant parties into negotiations, or becoming involved prematurely on the ground, where there is little chance of compliance and prospects for success somewhere else are not as daunting."[30] The language that began to creep into nearly all Security Council statements as a consequence of what happened in Somalia was that an operation was justified only so long as the parties of the conflict demonstrated a resolve to work toward political progress. The Security Council, for instance, emphasized how "the people of Somalia bear the ultimate responsibility for achieving national reconciliation and for rebuilding their country."[31] In this world of triage, where resources and energy are limited, the UN must make tough choices regarding who will get its attention and who will not. There were good reasons for this stand. The UN, stretched thin and facing a nearly inexhaustible number of potential crises, had to decide who deserved its attention, and one reasonable criterion is the active support of those whom it is helping.

Yet the shift in discourse and the emergence of more discriminating rules also reflected a desire to preserve the UN's reputation, to expend scarce resources and to put its credibility on the line only when there was a reasonable chance of success. Many at the UN headquarters perceived this increasingly despondent period as fulfilling their long-standing fears. From the very moment the UN stepped into the spotlight, many high-ranking officials approached these new opportunities with equal parts excitement and trepidation. Secretary-General Pérez de Cuéllar openly worried that opportunities brought the chance for failure, and cautioned that member states and the international community can be very unforgiving when failure is realized. Early in his term, Boutros-Ghali anxiously confessed that the "problem is how we can maintain this credibility and how we will not deceive the member states and the public opinion when they will discover that maybe we have not been able to cope with all the problems they ask us."[32] There are such high expectations, we are being asked to do so much, he continued, and all these new tasks might lead to the UN's overexposure and failures in the field. "So the problem is how we will maintain our credibility," he concluded.[33] The UN's most dire predictions were coming true: failures tarnished the UN's credibility, which in turn jeopardized its future. In response, the emerging thinking among many top UN officials was that the UN should put its good name on the line only when it had a reasonable chance of success. The rules of peacekeeping certainly made this desirable outcome much more likely.

These rules, then, provided a screening device that enabled the UN to accept operations that had a reasonable chance of success and reject those that did not. Roughly translated, the UN was interested in picking "winners," those places that had stability on the ground, and avoiding "losers," those places where stability was absent and humanitarian nightmares were present. This development not only was a pragmatic recognition of the possible but also was justified by a principled defense of the UN. These pragmatic and principled responses subtly transformed the victims of humanitarian nightmares into a possible threat to the organization.

Helping those who could not help themselves could suffocate the organization. Unlike medical triage, where the awful choices are guided by the principle of expending scarce resources on those who have the greatest chance for survival, in this instance the UN was now denying care because of the same fear a doctor might have when seen in the vicinity of a dying patient—it might lose its license to practice. The desire by the UN decision makers in New York to pick winners and to avoid failures meant that the UN was as interested in its own security as it was in human security. This represented an important shift in the discourse of peacekeeping, as officials in and around the UN took greater care to protect the organization's interests, reputation, and future. These rules represented an epoxy that bound together the desire to help with the desire to defend the organization and its ideals. Rwanda was born in these uncertain times.

2

Rwanda through
Rose-Colored Glasses

Many post-1995 histories of Rwanda have two defining characteristics. One is that they are written from the vantage point of the genocide, selecting and connecting the events, developments, and processes that seemingly merged to bring it about. Like forensic psychiatrists attempting to understand the mind and the environmental forces that produced the serial killer, these histories attempt to unlock the complex interplay between morphological and situational factors, the overbearing structures and the conjoining of chance events that produced this rare but deadly occurrence. The other characteristic is that they are written with an eye to correct what are seen as egregious misconceptions of the country's politics and history. These misconceptions were advanced by the media's coverage of the genocide or were pressing upon policymakers and causing them to arrive at mistaken understandings and to make misinformed decisions.

At the top of the list of misunderstandings to be corrected is the status of the "Hutus" and "Tutsis." During the genocide the popular press frequently referred to them as tribes. This was Africa, after all. But as many specialists have pointed out, these groups had none of the sociological, linguistic, or political characteristics of tribes. At the time, the more accurate writers described them as ethnic groups (but oftentimes used *tribes* and *ethnic groups* interchangeably and in the same story). Yet even these descriptions introduced a distortion, because they nearly always portrayed the groups as originating from distinct gene pools, whose characteristics were primordial and whose boundaries were fixed and sacrosanct. To illustrate the existence of these biological boundaries, many reports noted how these ethnic groups have distinct physical characteristics: the Hutus are short and squat and have Negroid facial features, while the Tutsis are tall and lean and possess angular facial features.

Specialists have gone to great lengths to correct these grossly inaccurate characterizations of the origins of these ethnic boundaries.[1] Far from descending from primordial roots, these two groups represent categories that have been socially constructed by a complex interplay of culture, politics, and economics. Those who are now in one category or the other can thank not their genes but rather the fluid mix of social processes that created and then institutionalized the separate identities. It might be that a group called the Tutsis descended from the north centuries ago, but it is not as if those who are now labeled Tutsis can trace their ancestral lineage to individuals who were part of that original trek or are absent "Hutu" ancestry. Racial profiling is a misleading predictor of ethnic identity, even if Rwandans themselves use these same physical markers to determine the ethnic identity of an individual. In fact, during the genocide Hutus were mistakenly killed because they had "Tutsi" features, and Tutsis were able to pass for Hutu because they had stereotypical "Hutu" features. As the sociologist W. I. Thomas noted, if objects are perceived as real, they will be real in their consequences.

The ethnic categories of Hutu and Tutsi predated colonialism, but without the same meanings or boundaries that they came to possess with colonialism. It was colonialism that institutionalized ethnicity and infused it with a perverse and distorted "scientific" belief system that naturalized the Tutsi destiny to rule over the majority Hutus. European rule descended on Rwanda in 1894, a century before the genocide, when a German count informed the king of Rwanda that Germany now controlled East Africa, including Rwanda. Germany ruled Rwanda and Burundi until 1916 (it was actually one administrative territory, called Ruanda-Urundi, and Rwanda was awarded a special status as an indirectly ruled kingdom), but lost its colonial possessions when it lost World War I.

Belgium took over where Germany left off, reinforcing and then solidifying Tutsi rule. In the late 1920s Belgium reformed the political system in a way that furthered the minority's grip on power. While the enthronement of minority rule was consistent with and had many of the same effects as a divide-and-rule policy, Belgium's sponsorship of Tutsi mastery was legitimated by its racist ideas about who was fit for rule. These ideas formed a "Hamitic hypothesis," derived from racist theories of evolution that purported to explain what Europeans perceived as pockets of "civilization" in "Black" Africa. In the evolutionary theory that was fashionable in Europe at the time, the belief was that the genetically superior Caucasians sat at the very top of the ladder and that other peoples could be ranked in descending order based on how closely they resembled Caucasian peoples in physical and morphological structure and the artifacts they produced. The signs of "civilization" in sub-Saharan Africa, the Europeans concluded, probably were created by a superior, "Caucasoid" race that had migrated from northern Africa. Because the Tutsis were perceived to have Caucasian features, the Belgians deemed them a superior people who were naturally superior to the less-evolved Hutus, and conferred on them ideological, political, and economic status. Being exemplary colonial administrators, the Belgians undertook an exhaustive census in 1933, used physical characteristics to determine who was a Hutu and who was a Tutsi, and then handed each person an identity card that fixed once and for all their ethnic calling. This "scientific" classification and its political institutionalization had a profound effect on Rwandan culture. Decades of such messages coming from all parts of society produced an indelible "reality" of Tutsi superiority and Hutu inferiority.

Although popular images of "tribal" and "ethnic" politics in Africa suggest a never-ending cycle of violence and warfare, the Hutus and Tutsis managed to exist relatively free of mass violence—until colonialism. At the time of the genocide, the popular media and many ranking decision makers portrayed the violence as the latest and bloodiest installment in a centuries-old pattern, an inevitable by-product of two rival ethnic groups crowded into the same, small geographic space and forced to compete over scarce resources and for power. Although Rwanda was no Rousseauean democracy, there is no evidence that the long-standing ethnic divisions degenerated into ethnic violence.[2] Instead, the coupling of ethnicity and violence is due largely to a colonization process that introduced myths of a superior race coming from the north to conquer an inferior native population (which in gross terms led to a feeling of entitlement and superiority among the Tutsis and a massive inferiority complex among the majority Hutu); and that institutionalized an ethnocracy.

Decolonization gave the Hutus the first opportunity to seek power and take revenge on the Tutsis. Beginning in 1947 the UN Trusteeship Council visited Rwanda on several occasions and produced a series of documents that were increasingly scathing toward Belgian rule and insistent that Rwanda should be given independence. As independence loomed, a central issue concerned its future constitutional fabric and relations between the majority Hutus and minority Tutsis. Views regarding the desirability of a democratic Rwanda predictably fell along ethnic lines. The Hutu population demanded majority rule and found the trope of democracy a convenient device to justify their bid for power. The Tutsis worried that "democracy" without "rights" would leave them impoverished and at the mercy of the Hutus. In anticipation of another UN site visit, a group of Hutus issued a proclamation demanding majority rule. This act triggered an intensification of the struggle for independence and ethnic rivalry.

In what came to be known as the "Hutu Revolution," from 1959 to 1961, a series of violent outbreaks convulsed Rwanda and resulted in the diminution of Tutsi political power, the flight of nearly 120,000 Tutsis to neighboring countries, and a rigidification of ethnic boundaries. Belgium responded to this political unrest and to a 1959 UN resolution calling for decolonization by switching to the Hutus' side and setting 1962 as the year for Rwandan independence. Elections were held in September 1961. Led by Grégoire Kayibanda's Parmehutu Party, Hutu-dominated parties won the vast majority of seats and stood on the cusp of taking political power.

When Rwanda achieved independence on July 1, 1962, it completed a stunning revolution in its external and internal relations. The mythologies that had legitimated Tutsi rule were now inverted like a photographic negative. The new mythology was that "foreign invaders" had descended from the north to impose an aristocratic dictatorship on the native peasantry. The majority Hutus now controlled political power, inferiority complex and all, and the newly installed President Kayibanda was more than willing to use ethnic terror and sow divisions to maintain his rule. A stunningly perceptive and prophetic 1961 UN Trusteeship Council report stated, "The developments of these last 18 months have brought about the racial dictatorship of one party. . . . An oppressive system has been replaced by another one. . . . It is quite possible that some day we will witness violent reactions against the Tutsi."[3]

Ethnic violence now became a central feature of Rwanda's politics. The Tutsi refugees in Uganda attacked the Hutu population and government, and the Rwandan government retaliated against the Tutsis, whom they gave the derogatory name of Inyenzi ("cockroach"). In November 1963 the Tutsis launched a series of border raids. The following month the government brutally responded, leaving anywhere from ten to twenty thousand Tutsis dead and nearly three hundred thousand in exile. The sheer scale and scope of the Rwandan government's campaign awoke a generally complacent international community. Although the accusations of genocide did not stick, for a time the world's attention was fixated on violence that compelled Lord Bertrand Russell to make comparisons to the Holocaust.[4] Ethnic violence remained a feature of Rwandan life over the next several years, though it never reached these levels.

In 1973 Major General Juvénal Habyarimana, a French-speaking Hutu from the north, took power in a military coup. The precipitating event was the 1972 ethnic violence in neighboring Burundi (which had a similar demographic breakdown between Hutus and Tutsis but where the Tutsis continued to hold political power). Political disturbances in Burundi quickly inflamed and left roughly two hundred thousand dead and an equal number of Hutus spilling into neighboring Rwanda in search of safety. President Kayibanda attempted to exploit the tragedy for political gain, began to move against the Tutsi minority in Rwanda, and asked Habyarimana to lead the campaign. Claiming that the counterinsurgency was too soft, Habyarimana turned his gun against the president. But instead of lowering the hammer against the minority, he essentially offered the Tutsis a deal: if they stayed out of politics, they could have a reasonably normal existence. The Tutsi minority now found itself guaranteed relative security if it "stayed in its place."

Habyarimana quickly consolidated his power. In 1975 he declared that Rwanda was officially a single-party state and that everyone belonged to the National Revolutionary Movement for Development (MRND). Habyarimana further reorganized political life and centralized his control using all means at his disposal, including the bureaucracy, the party, the church, and the military. Soon there developed a tight patronage system. Behind these institutional trappings and informal networks resided the *akazu*, the heart of the power structure, which translates literally as "little house." This tightly knit corpus included President Habyarimana and his wife's family and retinue.

Habyarimana's reign was noteworthy not only for its political stability produced by an iron glove but also by the upturn in Rwanda's development prospects. Even though it remained desperately poor, Rwanda earned a reputation of being a success story, in part because it was finally demonstrating some economic development in a region that was sadly lacking in any good news. One-party stability, the dampening of ethnic conflict, and modest economic progress invested Rwanda with a reputation for stability and hope. Outsiders routinely touted Rwanda as a model of efficiency and referred to it as the Switzerland of Central Africa.

Beginning in the late 1980s a series of reinforcing events bore down on the Habyarimana government and challenged its rule. First, Rwanda's economy worsened dramatically. Although it grew at a reasonable rate between the mid-1970s and the late 1980s, the dangers of dependence on a single export, coffee, became realized in the late 1980s when the combination of a drought and a decrease in international demand left Rwanda with a heavy debt burden. International financial institutions now flocked to Kigali to provide assistance and structural adjustment advice, finding in

Rwanda a relatively sophisticated administrative structure and a willing government that might be capable of implementing the reforms they proposed. This was hardly a "failed state," as observers at the time of the genocide described Rwanda.

Even though it was in the midst of an economic downward spiral, fighting a civil war, and attempting to house nearly three hundred thousand displaced people, Rwanda swallowed the economic medicine in slow but steady doses (managing to use some of the aid to buy weapons). The development industry's failure to incorporate the political variables that might complicate its economic models was also evident in its almost complete neglect of the worsening human rights situation. Sometimes there was talk about aid conditionality and "good governance," but for the most part it was business as usual.[5]

More immediately threatening to the Habyarimana regime were the societal pressures demanding political liberalization after nearly two decades of single-party rule, pressures that were receiving support from a post–Cold War wave of democratization. Because of external and internal demands, in July 1990 Habyarimana convened a national commission to explore solutions to the political crisis. Two months later the commission delivered its response: multiparty democracy. Although Habyarimana had little interest in devolving power, by June 1991 he yielded to the pressure and permitted multiple political parties. Within a few months, more than fifteen parties had registered, representing a span of political and ethnic positions, the most important of which was the Democratic Republican Movement (MDR), the chief opposition party.

Every action engenders a counterreaction, and the political liberalization led to reactionary moves by the ruling guard. The MRND transformed one of its youth groups into a militia and named it the Interahamwe, which literally means "those who go together." The Presidential Guard became increasingly agitated by the specter of sharing power and giving political voice to the Tutsis. In March 1992, yet another political party formed, the Committee for the Defense of the Republic (CDR). This radical, racist, Hutu party to the right of the MRND had the goal of keeping the Tutsis at bay. Its followers spewed the most vile anti-Tutsi propaganda and eventually staffed the infamous Mille Collines Radio that agitated for genocide. Increasingly audible were the first demands for an ethnically pure Rwanda.

The radicalization of Rwandan politics led to the continuation of politics by violent means. Massacres of civilians now happened with dreadful predictability. Most were directed at Tutsis, oftentimes justified with contrived claims by radical Hutu leaders that these attacks represented "understandable" reactions to the violence instigated by the Tutsis or to the discovery of secret plans by the Tutsis to attack Hutus. In retrospect there is little doubt that these attacks were instigated, organized, and directed by extremist politicians, but at the time the standard government line, rarely challenged by outsiders, was that these were spontaneous acts of revenge. Those with political power were increasingly fearful of losing their privileges, especially to arch rivals, and began to contemplate the use of all means necessary to defend the status quo.

At the same moment that Habyarimana found himself fending off domestic challenges, he was facing a major military offensive from a newly organized and powerful Tutsi-led Rwandan Patriotic Front (RPF). In 1988 the RPF formed as a political and military organization with the goals of repatriating Tutsi refugees and establishing a power-sharing arrangement with the Rwandan government. The RPF was largely formed by the children of Tutsi refugees who had fled persecution in the early 1960s. But they had not always found sanctuary. Certainly not in Uganda. Ugandan President Milton Obote had long used the Tutsis as a scapegoat, which is why they welcomed Idi Amin's power grab in 1971. The return of Obote to Uganda in the 1980s meant the return to persecuted status, and the Tutsis joined Yowen Museveni's National Resistance Army in his war against Obote, comprising almost one-fourth of his force and filling its top ranks. Although Museveni's victory momentarily made life easier for the Tutsis, soon the new president desired to dispel the image that his victory was helped by "outsiders" and accordingly, introduced various limitations on their political and economic life. By the late 1980s these Tutsis had the desire, the resources, and the military acumen to fulfill their dream of going home.

The war between the RPF and the Rwandan government began in October 1990 when the RPF inaugurated attacks against the Rwandan government that carried it into Rwandan territory. The RPF offensive exacerbated ethnic divisions and set the stage for further radicalization of politics. The invasion displaced nearly three hundred thousand terrified Hutus into makeshift camps, a future breeding ground for anti-Tutsi resentment. The RPF imagined that it would be received warmly by the Tutsis and most of the Hutus, who would see the force not as an alien invasion but as an army ready to liberate the Rwandan population from a despotic government. The RPF was sorely disappointed because few cheered and most, including the Tutsi population, rallied to the side of the government. Notwithstanding Tutsi loyalty, Habyarimana used the RPF invasion to play the "ethnic card" and to move against his domestic "enemies" in order to shore up his regime. Ethnic politics had remained relatively peaceful for almost fifteen years, but Habyarimana had now reawakened its underside as he denounced all Tutsis as collaborators and traitors.

Habyarimana requested and received Zairian, Belgian, and French military assistance. The French arrived on October 4, 1990, just three days after the RPF invasion, and quickly secured the airport and then provided wider military support. They stayed long after the goals of the intervention were accomplished, and France became Rwanda's patron. Exactly why France decided to cast its lot with a relatively poor, landlocked, unstable, and not particularly strategic country is something of a curiosity. The historian Gérard Prunier suggested that the French involvement was due to a long-standing fear of being encircled by the "Anglo-Saxons."[6] Since before the Fashoda crisis in 1898, when the British eliminated the French presence in the upper Nile, the French have been nearly paranoid about losing status and power to the vastly inferior Anglo-Saxons, and have viewed any slip in their status or power (particularly in Africa) as a consequence of an Anglo-Saxon conspiracy. Therefore, France saw the English-speaking Tutsi population (coming as they did from English-speaking Uganda) as part of that plot, one more attempt to topple a French-speaking country.

Almost anachronistically committed to the idea, the duty, of intervention in Africa, the French were ready to prop up a faltering dictatorship while asking for very little in return and very few questions in the process. France became involved intimately with almost all facets of Rwanda's military expansion and training. Relations between France and the Rwandan government became so cozy that a joke in diplomatic circles was that the French ambassador was not the French ambassador to Rwanda but rather the Rwandan ambassador to France.[7] The Habyarimana government recognized this nearly unconditional French support for what it was, and soon concluded that it was immune from any pressure to reform its policies. The military and financial pipeline was now fully opened, with some aid (perhaps intentionally) assisting the MRND and CDR militias, that is, those who became the instigators of the genocide. Rwanda was becoming rapidly militarized; the army expanded severalfold and the government became the third largest arms importer in Africa.

A deteriorating economy, political turmoil associated with the demands for immediate democratization, and the RPF invasion created a double movement of political compromise and reactionary politics. There was a growing culture of political opposition and expectation of the devolution of political power. Moreover, under pressure from key opposition parties, in April 1992 Habyarimana agreed to enter into serious negotiations with the RPF. A few months later, on July 10, the combatants signed a cease-fire agreement in Arusha, Tanzania, and then in August initialed a series of agreements that would later become known as the Arusha Accords. Several more protocols were added to the agreements over the next several months. Domestic opposition and a military invasion were pushing Habyarimana to take a more conciliatory stance toward his enemies. The combination of negotiations with the RPF and political liberalization increased the tension between Habyarimana and the political right. The MNDR and the CDR became increasingly agitated by Habyarimana's move to the political middle and the prospect of sharing power. Habyarimana's policies created unease even closer to home. The *akazu* itself was divided over whether to strike a conciliatory or a hostile attitude toward these changes. Increasingly suspicious of the president's moves, Madame Habyarimana and her brothers cozied up to the extremists, believing that any political compromise would force them to share the spoils of power. Precisely when the most violent of the radical right considered genocide to be a serious option is unknown (possibly around the end of 1992), but violence against civilians was already part of their repertoire of political protest. Habyarimana had to wonder whether he had more to fear from the RPF, the political opposition, the military, the right-wing parties and militias, or his wife and her associates.

Then in February 1993 the RPF launched a major military attack against the Rwandan government because of the latter's massacre of Tutsi citizens. The fighting continued throughout the spring of 1993 and ended only with a last-ditch military intervention by the French. This most recent offensive led to the displacement of another million people, meaning that one-seventh of the population was now homeless.

Unlike the situation in the past, when military stalemates led to stillborn negotiations and unstable cease-fires, the political and military conditions had suitably changed to improve the prospect of a lasting negotiated settlement. The RPF was running out of steam and did not suffer the illusion that it could defeat a Hutu government backed by a militarily powerful French patron. The Hutu government was increasingly aware that France stood between itself and defeat. But France was now telling its client that because it had no intention of playing bodyguard long into the future, the Rwandan government should begin negotiations in earnest, and that France would safeguard the government's core interests. The result was that both the RPF and the government were compelled to reach the compromises necessary to strike a negotiated agreement. They quickly established a lasting cease-fire and then began serious negotiations.

Many accounts of the pre-1994 period in Rwanda offer the critical observations summarized in this historical overview. These accounts perform a valuable service as they attempt to uncover the confluence of forces—civil war, economic deterioration, political liberalization, extremism, mutual "othering," and backing by a Great Power—that hurtled the situation headlong toward genocide. In doing so, they give substance to Max Weber's claim that any historical outcome is a product of conjunctural causation, a complex combination of the historically demarcated structural and situational factors that combine in unrepeatable and unexpected ways.

These accounts also suggest, importantly, that decision makers at UN headquarters were laboring under a superficial and at times incorrect reading of some basic features of Rwandan politics. Whereas policymakers tended to see Rwanda as a place of primordial ethnicity that was slowing ascending to the language of cooperation and conflict resolution, these accounts bring into clearer focus the dialectical development of the politics of accommodation and hatred. These analyses, in effect, project a split screen of Rwandan history, with one side showing the world as policymakers mistakenly viewed it and the other the world as it really was.

However welcome and essential these accounts are for generating a more complete understanding of the Rwandan genocide, they are, in some ways, irrelevant and even detrimental to the task of reconstructing the view from the UN. Such a reconstruction must include four essential features. First, policymakers can and should be easily forgiven if they did not possess an anthropologist's understanding of the culture or a historian's knowledge of the crooked path that made Rwanda what it was. They were not anthropologists or historians. In most cases, they did not even possess firsthand experience of Rwanda. The expertise of these officials and bureaucrats largely resided in another part of the world and in peacekeeping and UN affairs more generally. A desk officer at the UN or at one of the missions to the UN was not assigned to Rwanda alone, and high-ranking officials did not begin to follow events in Rwanda until after it became fairly certain that the country would receive a peacekeeping operation. Typically those following Rwanda also oversaw other operations or parts of the region, which meant that they attended to Rwanda only when it proved necessary. Because Rwanda was not a high-profile operation, it did not receive high-profile attention.

Second, the constant juggling of operations meant that there was little time to master Rwandan history or synthesize the discrete pieces of information that were consumed sporadically over time. Few had the luxury to obtain a detailed understanding of a conflict that was of marginal importance, and most had to satisfy themselves with an undergraduate lecture's worth of knowledge. Colin Keating, New Zealand's ambassador to the UN, recounted how he only came to understand that Rwanda was a ticking bomb after he decided to do some background reading the weekend before he was to assume the presidency of the Security Council in April 1994; only then did he realize how his previous votes had been cast in ignorance of the real situation.[8] Those who were dispatched to the field were selected because of their availability and not because of their deep knowledge of the conflict. The presumptive secretary-general's special representative was Macaire Pedanou, who had been the UN's chief representative to the Arusha talks. But because of emergency eye surgery, he was unable to serve and was replaced by a much less astute and knowledgeable diplomat.

Third, the scarcity of time produced a highly instrumental approach to information. To attempt to re-create what those in New York probably knew at the time requires an appreciation for what they also might have cared to know and needed to know at the time. It means, in short, putting aside the very complexity that historians and anthropologists have reproduced dutifully in their postgenocidal studies. Knowledge that was relevant was knowledge that could be applied quickly to understand and address immediate concerns. So, when Rwanda appeared on the UN's agenda, relevant information sought and produced pertained to the pressing issue: whether or not to approve a peacekeeping operation for Rwanda.

To address that issue required a certain level of knowledge regarding a select number of critical features of Rwandan politics. Bureaucratic knowledge, by necessity, flattens and shoehorns history into already established boxes and cubicles; information that is sought is information that conforms to already established modalities. That Rwanda's conflict was rooted in ethnic politics was important to know. The details regarding its socially constructed nature were irrelevant. It was clearly relevant that the parties had signed a peace treaty to end their conflict. The "culture of violence" that analysts have now exhumed was rarely part of the conversation because it could not be translated immediately into usable knowledge. Knowing something about the political landscape, particularly how liberalization and democratization had produced a competition among new political parties, was important. But there was no room for a detailed understanding of the political players and loose alliances on the two-page briefing papers given to high-ranking officials. The presence of radical parties that abhorred the idea of sharing power was relevant but not alarming. All political compromises generate their opponents, even extremists. Exactly who were the extremists in Rwanda was important information, but what mattered was that the government and the RPF appeared to be committed to the agreement.

Fourth, the broad categories that were used to diagnose and remedy civil wars and ethnic conflict also produced a way of seeing and knowing Rwanda. There is no "natural" way to think about Rwanda. The conflict in Rwanda might be conceived of as a "tribal conflict," an "ethnic conflict," or even a "class conflict." The violence in Rwanda might be understood as part of a "civil war," "age-old ethnic hatreds," or even a "messy political transition." While some categorizations are more accurate and closer to the truth than others, and people will debate over the nature of the objects that confront them, the culture in which they are embedded will shape how they come to understand those objects at that moment.

Bureaucratic categories and organizational boxes do more than simply separate relevant from irrelevant information. They also produce the social optics that policymakers and bureaucrats use to see the world. Before policymakers can act, they first must come to create a definition and understanding of the situation, and that understanding is mediated by how the institution is organized to think. For instance, the very vocabulary of the "failed state" was omnipresent at this moment, and many states in turmoil were given that label. This meant that the very Rwanda that development agencies found to be a model of efficiency only a few years before was constructed as a "failed state" by those in New York. This label would have important implications for how policymakers later came to describe the violence. How organizations categorize and carve up the world has a profound impact on how policymakers see the world.

Attempting to re-create the view from New York means that we have to take seriously the fact that heavily overworked individuals were overseeing an operation of marginal importance, were highly economical and instrumental in the knowledge that they sought to understand Rwanda and ultimately create policy toward it, and were using the categories available from the organizational culture in which they were embedded to do so. It means appreciating how past interpretations are projected into the present circumstances, and considering how the stock of knowledge and recent events that are organizationally (and not simply individually) lived and experienced structure the present demands and responses. Of course, individuals are more than willing to accept interpretations that prove convenient or to overlook interpretations that do not. But beginning with the view from New York helps us to understand how certain realities were readily accepted.

THE UN commenced discussions on Rwanda immediately after the RPF and the Rwandan government formally established a new cease-fire on February 22, 1993.[9] They, with the help of France, sought the UN's involvement in monitoring the cease-fire and giving momentum to the negotiations, which were to be held in Arusha. On March 7, following talks in Dar es Salaam, Tanzania, the two parties issued a joint communiqué that detailed and extended this initial cease-fire agreement. The joint communiqué also made clear that both parties believed that a UN monitoring force would be instrumental for maintaining the cease-fire and for promoting the Arusha talks, which were to begin the following week. Upon the recommendation of the secretary-general, on March 12 the Security Council authorized the secretary-general to explore how the UN might contribute to the peace process and the possibility of establishing a military observer force to monitor the cease-fire agreement. Boutros-Ghali dispatched a technical mission headed by his military adviser, Maurice Baril. Baril returned from his four-day trip in early April in favor of an observer force. Soon thereafter, Boutros-Ghali, with the permission of the Security Council, sent three representatives to the Arusha talks as part of a "goodwill mission." This team, along with other international observers at Arusha, were there to help the parties overcome difficult hurdles, to answer any logistical questions that might arise, and to prepare the groundwork for any future observer operation. Throughout this period Boutros-Ghali and the French kept reminding the parties that any observer mission was dependent on the parties making real strides in their peace negotiations and abiding by the cease-fire.

On May 20, 1993, three months after Boutros-Ghali agreed to send a technical team to explore the issue, he delivered an interim report to the Security Council recommending that it establish the United Nations Observer Mission Uganda-Rwanda (UNOMUR). As envisioned in the report, the observer mission's principal responsibilities were to reside on the Ugandan side of the border and monitor the cease-fire between the government and the RPF, to reassure the Rwandan government that no new military aid was finding its way from Uganda to Rwanda, and to "help to promote the negotiation process in Arusha and encourage the parties to actively pursue their efforts toward peace and national reconciliation in Rwanda."[10] Acting on the observations and recommendations of the report, the Security Council approved Resolution 846 on June 22. Eighty-one military observers and two dozen support staff were to begin deployment to the area within the next several weeks.

Although the Rwandan government and the RPF were pleased to learn that the Security Council was likely to approve an observer mission, and relieved when it finally did so, they continued to long for a more robust and wide-ranging UN operation. Early in their talks they communicated to the UN their desire for an "international force" to become deeply involved in the implementation of their agreements. On June 14, in fact, even before the Security Council had authorized UNOMUR, they wrote to the secretary-general to inform him that to implement their eventual peace agreement they would require a "neutral international force" as soon as the ink was dry on the signed peace agreement. In anticipation of such a peace treaty, the letter continued, they requested that the UN immediately send a reconnaissance mission to assess the needs of such an operation. Boutros-Ghali's response to this request was similar to earlier ones: he politely refused on the grounds that the UN would only consider such an operation and engage in a planning exercise after the parties had signed the final agreements. Although he conceded that it would take several months between the time a peacekeeping operation was formally requested and when one could land in Kigali, there were UN procedures to respect.

Months of demanding negotiations culminated in the Arusha Accords, signed on August 4, 1993, to great fanfare and greater relief. The accords had two protocols: one covering the integration of the armed forces of the two parties and the other containing a variety of issues, including ratification of human rights instruments and deletion of references to ethnic groups in official documents. These protocols, combined with earlier agreements, comprised an eleven-article peace agreement that included the rule of law, power sharing, transitional institutions, repatriation of refugees, and resettlement of displaced peoples. The accords also included a timetable for the projected twenty-two-month transition period, beginning with the establishment of transitional institutions within thirty-seven days after the signing of the agreement—that is, by September 10—and ending with democratic elections. On the surface Arusha promised a brighter, more stable, and democratic Rwanda.

The parties might have been "all smiles and songs" about their bright future together in a democratic Rwanda, but underneath they were quite fearful of the future because the extremists were venomously opposed to the accords. Accordingly, the proponents of Arusha insisted that an "international force" take an active role in implementing and monitoring the accords. As outlined in the accords, the force was (1) to help provide security throughout the country, for humanitarian assistance, and for the expatriate community; (2) to monitor the cease-fire agreement, which included the establishment and maintenance of a demilitarized zone (DMZ) around Kigali; (3) to investigate all reported infractions of the cease-fire agreement; (4) to help maintain public security by monitoring the activities of the gendarmerie and police; and (5) to assist with the demilitarization and demobilization and integration of the armed forces, a task that was expected to take seven to nine months and involve almost thirty thousand personnel on the government's side and twenty thousand for the RPF. The international force, in essence, was to provide security and create an environment that would give both parties the assurance that they could make cooperative moves without finding themselves duped and vulnerable.

The parties told Boutros-Ghali that they hoped that the international force would be on the ground before September 10 so that it could help facilitate and oversee the establishment of the broad-based transitional government (BBTG) that was due on that date. Boutros-Ghali (and other international officials involved in the negotiations) broke the news to them that such a request was impossible. Patiently they gave them a minilesson in the highly cumbersome UN procedures. First, a UN team must be dispatched to determine the practicalities, modalities, and resource needs for an operation. Then this team reports to the secretary-general, who writes a report and recommendations for the Security Council. Then the council debates the report and passes a final verdict. If the Security Council approves an operation, then various UN committees examine the features of the operation that have budgetary implications, and the secretary-general begins to solicit troop contributions from member states and to assemble a staff, which can be very time-consuming, depending on how complex the operation is. In other words, the parties should not expect to see the first blue helmet in Kigali until late October—six weeks after the projected establishment of the transitional government. Although the UN might not be able to move as quickly as the Rwandans hoped, Boutros-Ghali warned that that was no excuse for the parties not to fulfill their obligations and meet the first deadline of September 10. Indeed, their failure to do so might be interpreted by the council as evidence that the parties did not have the will to stick to their agreements and thus reason to vote against the proposed operation.

A week after the parties signed the Arusha Accords, a different part of the UN system generated a report on the human rights situation in Rwanda. Following up on a visit to Rwanda completed several months before, on August 11 the special rapporteur on extrajudicial, summary, or arbitrary executions, Waly Bacre Ndiaye, released his findings. Toward the end of this report, which portrayed a disturbing picture of the human rights situation, was a section titled "The Genocide Question." It stated, "The question whether the massacres described above may be termed genocide has often been raised. It is not for the Special Rapporteur to pass judgement at this stage, but an initial reply may be put forward." The section proceeds to outline the definition as provided by Article II of the Genocide Convention, and then concludes that it is very clear that

the victims of the attacks, Tutsis in the overwhelming majority of cases, have been targeted solely because of their membership in a certain ethnic group, and for no other objective reason. . . . Article II, paragraphs (a) and (b), might therefore be considered to apply to these cases.[11]

The rapporteur was clearly alarmed by a pattern of violence that was not directly related to the civil war but rather had a different and more sinister source, and his summary was a warning for all to see. If only anyone had seen it. Delivered in another part of the UN bureaucracy, the report was not heard in the Security Council and did not come to the attention of those who were to plan the peacekeeping operation.

What might have been the likely effect of such a report, with the passage on genocide properly highlighted, on the proposed peacekeeping operation? At the least, probably not much; at the most, it might have halted any plans right then and there. No one remotely knowledgeable about Rwanda would have been shocked by the reports of civilian killings that had an ethnic component. And while the report's detailed account of the human rights situation was graphic and disturbing in its totality, the situation was not unknown to those even remedially familiar with the domestic situation.

The obvious solution to these killings and the general ethnic conflict was to get the parties to reach a negotiated solution and establish a multiethnic and democratic Rwanda that was committed to the rule of law. That was the very purpose of the recently signed Arusha Accords. It was hoped that the human rights situation was about to improve. However, if the implication of the report was that the parties were making grand promises of reconciliation but that the Habyarimana government was intending to continue its terror campaign against the Tutsis, then the council might have concluded that there was no basis for peacekeeping. And, what if the Security Council had zeroed in on the "genocide" passage? Then almost assuredly the peacekeeping operation would have been called off as premature, and it would have been replaced by a strongly worded statement by the council that such actions would be dealt with severely. But no such discussions ever took place in the council because the human rights report, delivered in a separate part of the UN, never found its way into its proceedings.

Boutros-Ghali dispatched a technical team to Rwanda, which arrived on August 19 and stayed for twelve days. The team was headed by Brigadier General Roméo Dallaire. Dallaire, in fact, had been tapped to be UNOMUR's commander. But the Arusha Accords were signed much more quickly than the UN expected, and since the UN knew of Dallaire's availability and destination for the area, it designated him the presumptive force commander of the likely peacekeeping operation (UNAMIR) and asked him to head the reconnaissance team. A highly regarded Canadian general with prior experience in multilateral operations, the forty-seven-year-old Dallaire had a reputation as a cultured but straight-shooting, hard-working, energetic, and determined individual. As someone who had been schooled in the North Atlantic Treaty Organization (NATO) and traditional military operations, however, his qualifications for the job did not include a deep knowledge of Africa or Rwanda. He later recalled his reaction when he was first approached about leading the UNOMUR operation: "When I got the call, I said, 'Yes sir, that's in Africa, right?'"[12] Others on his team were not that much better versed on the ins-and-outs of Rwanda.

Before going to Kigali, the technical team stopped in New York to process the requisite paperwork and to receive their predeparture briefing, spending much more time on the former than on the latter. The briefing consisted of hasty and not very informative meetings and a two-page informational sheet from the Department of Political Affairs that provided a synopsis of Rwandan history, the recent conflict, and the central figures and political parties involved in the current process—but no analysis.[13] Most important, they were informed that while there was a continuation of some violence on the ground, it was sporadic and not a real threat to the cease-fire agreement. Handed a Michelin map of Rwanda and a copy of the Arusha Accords, which Dallaire and his military attaché quickly discovered was littered with gaps and contradictions, this motley and thoroughly unprepared group flew off to Kigali.[14]

What they found largely confirmed what they were told to expect. Everyone they met was upbeat and confident about the future, and insistent that the UN's presence was absolutely essential if the country was going to turn the corner on its violent past. What they did not know, because they did not have a deep understanding of the Rwandan conflict, was that they only met moderates and did not meet a single extremist during the entire trip. Generally impressed by what he saw during his stay, Dallaire confidently predicted upon his exit that the "restoration of order and stability in the country makes it possible to deploy international peacekeeping forces here soon. These forces will supervise the fulfillment of the peace agreement and the transit of the country to democratic rule."[15] On his way back to New York, he emphatically proclaimed that "[t]he people do not want war any more. . . . The situation is calm and everybody has a clear desire for peace."[16] According to a member of the team, everyone in Rwanda whom they met gave them a hearty welcome and told them that they wanted the UN "yesterday." Given such a reception and encouragement, that same member recalled, "our report was that this was a winner mission, where the UN can redeem itself, that there is a peace agreement with some holes but that everyone is behind it." He further reflected that "we knew that the UN badly wanted a win, and we told them that this was it."[17]

Once the Dallaire team had completed its visit, the Rwandans became increasingly anxious for a peacekeeping operation, particularly as the September 10 deadline approached and then passed without the establishment of the BBTG. On September 15, Boutros-Ghali received a joint RPF-government delegation. The delegation pleaded for the immediate deployment of 4,260 troops, on the grounds that time was of the essence and that it was highly unlikely that the BBTG would be established until there was a peacekeeping force on the ground. The secretary-general repeated his prior counsel that even if the Security Council authorized a force today, it would take two to three months before peacekeepers actually arrived in Rwanda. So, hold tight and stick to your agreements, he advised. This was the same advice he delivered almost a month before in response to a similar request from President Habyarimana. Nevertheless, the council was very impressed by this unified and concerted pitch for a peacekeeping operation by these two former enemies, taking it as the best sign possible that there existed a true commitment to peace.[18] One-half of the duo later confessed that their passionate plea stemmed largely from the recognition that every moment delayed was a moment gained by the extremists who were opposed to Arusha and the UN's presence. To the Security Council, however, they presented themselves not as running out of fear but rather as running toward the vision of multiethnic and peaceful Rwanda.[19]

Meanwhile, the secretary-general and DPKO were busily drafting the secretary-general's report, which was based heavily on the assessment team's findings and occasional advice from several member states. The team wanted a force just shy of five thousand troops, which they believed was the minimum required to do the job and to provide sufficient coverage of Rwanda. However sympathetic the Secretariat might have been to the military logic behind the request, it told them to think about a more realistic number, say about half the proposed figure. In the context where high-profile and highly fluid operations were being shortchanged of peacekeepers, where it was becoming increasingly difficult to find peacekeepers now that there were almost seventy thousand deployed in sixteen operations around the world, and where the Security Council was becoming increasingly edgy concerning the high cost of peacekeeping, five thousand might have been advisable from a military standpoint but it would never pass the political test. The Secretariat ultimately recommended a force structure of 2,548, anticipating that the Security Council (that is, the United States) would object to any higher number because of the cost.[20] Running the operation with half the troop strength believed to be required would have operational consequences. In order to monitor all of Rwanda, this skeletal force would have to spread itself thin. This would not be a problem if UNAMIR was only expected to show the flag but quite worrisome if it was to use force.[21] But no such force was expected because this was a Chapter VI mission that operated with the consent of the parties and was to oversee a straightforward operation, and if civil war returned, then the mandate was finished and the operation would simply fold.

On September 24, Boutros-Ghali presented his report to the Security Council. The proposed force of 2,548 peacekeepers, and various civilian and military personnel and a handful of civilian police, would be assigned an array of tasks that broadly corresponded to the functions outlined in the Arusha Accords. Much of the report was based on the findings of the reconnaissance mission.

A critical feature of the operation, and one that would loom especially large in a few months, concerned the security practices available to UNAMIR. From the outset, General Dallaire envisaged that UNAMIR would engage in a range of operations that would provide the stable environment necessary for the political transition. His logic ran as follows. The parties would only have the confidence to undertake this risky transition if they could be reasonably assured of their security during the process. UNAMIR's job was to provide that security. Toward that end, it had to be prepared to undertake a range of operations. Based loosely on the Canadian contingent's recent experiences in Croatia, Dallaire proposed the establishment of a Kigali Weapons-Secure Area (KWSA), to be negotiated by the parties. In this area UNAMIR would be allowed to establish roadblocks, checkpoints, and other barricades in order to collect illegal weapons; to monitor closely the movement of all forces from both parties; to confiscate all illegal weapons, especially those possessed by militias; and to undertake other practices as needed to provide for a secure environment. Importantly, he believed peacekeepers did not have to wait for the weapons to come to them but that peacekeepers could go get the weapons if they posed a possible security threat. Dallaire's language was included in the secretary-general's report to the Security Council.

The report also noted that UNAMIR would have four phases. Phase One, to last roughly ninety days, until the end of the year, included the immediate dispatch of an advance team of roughly forty-six personnel, including twenty-five military staff, to help establish the security area in Kigali and oversee the establishment of the transitional government. The hope was that the initial advance team would be joined by fourteen hundred peacekeepers by the end of the year. At this point, UNOMUR would be folded into UNAMIR, though it would remain semiautonomous for a period of time. Phase Two was to begin the moment the transitional government was established, would include providing for a weapons-free zone around Kigali, and would end after three months with the beginning of the preparations for the military demobilization and integration. At that point UNAMIR was expected to be at full strength. Phase Three would last around nine months and revolve around the military portions of the agreement and the continued monitoring and enforcement of the safe zones. Phase Four would kick in around late 1994 and oversee the completion of the military demobilization and integration and plan for elections. During this ten-month phase the UN operation could be reduced significantly because of the increasingly secure and peaceful environment.

If all had gone according to plan, the UN would have successfully shepherded Rwanda's transition from civil war to civil society by the end of 1995. In keeping with the tenor of the times, the secretary-general closed his report with two warnings: first, the parties must comply with the letter and the spirit of the Arusha Accords, and the role of the UN was to assist the parties in their efforts to make peace, not to make peace for them; and second, "at a time of unprecedented financial constraints facing the United Nations, it is imperative that Member States be prepared to assume the obligations resulting from the new mandates they entrust to the Organization."[22]

The Rwandan operation was formally brought to the Security Council's attention at the very moment it was beginning to suffer a political hangover from excessive wear, was going through a hellish few weeks, and was about to be hit by the Somali tsunami. In fact, the ten days between the day the secretary-general submitted the report on September 24 and the day the Security Council voted to authorize the operation on October 5 was unusual in the level of intensity and anxiety at the UN. The day after the report was delivered, several Americans were killed in a helicopter crash in Somalia, unleashing an outcry in Washington and increasing the pressure to alter the United States', and thus the UN's, policy toward Somalia. Two days later, President Clinton delivered his "tough love" speech to the General Assembly. In a private meeting with Boutros-Ghali a few days later, representatives of the permanent members of the Security Council reiterated the need to be less generous and more discriminating. And then on October 3, at the very moment that the Security Council was debating the proposed operation, American Rangers were dying in Mogadishu and American foreign policy toward the UN was about to enter its blue period. These were only the highlights. The Security Council was in near-constant session, meeting on a variety of issues related to international peace and security.

It was in the context of this dour climate and this crowded agenda that the Security Council debated yet another operation, this one in Rwanda. Although there was some grumbling that the last thing the council needed at this moment was another operation in Africa designed to quell ethnic conflict, several factors nearly foreordained its authorization of the proposed operation. To begin with, a Rwandan operation had been in the works for several months, beginning with the establishment of UNOMUR, and was virtually promised if the parties did their part and signed a sweeping settlement. Moreover, although proposed operations do not necessarily require sponsorship by a Great Power, it helps. It certainly helped here. France vigorously lobbied for the operation, something it believed was necessary to end the civil war and desperately wanted in order to extricate itself from the situation. Hence, it would be difficult for the council to deny the operation. If the United States put up a fuss and objected to the operation, then it could anticipate that France would return the favor sometime in the near future, for instance, when the United States forwarded new measures on Haiti. While there was no explicit quid pro quo between the United States and France, certainly each worried that challenging an operation desired by the other might encourage diplomatic revenge when the tables were turned.

Furthermore, Rwanda fulfilled the basic conditions for an operation: a stable cease-fire; a peace treaty that had the support of the parties; and accords that promised national reconciliation, a democratic Rwanda, and to make ethnic hatred a legacy of the past. To introduce new criteria at this point would have been an extraordinary departure. The United States was the country most likely to object to the peacekeeping operation because it was making most of the noise about the increasing number and cost of peacekeeping operations. But the U.S. Mission checked the conditions in Rwanda against the criteria circulating in the draft version of PRD-13, and concluded that there was no basis for voting against the operation.[23] Stating the positive case, the Canadian Mission to the UN cabled to Ottawa that from the Security Council's view, the Rwandan operation was a model for the future.

There also was the hope that this would be a successful operation. Indeed, Rwanda was presented as an "easy" operation. *Easy*, in this context, did not mean the absence of obstacles or the certainty of a success with little effort, but rather that the parties had demonstrated their commitment to an agreement that looked practical and had reasonable goals and a steady timetable. After the operations in Cambodia, Somalia, and the former Yugoslavia, a nice "quiet" operation was exactly what the Security Council wanted to restore its besmirched image. This was how Rwanda was presented, a view intimated in the secretary-general's report, pushed by the secretary-general himself, and enthusiastically supported by the Rwandan government's patron, France. The very fact that a joint government-RPF delegation had come to New York to appeal for an operation impressed the Security Council and further enforced the belief that with relatively little effort the UN could do right and gain some good publicity.[24] As Colin Keating reflected, the prospect of a successful operation "was like manna from heaven."[25]

It also helped that few really knew much about Rwanda. Although in Rwanda nearly everyone was quite anxious about the agreement's prospects, hardly a hint of that anxiety found its way into the Security Council's debates. "We knew nothing of the true reality," Keating later confessed.[26] France delivered confident reassurances that the parties were committed to see the accords through until the democratic end, and the joint delegation presented itself as the embodiment of the new thinking found throughout Rwanda.

The cross-examinations coming from those on the Security Council concerned not a detective's investigatory skills or a historian's knowledge but rather a politician's working understanding of Rwanda's recent past and a bureaucrat's concern with making sure that the proposed operation satisfied the minimal conditions. After having authorized nearly a dozen peacekeeping operations over the previous several years, the council had developed something of an algorithmic set of questions to determine whether or not an operation should be authorized. These questions included the following: How stable was the peace treaty? Were the parties committed to the agreement and the rule of law? How stable was the cease-fire? Were the projected responsibilities for the UN force reasonable? Would the operation operate under Chapter VI or Chapter VII? Were there resources to match the tasks assigned to the UN operation? What would be the length of the operation? These questions were addressed with brief, reassuring answers. The council understood that all transitions are messy and require courage, determination, and no small amount of luck, but felt reassured that the basics were in place.

A matter of central importance concerned UNAMIR's concept of security operations. The recommendation of the secretary-general, which was based largely on the findings of the technical mission, was that UNAMIR would provide the necessary security through the establishment of a weapons-secure area. Toward that end, it would vigorously patrol the area, control the movements of militias and combatants, and confiscate illegal weapons. According to the vernacular of the day, this put UNAMIR somewhere between Chapter VI and Chapter VII. It was not a Chapter VII operation because it was operating with the consent of the parties. Yet it was beyond classic peacekeeping because it envisaged peacekeepers as more than mere monitors and as actively confiscating weapons.

But how active was active? The council purposefully introduced language into the mandate that was intended to give the force commander some wiggle room, according to Keating.[27] Otherwise, he continued, it never would have adopted words to the effect that UNAMIR was to contribute to the establishment of a weapons-free zone in Kigali. But how far could the force commander go? At this very moment when Somalia was at the forefront of its collective fear, the council implicitly rejected the idea of a vigorously enforced disarmament program. Such language would have taken the mandate a step closer to an enforcement operation and probably beyond the dreaded "Mogadishu line." The implication was that UNAMIR could seize weapons that came to them—those that were in a public space or happened to cross its path. Anything else, even if those actions were inimical to the contribution of a weapons-secure area, was probably beyond the mandate. All of this was implied in the council's deliberations. Importantly, none of this nuance or subtext was ever communicated to the force commander. Dallaire took up his post in Kigali with the assumption that his proposed recommendations had been authorized in toto by the council.

The council's debate became testier when it moved to the topic of force structure and size, for these items had immediate budgetary implications. All council members were aware of the impoverished condition of peacekeeping and that the larger the operation, the more expensive it would be. All peacekeeping operations were run on the cheap and on assumptions that all would go well and the parties would have a reservoir of trust and self-restraint. Rwanda was not going to be an exception, and the unified presentation by the parties that they were happily reconciled to a multiethnic state and the power-sharing agreement meant that this operation required very little UN presence. In other words, it should be an inexpensive one.

The countries that were most sensitive to the cost of the operation were those that were expected to pick up the largest part of the bill. In short, the United States, which according to the UN's assessment rate would absorb one-third of the total cost. The Clinton administration was less worried about its total share, which amounted to $20 million, than the fact that it would have to justify the operation and its cost to an increasingly hostile Congress. Congress would want to know why the UN was setting up another operation and why it cost as much as it did. Therefore, while in principle the United States favored the Rwandan operation, in practice it objected to any proposal that might give Congress yet another opportunity to scrutinize Clinton's foreign policy. This political touchiness led the United States to suggest that a token force of five hundred might do the job, but after this proposal landed like a thud, it quickly retreated to the proposed number of 2,548.[28]

Still, the United States' "bottom line" attitude led it to insist that the Secretariat consider ways to introduce a sliding deployment, one that could expand and contract depending on the phase of the operation. Objections were raised that writing into the mandate any set figure would unnecessarily micromanage the operation and perhaps leave it so ethereal that it would be unable to do its job. The compromise language that found its way into Paragraph 9 of the final resolution was that the Security Council "invites the Secretary-General to consider ways of reducing the total maximum strength . . . in particular through phased deployment without thereby affecting its capacity to carry out its mandate, and requests the Secretary-General, in planning and executing the phased deployment, to seek economies and to report regularly on what is achieved in this regard." The White House was pleased to have language to show Congress that it was determined to reduce costs where and when possible.

On October 5, 1993, the Security Council voted in favor of Resolution 872, which established UNAMIR, the eighteenth operation authorized by the Security Council in the previous five years. The statements made by council members accompanying the formal vote were exaggerated in the fashion typical for the moment: there was lofty praise of the Rwandans and back-patting congratulations to themselves for helping to lift the peace process and to provide the chance for a democratic Rwanda. Yet they also used the occasion to issue warnings and to reveal fears. After the Security Council formally voted to approve the operation, Edward Walker, the deputy U.S. ambassador, said, "It is now up to the Rwandans themselves to ensure that the transition to democracy moves forward. . . . We are pleased to note that this resolution has a tightly focused mandate. This body's continued support will depend in large measure on demonstration of substantive progress towards implementation of the peace agreement."[29] The council's responsibilities, in short, were qualified and contingent on the behavior of the Rwandans. UNAMIR was deployed naively and was undernourished, a deadly combination, a gift from member states who hoped for a quick victory and were willing to take shortcuts to get there.

The council's debate on Rwanda encapsulated the collectively held image of a UN whose promise was rapidly collapsing before their eyes. Desires to promote international peace and security and to help fallen states reclaim their lives still persisted. But there was no ignoring the fact that the UN had grasped beyond its reach and was now suffering for it. The previous two weeks—with various world leaders telling the UN to restrain itself, and the deaths in Somalia—had convinced even the most wide-eyed champions of the UN of its precarious state. Because of reclaimed principles and pragmatic responses, UN officials in New York were now reconciling themselves to more scaled-down and modest times. The Security Council would have to learn to say no when the conditions were not ripe, to turn a blind eye to various calamities that might have stirred it only a year before, and to learn to do more with less and expect the parties to make up the difference through their goodwill and behavior. No more could the Security Council leap before looking. The Security Council, never one to spoil an operation, would now have to become even more insistent that all operations would be run on the cheap—and be cheaper than ever. This council would also be much less patient and forgiving. The delays and missteps that could be reasonably expected would no longer be tolerated.[30] The UN's duties and obligations were dependent on the follow-through of the parties.

Rwanda might have been grandfathered into the UN's protection umbrella, but other candidates for the UN's assistance were not so fortunate. Three weeks after the Security Council established the operation in Rwanda came the opportunity to establish an operation in neighboring Burundi. On October 21, army officers assassinated Burundi President Melchior Ndadaye, leading to an ethnic bloodbath and tens of thousands dead. From the very beginning of the crisis, there was talk of a possible peacekeeping operation to halt the civil war and protect civilians, with the strong insinuation that because Burundi and Rwanda were estranged twins that had similar life histories and faced similar predicaments, they deserved equal treatment. From the vantage point of the Security Council, these countries might resemble each other in many ways, but in one crucial respect they differed: there was a working cease-fire in Rwanda and none in Burundi. Living in the immediate shadows of Somalia, many members of the Security Council argued against intervention on the grounds that there was "no peace to keep" and that the UN needed to avoid obvious quagmires.

The decision not to intervene in Burundi symbolized a shifting sentiment at the UN concerning the feasibility and desirability of humanitarian intervention. Those who opposed intervention contended that such crises are a by-product of wars, wars are defined by instability, and a modicum of stability is a precondition for effective peacekeeping. The UN could only be effective when there was a peace to keep. Most officials in New York sighed with relief when the Security Council opted to abstain from the conflict in Burundi and let the killing proceed.

3

"If This Is an Easy
Operation . . . "

I didn't know much of the Rwandan language. But they taught
me that the word MINUAR [the French acronym for UNAMIR]
actually has a meaning in Kinyarwandan. The word means that
your lips are moving, but they don't really say anything. And
that's what we were from the beginning. After a few weeks the
extremists knew we had no power.

COLONEL LUC MARCHAL, head of the Belgian contingent[1]

As instructed by the Security Council in the October 1993 resolution
that established UNAMIR, in early January 1994 the secretary-general reported on the status of the operation and the peace process. The report intimated that while the UN was generally holding up its obligations, the
same could not be said of the Rwandans.[2] The UN deployment had been
running behind schedule, an all too common feature of most operations,
but was now in place. Dallaire arrived in Kigali on October 22, joined five
days later by twenty-one other military personnel. The first UNAMIR
troops entered Kigali in early November. A few weeks later, on November
23, Special Representative Jacques-Roger Booh-Booh took up residence in
Kigali. (The former foreign minister of Cameroon and a personal friend of
Boutros-Ghali, Booh-Booh quickly earned a reputation for being an ama-
teur and having Hutu leanings.) The Kigali battalion, composed of Belgian
and Bangladeshi forces, arrived in the first part of December, allowing the
remaining French forces to depart. On December 24, UNAMIR secured
the parties' signatures to the mutually negotiated Kigali Weapons-Secure
Area (KWSA) agreement, essentially a demilitarized zone. This central doc-

ument paved the way both for UNAMIR to step up its security role and for the arrival of the RPF battalion on December 28. Rwanda now hosted 1,260 UN military personnel from a dozen different countries.

The Arusha Accords were still running in place, however. Perhaps the grandest achievement was that the cease-fire had held despite several ominous overtures. Although there were intermittent reports of cease-fire violations along the northern border, both sides demonstrated some self-restraint, presumably because neither relished the resumption of war. Ethnic violence continued, leaving scores dead and wounded. Once UNAMIR was on the ground, the secretary-general's report stated, it had begun to react to the outbreaks of violence, offering a calming voice and reminding the parties about the need to stick to the accords.

More alarming was the ethnic conflict in neighboring Burundi in late October. At the time, everyone held their collective breaths, expecting that it would trigger a similar confrontation in Rwanda. Instead it appeared to act as a "there but for the grace of God" moment as both sides held their fire. That the cease-fire had prevailed in the face of all these flash points, the secretary-general suggested, was something of a victory given the alternative, more disconsolate scenarios, and could be read as a concrete indication of the parties' commitment to Arusha. "Progress" in such contexts is measured in relationship to grisly but unrealized futures and not to missed appointments on some idealized schedule for peace.

Yet the failure of the parties to establish the transitional government was a major setback and contributed to a view of a paralyzed Rwanda. The cornerstone of the Arusha Accords was the transitional government, which by January 1994 was supposed to have been more than three months old. But it was still nowhere in sight, and the politicking that was to have been settled during the treaty negotiations was still in full throttle. The stumbling block was the composition of the new government. Habyarimana insisted that the CDR—the virulently anti-Tutsi extremist party that was rumored to have been behind many of the ethnic killings over the previous several months and that was viscerally opposed to the Arusha Accords—be included in the coalition. He argued that the CDR was less of a threat inside than outside the government, a position publicly seconded by Booh-Booh. The RPF and other liberal parties steadfastly rejected its inclusion. The continuation of this discussion regarding the CDR's future role delayed the establishment of the transitional government and effectively allowed the CDR to play a spoiler role whether or not it was in the government.[3] Because the transitional government had not yet been established, the national assembly and other political objectives were circling, unable to land.

The security situation was, in fact, more dangerous than what the secretary-general's report suggested. The violence in Burundi in late October displaced thousands of refugees, who were now camped in southern Rwanda and were complicating the already difficult humanitarian and political situation. To respond to this exigency, UNAMIR shifted some of its observers to the south, emaciating further an already thin force in other high-risk areas. In order not to jeopardize its monitoring capacity in these sectors, UNAMIR requested an increase in the number of military observers. The secretary-general omitted from his report UNAMIR's appraisal of an increasingly dangerous security situation in the south and the request for supplementary humanitarian assistance. This omission is attributed largely to his desire to avoid alarming an already edgy Security Council and to forward only recommendations that he believed the council was likely to accept.[4] However, he did advise reinforcing the military force on the northern border in order to keep the combatants apart. Rwanda might have been an easy operation in October, but it was making a strong bid for reclassification.

The report and the council's discussions dwelled on the failure to establish the transitional government. Headquarters was obsessed with this government to the point that it became viewed as the taproot for all future positive developments. The transitional government was the surest indicator of the overall health and progress of the operation. Until the transitional government was established, the operation was, by definition, a difficult one. The establishment of the transitional government would elevate a struggling operation into the ranks of the successful. It would unleash other essential features of the peace process. It would reduce the violence. In this no-man's-land between a civil war and civil peace, a thin layer of stability masked an underbelly of violence.

The general assessment was that the failure to establish the transitional government was contributing to the deteriorating security environment, which in turn was hamstringing the establishment of the transitional government. The only way to escape this violent chicken-and-egg dilemma was to insist that the parties honor the cease-fire agreement and immediately establish the transitional government. The council viewed the transitional government as something of a miracle cure, a combination of political epoxy, vanishing cream, and rejuvenator.

There was little question that the secretary-general would recommend and the council would vote in favor of extending the mandate. Never before had the council suspended an operation because of delays in implementing a peace agreement. And there was no good reason for the council to do so now, particularly since the delay was only a few months, which was relatively insignificant when compared to the delays typical of transitions of this sort. Moreover, the unstated but quite reasonable fear was that if the council terminated the operation because of a lack of progress, then it could expect the resumption of war. Better to remain patient than to act hastily and be blamed for the bloodshed. Still, during the meetings the council scolded Rwanda for failing to live up to its agreements, and hinted that it might not be as quick to renew the operation in March if the transitional government was still a fiction and not a fact.

The council's growing impatience was communicated to Rwanda in the most direct way imaginable. Beginning on January 1, 1994, Rwanda became the newest member of the Security Council. Although in retrospect it is curious that a country that was the site of a peacekeeping operation should be a member of the council, at the time this development received little attention. After the standard welcome to this august body, the next sound Rwanda heard was a council annoyed by its failure to carry out its promises.

JUST how complex and potentially lethal the political and security situation was became clearer to a handful of UN officials on January 11, 1994, just five days after the council renewed UNAMIR's mandate. Ever since his arrival in Kigali on October 22, 1993, Dallaire had been receiving a sobering education in Rwandan politics. He landed in generally high spirits, saluting the Rwandans for having the courage to begin anew and pledging his energies toward assisting them with their difficult task. But his initially optimistic assessment was increasingly plagued by gnawing fears that Rwanda was not ready for peace at any price. There was the continuing failure of the parties to follow through on their initial political agreements. More disturbing was the violence on the ground. In November and December there were several large-scale attacks on civilians that left scores dead and injured. In each case, UNAMIR attempted to intervene to defuse tensions and keep the accords in place. Then on December 3, a senior group of Rwandan military officers sent a letter to Dallaire and diplomatic missions that warned of a "diabolical" plot to scuttle the Arusha Accords. Another violent episode occurred on January 8, 1994, that had sinister overtones. Dallaire and other UNAMIR officials were now keenly aware that they were supervising a highly explosive situation and were increasingly suspicious that there existed a well-established and politically powerful clique that wanted to scuttle the accords and were willing to deploy violence to do so.[5]

Those fears were substantiated by an informant, known as "Jean-Pierre," who was introduced to UNAMIR by a "very very important government politician" (it was later learned that Jean-Pierre was Jean-Pierre

Twatzinze and the politician was the prime minister–designate, Faustin Twagiramungu). The informant claimed to have personal ties to the palace and the Interahamwe, and was personally involved in the crusade to derail the accords.

According to Jean-Pierre, well-positioned and cruelly motivated Hutu elites were busily transforming the Interahamwe, whose previous function had been to protect the president and Kigali from the RPF, into a machine of extermination. All Tutsis, not just members of the RPF, were marked. This was why the informant decided to expose the conspiracy; while he opposed the Arusha Accords and sharing power with the RPF, he was outraged by the planned extermination campaign. To transform the plan into reality, the Interahamwe was busily stockpiling and distributing weapons, creating lists for assassination, and organizing hit teams. The whole idea, according to Jean-Pierre, was to create a "killing machine because the objective was very clear for everybody—kill, kill, kill."[6] The ethnic cleansing would begin the very moment the political deadlock ended and the transitional government was established. Although the Interahamwe believed that it could successfully confront the RPF and its Tutsi allies, it did not want to fight a two-front war with the UN. To remove the UN and that very possibility, the Interahamwe plotted to assassinate Belgian peacekeepers, an act that was predicted to provoke not swift retaliation from UNAMIR but rather its hasty retreat. Somalia certainly provided a positive role model in that regard. The informant offered to take UNAMIR to the weapons caches, which happened to be at the headquarters of the president's party. Time was of the essence, urged the informant, because the weapons were to be distributed in the very near future.

Dallaire was shaken by the news. Under normal circumstances, this information might have seemed too depraved and audacious to be believable, but Dallaire took it seriously because it tapped into his (and others') fears and suspicions.[7] Here was evidence that the Rwandan political and military elite were busily preparing for war and butchery while mouthing reassuring statements of their continued commitment to the peace process.

Dallaire hurriedly cabled UN headquarters, addressing General Maurice Baril, DPKO's military adviser and a comrade from the Canadian military. Titled "REQUEST FOR PROTECTION OF INFORMANT," this compact and carefully worded cable conveyed the informant's startling report, including the news that "since unamir mandate he [the informant] has been ordered to register all Tutsi in Kigali and suspects it is for their extermination. Example he gave was that in 20 minutes his personnel could kill up to 1000 Tutsis."[8] He concluded the two-page cable by questioning the motives and sincerity of the informant and raising the possibility that the informant's offer to guide UNAMIR to the weapons caches might be a trap. "After all, this informant had blood on his hands and it was not clear why he suddenly had a change of heart," Brent Beardsley, Dallaire's executive assistant, recalled thinking at the time.[9] Still, Dallaire thought the information credible enough that he notified DPKO that while he checked out the informant's story, he intended to begin planning the raid, which he hoped to carry out within the next thirty-six hours. Dallaire needed advice, however, on how to handle the informant's request for protection. Understandably, the informant now feared that he and his family would find their names on the lengthening list of individuals to be assassinated. "This HQ does not have previous UN experience in such matters and urgently requests guidance." The cable closed with an urgent call for action: "Peux ce que veux. Allons-y."[10]

Several top officials of DPKO, including Iqbal Riza (the assistant secretary-general for peacekeeping), Baril (DPKO's military adviser), and Hedi Annabi (DPKO's chief of the African section), gathered that evening to discuss the cable. They decided to order Dallaire to junk his plan for seizing the weapons caches, to relay the information to the American, French, and Belgian embassies in Kigali (members of the contact group), and to deliver a strongly worded demarche to President Habyarimana regarding the seriousness of the allegations.

Paragraph 1 opened with an unambiguous directive: "We have carefully reviewed the situation in light of your MIR-79 [coding of January 11 cable]. We cannot agree to the operation contemplated in Paragraph 7 of your cable, as it clearly goes beyond the mandate entrusted to UNAMIR under resolution 873 (1993)." Instead, Dallaire was instructed to go to the president and tell him to halt these "subversive activities" and recover the weapons. Dallaire then was to report within forty-eight hours whether such action has been taken. To reinforce the severity of the transgression, Dallaire was advised to inform the president that if violence did occur, "you [UNAMIR] would have to immediately bring to the attention of the Security Council the information you have received." As far as protecting the informant, this went beyond UNAMIR's mandate, but Dallaire was authorized to reassure him that his identity and contacts would not be revealed. Just in case Dallaire had not gotten the message, DPKO closed the cable on the following note: "If you have major problems with the guidance provided above, you may consult us further. We wish to stress, however, that the overriding consideration is the need to avoid entering into a course of action that might lead to the use of force and unanticipated consequences. Regards."[11]

Ever since it was uncovered, the January 11 cable has come under a critical gaze, viewed as the first and most obvious warning sign of the looming genocide and one that DPKO inexplicably ignored. How could DPKO have been so oblivious to such a starkly written warning sign, a scarlet message of danger to civilians, to the peace process, and to peacekeepers? How was this stunning cable, with its graphic cataloging of detailed plans of violence and sedition, not a prelude to forceful action? Why did DPKO fail to immediately inform the Security Council of this message?

DPKO officials admit that "mistakes were made" and that if they had known then what they know now, they would have acted differently. But they have defended their actions by referring to extenuating circumstances that they insinuate explain if not excuse their behavior. Their defense typically begins by insisting that the cable be placed in its proper context. While they and their critics stare at the same texts, there is one critical difference that accounts for their distinct responses: their examinations are occurring at radically divergent historical moments. The critics of the UN have the advantage of hindsight and the ability to start with knowledge of the genocide, return to the January 11 telegram, and then draw a direct link forward to the genocide. Such historical promiscuity transforms a troubling cable into a chillingly accurate prediction of the future that could hardly be missed. But, as UN officials defensively and rightly note, they did not have the luxury of retrospective wisdom. If the telegram is wrenched from its historical and organizational context, then it is an unimpeachable warning sign that cannot be ignored or misinterpreted. Once it is properly situated, however, then its Nostradamus-like qualities disappear. The cable should be read as they read it then, they insist, which means recovering its uncertainty, the restrictions imposed by the mandate and the council, and the recent historical events that shadowed and colored what was politically doable and desirable.

So, what did DPKO know? What could it have known? What more could it have done? Before these questions are addressed, it is important to note that those at UN headquarters who were directly involved in these events have been reluctant to divulge the details of their discussions. When they have spoken, moreover, their descriptions of events typically take the form of excuses that are intended to respond to the accusations of negligence. These descriptions make the attempted reconstructive exercise slightly less speculative than Kremlinology during the days of the Cold War but certainly much less informative than one might desire. Fortunately, cables subsequently were leaked and entered into the public domain, and many UNAMIR officials who were on the transmitting end have been willing to speak. The picture that emerges is that DPKO's "mistakes" were shaped by the combination of a peacekeeping culture of consent and impartiality, a mindset that allowed the fear of civil war to consume all other possible forms of violence, and the post-Somalia haze that left them panicked about their next (mis)step. They were certainly limited in what they could know and do. But those limits proved comforting to individuals who wanted to play it safe because they worried about the UN's survival.

DPKO was distressed by the cable because it portended danger. Yet UN officials, in their attempt to defend their seemingly cavalier attitude toward the violence predicted by the cable, have suggested otherwise. Riza claimed that this was "a normal cable . . . [and] there are a number of cables that we get of this nature."[12] Boutros-Ghali reflected that while reports such as those contained in the January 11 cable are treated with "utmost seriousness by UN officials, [they] are not uncommon within the context of peace-keeping operations."[13] DPKO apparently knew how to read this cable because of prior experience dealing with similar communiqués from other operations. Peacekeeping operations, by definition, are located in places where violence is present or an imminent possibility, and Rwanda as a peacekeeping operation was no different except perhaps in terms of the level of violence. By defending their actions in this manner, UN staff give just cause to those who paint them as perfect organizational men who cannot think "outside the box." Along these lines, Philip Gourevitch observed, "Essentially, the response of the peacekeeping headquarters in New York at the UN . . . was to treat this fax as a routine bureaucratic matter. It set off no special alarm bells that rang loudly. It was not disseminated. . . . It was treated as a routine bureaucratic matter."[14]

But it is not true that the telegram was given the bureaucratic treatment and rang no alarms. It was rare to hastily convene a meeting at the end of a long day on a relatively minor peacekeeping operation. And over the next several days, as indicated by the flurry of cables, DPKO officials continued to give serious attention to the news coming from Kigali. This happened because the cable *was* unusual. The magnitude of the violence it predicted was out of the ordinary, as Riza himself conceded.[15] And if DPKO failed to comprehend the gravity of the situation from that one cable, the next few days of urgent telephone calls from Dallaire surely would have cleared up any misunderstandings. The Interahamwe was possibly planning a campaign of ethnic cleansing against the Tutsi population, Dallaire told headquarters on several occasions.[16] At that point, according to Dallaire's aide, the force commander used the language of ethnic cleansing (and not genocide) to describe the threat. Thanks to Bosnia, he continued, they had learned to describe these possibilities with the vocabulary of ethnic cleansing and not genocide.[17] While *ethnic cleansing* can refer to a range of hideous policies, including forcible displacement and selective killings,

UNAMIR explicitly associated the concept with specific practices—the gathering of lists, the targeting of Tutsi civilians, and plans of an extermination campaign. DPKO was now being made aware that not only were the Arusha process and the cease-fire in danger, but also there was a distinct possibility of ethnic cleansing in its most extreme form.

Yet, it does not appear that the predicted violence became the object of DPKO's immediate concern. If DPKO officials did not give it "the attention it deserved," it was because their eyes and fears were trained on another object. The immediate danger involved not what the Rwandans might do but rather what Dallaire intended to do. Predictions of violence, even violence directed at civilians and peacekeepers, were not uncommon. It *was* highly irregular for force commanders who headed underequipped operations to seize arms caches in politically sensitive locations. Because Dallaire had declared his intention to strike within the next thirty-six hours, DPKO had little time to respond. Evidence that this was the source of their anxieties can be found in the critical opening and closing paragraphs of the responding cable, which instructed Dallaire to drop his planned raid. DPKO reminded him, in the most direct language available to UN civil servants, that this was a peacekeeping operation, not a peace enforcement mission, that he was to operate with the consent of the parties and not with coercion, and that his mandate prohibited him from undertaking the very action he now proposed. Although Baril later denied that anyone at DPKO thought Dallaire was a "cowboy," they certainly wanted to remind him that he was a peacekeeper and not a soldier.[18] At this moment DPKO was more fearful of Dallaire than of the extremists.

DPKO officials assert that they had little choice but to call the raid off because of the restrictions imposed on them by the mandate, the peacekeeping rule book, and the council. The mandate prohibited the very actions Dallaire proposed. Riza observed, "We have to go by the mandate we are given by the Security Council. It's not up to the Secretary-General or the Secretariat to decide whether they're going to run off in other directions."[19] Under the mandate, UNAMIR was to "contribute to the security of the city of Kigali, *inter alia*, within a weapons-secure area established by the parties in and around the city."[20] According to Riza, himself a veteran of the UN operation in El Salvador, this meant that UNAMIR's mandate permitted it to *assist* the parties in establishing a weapons-secure zone, not to "go and recover weapons" on its own.[21] The verbs *assist* and *contribute* signaled, therefore, that UNAMIR could be an active presence in the streets and had some discretion concerning how robust a presence it would maintain. But the spirit of the mandate did not envision UNAMIR storming into residences or party headquarters to seize weapons. UNAMIR could inform the local authorities that it had knowledge of illegal stocks, a clear cease-fire violation, but it could only seize the weapons if given prior authorization to do so by the parties.

DPKO's response to Dallaire also was consistent with the principles of consent and impartiality, the hallmark of a Chapter VI operation. Peacekeeping is defined by these principles. Those who might have wanted to argue in favor of Dallaire's plan now had to argue against these principles, which had become further ingrained by the situation in Somalia. Furthermore, UNAMIR's rather minimal force structure certainly did not inspire confidence that Dallaire's exercise was militarily advisable. In comparison to UNAMIR, UNOSOM was heavily outfitted and generously equipped, and UNOSOM faltered under more favorable circumstances. UNAMIR, in short, would have to rely on the consent and full participation of the very individuals who were storing and hiding these weapons. However self-defeating this might appear, it was unquestionably consistent with the mandate and the principles of peacekeeping.

But Dallaire held a decidedly different interpretation of the mandate, one that made such operations both permissible and necessary. His view was that UNAMIR was being asked to help provide the security that would facilitate the implementation of the Arusha Accords. The KWSA was a piece of this logic and process. According to Dallaire, it was a "purpose-built" concept that was intended to provide security in Kigali and to allow UNAMIR to "push the envelope"—that is, use force if need be in those areas where there was substantial movement of people and the danger of violence.[22] At this critical juncture, UNAMIR had to provide the security that would enable the parties to take the necessary political leap. A newcomer to the culture of the UN, Dallaire presumed that words like *assist* meant that UNAMIR could undertake activities that were consistent with Arusha and that provided for security. If he did not know that words like *assist* were pronounced with a passive inflection, it was because, as incredible as it seems, no one at headquarters bothered to have an extended conversation with him about headquarters' understanding of what was and was not permitted by the mandate.[23]

In keeping with his interpretation and the recently signed KWSA, Dallaire had UNAMIR, beginning in late December 1993, step up its security presence, seizing weapons at roadblocks and confiscating weapons of illegal militias regardless of their location in Kigali. Dallaire dutifully reported these developments in situation reports to headquarters. For instance, in a January 4, 1994, cable he wrote, "UNAMIR ensured the Kigali Weapon Secure Area so far and is ready for appropriate action in case of violation. FC implemented the first offensive ops [operations] planning against armed political milities [*sic*] and suspicious area. No results so far."[24] Now he had learned that an illegal militia that wanted to scuttle the accords and kill civilians was stockpiling weapons for that very purpose. This was a clear violation of the KWSA and a menace to Arusha. Accordingly, Dallaire decided to seize the weapons. There was nothing controversial about this measure, in his opinion. This type of action was authorized by the mandate and the KWSA, and it was UNAMIR's very raison d'être. Similarly, Colonel Luc Marchal, who headed the Kigali sector battalion, stated categorically that the mandate did permit the seizure of weapons. "For me, my responsibility was the enforcement of its provisions."[25]

When Dallaire shot off his cable, he was not expecting headquarters to comment on his plan to seize the weapons but rather was looking for guidance regarding how to handle the informant's request for protection. Therefore, he was astonished when DPKO denied a request that he assumed was well within his mandate and demanded by the circumstances. The nature of its denial and the reasons it gave made it clear to him that he and DPKO were "not part of the same philosophy." While he conceded that there was a risk of failure, that risk was clearly outweighed by the risk of doing nothing and allowing the threat to the operation and the civilians to accumulate.[26]

Over the next several days, Dallaire and headquarters held heated exchanges over its refusal to permit this action. Acting like a man who believed he was being misheard, Dallaire kept presenting the same information in new ways, though always insisting that his plan was within his mandate and that UNAMIR had to provide security if Arusha was to have a chance. DPKO was not buying the same argument in a different guise, repeatedly insisting that his request was outside the mandate and any reasonable interpretation of "assist."[27] Dallaire saw his plan as a natural extension of his previous actions and consistent with the KWSA. DPKO saw his plan as an abrupt departure from anything that had been done previously and outside what would be permitted by the mandate or a Chapter VI operation.

Instead of passing along this information and the decision to the council, DPKO made the call without its input. The council certainly does not want to weigh in on all aspects of a peacekeeping operation, and assumes that the Secretariat will implement the council's wishes and handle the day-to-day matters. And so DPKO and Boutros-Ghali might have presumed that this matter could be left to their discretion.[28] DPKO also might not have wanted to approach the council because of Rwanda's presence; once it informed the council, then Habyarimana would be tipped off about UNAMIR's information and intentions (though the result would be exactly the same once Dallaire delivered his demarche to the president). More pressing, perhaps, was DPKO's expectation that Dallaire's plan would unnerve a Somalia-obsessed council. Bringing this information to the council also would have made it even more distrustful of the parties' intentions toward Arusha. The council would have been highly disturbed by the news that the security situation was even worse than it was led to believe, that parties close to the president might be conspiring to destroy Arusha and harm peacekeepers, and that the best way to salvage the situation was to have a malnourished force raid weapons caches. Little good would come from asking the council to consider an "enforcement" operation that DPKO knew would be rejected out of hand.

This did not mean, however, that DPKO was resigned to a course of action that it thought was ill-advised. Various reports have suggested as much—that DPKO would have preferred to ask for the resources and the permission for robust action but decided not to because it knew the council would say no.[29] This observation happens to be a truth convenient to the Secretariat because it shifts the locus of responsibility to the Security Council and portrays DPKO as cowed into a passive and impossible position. That does not make it wrong. After all, DPKO did have good reason to come to this conclusion.

Yet DPKO also appears to have decided independently against Dallaire's plan. When DPKO received the cable from Dallaire, its immediate response was to focus not on the threat to peacekeepers but rather on Dallaire's planned action and its threat to the operation and the UN. Riza suggested this very possibility. He said that his immediate reaction to Dallaire's telegram was, "Not Somalia again. . . . We're talking about this cable having come in January,"[30] just months after the Pakistani and American soldiers were killed as a consequence of their efforts at forced demilitarization in Somalia—that is, Dallaire's operation bore an eerie similarity to Somalia. Somalia redux.

From DPKO's perspective, Dallaire's plan resembled the forced disarmament that had been the undoing of UNOSOM, and they feared that the Interahamwe would give an Aideed-like response to a UNOSOM-like provocation. How many peacekeepers, and civilians caught in the firefight, would die from a possible retaliation? And what about the future of UNAMIR? Somalia began to fall apart when peacekeepers began to go after the opponents of the peace process. Dallaire might have believed that he was within his mandate, but a raid gone awry might mean the very end of the mandate and do further damage to the UN. Responding to Dallaire, who was livid that DPKO had denied his operation, Baril told him to settle down and recognize that from New York's view, his planned raid had Somalia and "mission creep" written all over it.[31] This peripheral peacekeeping operation, of the kind that typically drew scant attention, might suddenly become (in)famous for all the wrong reasons.

DPKO officials could imagine the consequences of warlike action more easily than they could the benefits of a victorious operation. From their vantage point, Dallaire's plan resembled the events in Mogadishu that had spelled the demise of the operation and hastened the UN's fall from grace. They personally and recently had lived through these experiences. They watched a humanitarian mission creep into an enforcement operation. They had to stew in relative silence as the United States abruptly announced its departure from Somalia. Ever since the announcement in October 1993, they had been receiving a steady stream of American officials planning the departure. They had to listen to officials in Washington and others admonish the staff at the UN headquarters for having grandiose plans and not realizing peacekeeping's inherent limitations. They understood from firsthand experience the price of risky action. Kigali would not be allowed to become Mogadishu by another name.

So DPKO arguably leaned on these rules, not simply because they were appropriate for the circumstances but also because they minimized the risk to the institution. In a highly revealing moment that implies that perhaps Dallaire was not laboring under a highly idiosyncratic interpretation of the mandate, Riza stated, "*We were cautious in interpreting our mandate* and in giving guidance because we did not want a repetition of Somalia. . . . We could not risk another Somalia as it lead [*sic*] to the collapse of the Somalian mission. We did not want this mission to collapse."[32]

The living lessons of Somalia, and not the explicit parameters of the mandate, chilled DPKO into a cautionary posture. "DPKO, therefore, emphasized that the responsibility for the maintenance of law and order must remain with the local authorities and that, while UNAMIR could *assist* in arms recovery operations, it should avoid entering into a course of action that might lead to the use of force and to unanticipated repercussions."[33]

Dallaire's proposal scared the hell out of DPKO officials, giving them night sweats as it triggered visions of a UN version of a "China Syndrome," where one raid gone bad leads to the collapse of a mission and the meltdown of the UN. UN staff feared that any more failures might spell the end of peacekeeping, particularly so if those failures were prodded by overzealous force commanders. There was a chance that the raid might succeed and demonstrate the mettle of UNAMIR. But that had to be balanced against the risk to the peacekeepers, the operation, and all of UN peacekeeping if the operation failed. While Dallaire kept insisting that DPKO's fear of failure had to be balanced against the risk of doing nothing and waiting for the inevitable return of violence, DPKO had a much easier time calculating the consequences for the UN and the mission of a raid gone bad than the benefits of a raid gone right.

DPKO's construction of Dallaire as a threat provides a possible clue as to why it apparently minimized the predicted threat to civilians. If DPKO read the cable as saying "the most important political power in Rwanda is planning to kill peacekeepers and tens of thousands of civilians," then its instructions to Dallaire to tell the palace that there was a "cease-fire violation" and rumors of "subversive activities" would be more than absurd. It also probably would have led to severe cognitive dissonance. DPKO officials would have had to deal somehow with the incredible gap between the gruesome predictions and their own sanitized response.

By categorizing the violence in a way that achieved consistency with its proposed plan of action, DPKO was able to maintain policy coherence and cognitively support its impartial stance. Organizations like the UN have a limited number of responses to any situation or demand, and the UN almost always starts with the principles of consent and impartiality. Only after the response is selected does DPKO classify the violence. "This is a standard cable." "We have heard all this before from Rwanda and other operations." "Dallaire is overstating the situation because he is new to peacekeeping." Response precedes stimulus. That individuals define the problem after they have selected the solution is not that unusual, and is, in fact, quite a routine feature of bureaucracies and organizations. While Dallaire was fairly crystalline concerning the nature of the violence, seasoned UN officials who were used to dealing with messy transitions might well have downplayed predictions coming from someone like Dallaire, who was viewed as overly energetic and who was new to peacekeeping and Africa.

UNAMIR immediately carried out the only actions DPKO permitted, holding a meeting with the president to inform him of the seriousness of the charges and the need to take countermeasures within forty-eight hours, and transmitting the information to the representatives from France, Belgium, and the United States. Booh-Booh immediately met with Habyarimana. According to the special representative's reporting cable to UN headquarters, the president appeared alarmed by the tone of the demarche and denied any knowledge of the activities. In a statement that simultaneously revealed how astute Dallaire was of the likely consequences of this demarche and how willing Booh-Booh was to tell headquarters what it wanted to hear, Booh-Booh wrote, "The President and the MRND seemed unnerved and is reported to have subsequently ordered an accelerated distribution of weapons. My assessment of the situation is that the initiative to confront the accused parties with the information was a good one and may force them to decide on alternative ways of jeopardizing the peace process, especially in the Kigali area."[34] Because of the imposed guidelines, UNAMIR had contributed to the very outcome it wanted to stop. This episode also did little for UNAMIR's reputation. The effect, as Beardsley put it, was to announce to the Hutu power elite that UNAMIR was a "toothless tiger."[35]

Dallaire shared the information and his assessment with the contact group, the United States, France, and Belgium. Dallaire's impression from these meetings was that they were not overly surprised by the news, which probably reflected the fact that each had active intelligence networks in Rwanda that had been getting whiffs of diabolical plots.[36]

France had the least reason to look shocked. It had developed intimate knowledge of the political and military situation because of its extensive contacts with the palace and many who counted themselves as part of the Hutu power elite. In retrospect, some French officials concede that by late 1993 they should have seen the violence coming.[37] But even the noted historian Gérard Prunier, who is generally relentless in his criticism of the French, wrote that it was difficult for "Westerners—and especially for French Cartesian minds—to make a meaningful connection between . . . obscure cultural allusions and the magnitude of the horror being planned."[38] Although the French might not have been able to foresee the genocide, they knew that Habyarimana's regime and those close to the president were responsible for human rights violations. Not only did the French fail to use their leverage to demand that Habyarimana do what he could to stop these violations, but also they continued to provide cover for the regime in various diplomatic fora and to allow their military advisers to train and equip the Rwandan army and right-wing militias. In addition, they convinced other Western states to pull their punches at various moments, including the contact group's demarche after the January 11 telegram, when France convinced its colleagues not to raise the most serious of the charges. It was business as usual.[39]

During this period officials at the American embassy in Kigali focused on the necessary establishment of the transitional government, tended to associate the predicted violence with a possible civil war or ethnic conflict, and steadfastly declared that the only possible resolution to the conflict was the immediate establishment of the BBTG. There is no evidence, moreover, that anyone in Washington imagined that a breakdown in the political process would lead to genocide. Of all the agencies in Washington, the State Department's African bureau was most on top of the situation, but it tended to minimize the most incredible rumors of wide-scale massacres coming from Rwanda because it had heard these rumors for a while.[40] The State Department's Bureau of International Organization Affairs was more interested in the overall health of the UN than it was in one peripheral operation. Therefore, it was unlikely to push risky action in Kigali if it might jeopardize broader strategic goals. There is little evidence that American officials in Kigali or Washington believed that Dallaire's proposed military operation was prudent, which is not terribly surprising given the fact that this was another part of Africa and was occurring only a few months after the debacle in Somalia.[41] For instance, Brussels called National Security Adviser Tony Lake to plead for more troops and a more generous interpretation of the mandate. His response was that UNAMIR was large enough for its observer mission and would never have enough troops if it were to be turned into an enforcement operation.[42] Officials in Washington had one answer for the security situation and Rwanda's ills: establish the transitional government. This answer not only was obvious but also was the safest politically. The National Security Council paid little attention to Rwanda and wanted to keep it that way, and this was best assured by not doing anything rash.

Belgium was the only member of the contact group to decide that this new information and growing insecurity required a stronger military presence. The Belgian contingent in Rwanda was keeping Brussels informed of the information being uncovered by its extensive intelligence networks. Hearing reports of impending massacres, knowing that the situation was rapidly deteriorating, and convinced that deterrent operations alongside an augmented presence were the only way to arrest the slide, Belgium pressed Boutros-Ghali to give a more generous interpretation of the mandate. On February 11, 1994, the clearly frustrated Belgian Foreign Minister Willy Claes wrote to Boutros-Ghali to implore him to permit UNAMIR to take a "firmer stance" and to warn that the failure to do so might lead to a situation where "UNAMIR might find itself unable to continue effectively its basic mission."[43] Officials in Brussels also tried without success to convince France and the United States that the gravity of the situation required a more direct response.[44] Anything short, some Belgian officials worried, would only feed a humanitarian nightmare. Belgium was the only member of the contact group that believed that UNAMIR had to risk bolder military action in order to avoid a bleak future.

OVER the next several months Dallaire agonized over the rapidly deteriorating security situation. The violence gave no indications of dissipating. Killings and political assassinations became routine, and a general culture of violence splashed across the airwaves and in newspapers and speeches. UNAMIR kept headquarters fully apprised of the disintegrating security environment. In a February 2 cable, Booh-Booh recounted the "violent demonstrations, nightly grenade attacks, assassination attempts, political and ethnic killings."[45] By the end of February the violence had become so chronic and fierce that UNAMIR began to despair that the parties had turned fully away from the Arusha Accords and toward bloodshed.

UNAMIR astutely feared that its anemic presence was an unwitting contributor to the growing instability. Both the proponents and the opponents of the accords were taking their cues from UNAMIR, acting in ways that seemed to propel the country down a violent path.[46] Because the extremists now believed that UNAMIR was unwilling or unable to respond to attacks and violations of the mandate, they determined that they could adopt more violent means without risking a forceful response.[47] If once restrained by the fear that UNAMIR might meet violence with force, extremists now speculated that the UN would rather retreat than fight, which encouraged them to think more grandly—that is, violently. Dallaire understood that the extremists were testing UNAMIR's resolve and that it was failing miserably.[48]

The proponents of Arusha also altered their behavior because of UNAMIR's presence. Whereas once they feared that they would pay with their lives if they spoke in favor of a multiethnic Rwanda, the moderate politicians were increasingly speaking their minds because they believed that UNAMIR would protect them from any physical backlash from the extremists.[49] As Dallaire later reflected, "The UN mission, and later the very civilians whose lives it was intended to secure, fell victim to an inflated sense of optimism which I myself participated in formulating, thereby creating high expectations which the UN did not have the capacity to meet."[50]

UNAMIR's presence and posture, therefore, produced a tragic though unintended dynamic. The moderate politicians acted on the faith that UNAMIR would protect them against the Hutu extremists. So they began to speak publicly and critically of the Hutu regime and Hutu power. As they did so, the extremists became increasingly fearful that they were about to lose political power and increasingly determined to use violence to keep it. And because of recent events the extremists came to believe that their violent actions would go unanswered by UNAMIR. Clear in retrospect, but not fully appreciated at the time, was that as the parties who favored the Arusha Accords began to act with more urgency out of their fear of the extremists, the extremists began to accelerate their own plans. Like political quicksand, the increasingly frantic motions toward Arusha at the surface produced a demonic but concealed opposition just underneath.

Aware that its passive behavior was encouraging the very violence UNAMIR was sent to stop, Dallaire concluded that only a firmer stance would correct the downturn. It was imperative, Dallaire recalled, that

UNAMIR keep the Interahamwe off balance, which meant it had to take the initiative and cease being so reactive.[51] In an attempt to make such action less threatening to headquarters, UNAMIR intentionally dropped any further references to "offensive" operations and strategically and consistently adopted the language of "deterrence." In the same February 2 cable in which Booh-Booh chronicled a quickly crumbling security situation, he wrote that UNAMIR is

> receiving more and more credible and confirmed information that the armed militias of the parties are stockpiling and may possibly be preparing to distribute arms to their supporters. . . . Each day of delay in authorizing deterrent arms recovery operation will result in an ever deteriorating security situation and may if arms continue to be distributed result in an inability of UNAMIR to carry out its mandate in all aspects . . . and create a significant danger to the safety and security of UN military and civilian personnel and the population at large.[52]

UNAMIR concluded that selective "deterrent" operations, including the seizure of arms caches, were necessary. Such deterrent action would not only fulfill the requirements of the mandate but also ensure the continued safety of UN personnel.[53]

Boutros-Ghali and DPKO were not swayed by any of these tactics, assessments, or demarches, reminding Dallaire of the meaning of consent and enjoining UNAMIR to act only in concert with the Rwandan parties.[54] The Secretariat's insistence that UNAMIR adhere to the principle of consent also shaped its restricted notion of the rules of engagement (ROEs).[55] Although the ROEs did provide UNAMIR with language to protect civilians from ethnically motivated crimes, in January the UN began insisting on a much more narrow interpretation that permitted the discharge of weapons only when peacekeepers were attacked or threatened directly. As a consequence, Dallaire repeatedly ordered his troops to negotiate with the parties and to seek their consent at all times.[56] The reason for this response, one DPKO official observed, was that the Secretariat was unwilling to cross the Mogadishu line.[57]

Dallaire was equally adamant that he was only proposing action that was permitted by prior agreements, that it was necessary to keep the extremists at bay, and that working jointly with the Rwandan forces was self-defeating because they either were unwilling to conduct such operations or did not have the capacity to do so. Eventually UNAMIR did conduct a few joint operations with the local authorities. However, they proved largely ineffectual because of the gross incompetence of the Rwandan authorities. Perhaps they were even feigning incompetence as a way of undermining the operations, and UNAMIR's plans were almost always leaked to the Interahamwe.[58]

Between January and April 1994, Dallaire's cables and telephone conversations with headquarters emphasized that the fraying situation was proving too much for UNAMIR's meager resources.[59] Indeed, the bulk of UNAMIR's cables focused less on the security environment than it did on the outrageous logistics situation. From the very beginning of the operation, UNAMIR had a difficult time getting the basic supplies required for the operation, including eating utensils. One story is that after months of begging for flashlights, they finally arrived. But without batteries. When UNAMIR cabled headquarters to ask about the batteries' whereabouts, it was told that there was money for flashlights but not batteries. At a later moment UNAMIR ran out of paper and was unable to file more situation reports.

The peacekeepers who were arriving in Kigali were hardly battle-tested and barely trained. Often they came without supplies, including basic items like boots, and expected a barren operation to give them the essentials. What limited military equipment UNAMIR received was generally shoddy. UNAMIR requested twenty-two armored personnel carriers (APCs); they received eight, only five of which were roadworthy. Only Belgium arrived with APCs. The Bangladeshi contingent was supposed to operate the other APCs, which were Russian vehicles with Russian-language manuals that were indecipherable to all, but neither they nor the APCs were up to the job. What UNAMIR was experiencing was scandalous even by the relatively low standards obtained for most operations. Dallaire was busily cabling New York with increasingly urgent demands for military supplies and logistical support. He bitterly recalled that "[s]eventy percent of my and my principal staff's time was dedicated to an administrative battle within the UN's somewhat constipated logistic and administrative structure."[60] A logistics situation that severely limited its ability to carry out the mandate would prove life-threatening in a very short time.

The view from New York was that the establishment of the long-promised transitional government was the only way to arrest the deteriorating security situation and get the peace process back on track. There was no other possible way ahead or out. This single-mindedness was in clear operation when Boutros-Ghali met a special envoy sent by President Habyarimana on March 1. Even though the month of February was crammed with cables from the field warning of an ominous security situation and threats to the peace process and civilians, Boutros-Ghali never raised the issue of human rights violations, instead concentrating on the transitional institutions.[61] In New York the constant focus of conversation was the failure of the parties to establish the BBTG.

The UN began pushing for the establishment of the transitional government with every imaginable consensual tactic at its disposal. UNAMIR was involved in the continuing negotiations, ready to lend a hand and nudge the parties forward. Members of the contact group made similar diplomatic interventions. The United States, for instance, sent a high-level delegation from Washington to deliver personally the message that it was imperative that the parties pick up the pace and that patience on the part of Washington and New York was wearing thin.

The UN also began to use unorthodox tactics. As soon as the political process began to sputter and stall, the Security Council and the Secretariat began to threaten to close down UNAMIR. At first this threat was whispered discreetly. But as the process dragged on, they wielded the threat more openly and directly. On January 14, Boutros-Ghali told Booh-Booh that he should meet with Habyarimana and inform him that it was imperative to resolve the political deadlock. Each day's delay cost the UN thousands of dollars, and such delays invariably caused Rwanda problems with the Security Council too.[62] In a telephone call soon thereafter, Boutros-Ghali personally delivered the message to Habyarimana that "unless there was progress the United Nations would be obliged to withdraw its presence."[63] After the parties missed another deadline for establishing the BBTG, on February 17 the Security Council issued a statement saying that its continuing involvement in Rwanda was contingent on the parties' following through on their promises. In his March 1 meeting with Habyarimana's emissary, Boutros-Ghali threatened to withdraw UNAMIR unless progress was achieved, emphasizing the competing priorities of the UN, and saying that "UNAMIR could be withdrawn within 15 days unless progress was forthcoming."[64] These threats and cajolings were not having their desired effect.

———————

THE Secretariat began preparing its report on Rwanda against the backdrop of distressing times at the UN. Earlier that month, Boutros-Ghali submitted "Improving the Capacity of the United Nations for Peacekeeping" to the Security Council, a document that bounced between ways to improve peacekeeping and ways to arrest what appeared to be its declining popularity after five years of distended growth coupled with failures in the field. Also, the remaining American forces were departing Somalia. While the transition was going reasonably well, there was little expectation that this operation, which was once supposed to be a showcase for the UN's talents, would suddenly turn around. UNPROFOR had been going through a particularly rocky few months. The UN no longer looked for good news but only for ways to minimize more of the bad news. And now the secretary-general was preparing to report on a stalled operation that only a few months before had been dubbed a surefire winner that would redeem the UN's reputation.

Perhaps the most notable feature of the secretary-general's report was its presentation of the security situation. It painted a deteriorating security situation, one that had worsened since the arrival of UNAMIR. In addition to banditry, "January and February [1994] saw increasingly violent demonstrations, roadblocks, assassinations of political leaders and assaults on and murders of civilians."[65] This violence, the report observed, was common to political transitions from civil war to civil peace and its intensity in this instance was due to the paralysis in the peace process. The remedy was the immediate establishment of the transitional government. While UNAMIR staff agreed with the remedy, they also gave the violence an ethnic and extremist face, a feature omitted by the report.[66] Perhaps the Secretariat's willingness to smooth over the ragged edges of the security situation had to do with its desire not to alarm an already edgy Security Council.

The secretary-general's subordination of the ethnic dimension to a political process and its insistence on a political solution to the domestic conflict also reflected its long-held understanding of the nature of the conflict and the UN's contribution to its resolution. Rwanda was still viewed through the lens of a civil war. The ongoing violence was associated with a stalled transition process that might backslide into a civil war. That the explosion of violence might degenerate into mass killings was always a possibility. But that the resumption of a civil war would become the cover and pretext for an extermination campaign was hardly imaginable. Certainly not by UN officials. Nor even by the most savvy and knowledgeable Rwandans. While most Rwandans figured that ethnic violence was a distinct possibility, few imagined massive crimes against humanity. Violence, yes. Genocide and extermination, no.

The report emphasized the political solution to the security situation and observed that there might be, at long last, good news to report. Though acknowledging the months of a repeated cycle of hopeful rumors followed by disappointment mixed with frustration, it nevertheless stressed that the RPF and the Rwandan government were reporting that they were close to an agreement on establishing the transitional government. Perhaps in the next few weeks. Boutros-Ghali recommended that the Security Council renew the mandate and give the parties more time to make the leap forward. But he also insinuated that the previous threat to close down the operation was having its desired effect, and the council should give notice that this would be the last extension absent sustained progress.

The increasingly exasperated Security Council was now being asked to renew UNAMIR's mandate. Although most renewals have an almost scripted quality, this one proved to be highly contentious and controversial because of the threat to terminate the operation if the BBTG was not established. The council's discussions focused on whether this was a "drop dead" date and whether any additional resources should be spent on the operation. The United States vociferously argued against renewing the operation, with some in the Clinton administration believing that this was a useful threat to move the process along and others being quite sincere in their intentions. In the council the United States argued that enough was enough and that the UN should cut its losses and save its resources for a more worthy operation. If the extremists were too powerful, it continued, then perhaps the UN had no business being in Rwanda because the Arusha agreement was not worth the paper on which it was written. There was an additional, long-term payoff to be gained from following through on a threat to withdraw: those who were awarded operations would now understand that the UN had limited patience and meant what it said. This would not be such a bad reputation to have.

The United States was not only looking out for the UN's welfare. It also calculated that such a tough stance would reap political dividends at home. This tough love approach would allow the Clinton administration to demonstrate through word and deed that it could be a hard-headed advocate of peacekeeping. Now Clinton officials marching up to Capitol Hill would be able to point to a concrete instance of their ability to say no to peacekeeping when certain conditions had not been met. Of course, what was true about Rwanda was true of any number of other operations, but Washington had no strategic interests at stake or any powerful domestic constituencies to fear. It could safely make an example of Rwanda.

Although many in the council recoiled at the American stridency and hypocrisy, there was general agreement with many of its claims. A peacekeeping operation was a privilege and not a right. The parties had to stick to their agreements. The failure to do so could lead to repercussions, including the threat of withdrawal. The fact of the matter was that the UN had few levers to persuade or punish the parties into implementing their agreements. While the council was now playing the withdrawal card, it was unclear whether it would be truly prepared to follow through on the ultimatum. To carry out such a threat would have been unprecedented. And many believed that it should take much more than a several-month delay to provoke the council to close down an operation. Still, the United States and the United Kingdom won the council over to the unprecedented idea of renewing the operation for a four-month period, with a likely review after six weeks if the transitional institutions had not yet been established.

The United States found itself completely isolated in its objection to the Secretariat's recommendation that UNAMIR be given another forty-five civilian police. UNAMIR urged this injection because of the deteriorating security situation.[67] Although to most on the council, forty-five was not a lavish number and seemed reasonable given the situation, the United States opposed even considering the expenditure of more resources until the transitional institutions had been established. Otherwise, the United States insisted, the UN would be "rewarding" the Rwandans for "bad" behavior. Behind this high-minded rhetoric were more base considerations. Once again, the White House feared that if it authorized this request, then at some time in the near future it would have to explain to someone in Congress about the appropriation of more funds for an operation in the middle of Africa that no one cared about and that had not yet completed the most simple steps in the transitional process. Although others in the Security Council and the Secretariat feared that the penny-pinching and shortsighted United States was harming the mission, the United States would not budge and won the desired language.

The Security Council voted an extension on April 5, just as the mandate was about to expire. The council's threat to close the operation unless the transitional government was immediately established, as well as a diplomatic offensive in Kigali in late March, convinced Habyarimana that he had run out of stalling tactics and had to take the next step forward. He flew off to Arusha, Tanzania, to finalize the transitional government just as the council was voting to extend the mandate.

4

The Fog of Genocide

The first scent of hell materialized the day after the Security Council voted to renew the UNAMIR mandate. On the evening of April 6, 1994, President Habyarimana was flying back from Dar es Salaam, Tanzania, where he was rumored to have put the final pieces in place for the BBTG. But the Mystère Falcon jet carrying him, Burundi President Cyprien Ntaryamira, seven senior members of the Rwandan government, and a French air crew was shot down as it approached the Kigali airport. At 8:30 P.M., the plane crashed onto the grounds of the presidential palace, killing everyone on board. The crash acted like a signal; forty-eight minutes later, the Presidential Guard erected the first road blocks and were immediately joined by the Interahamwe. Shortly afterward, the conspirators fanned out around the city, picking up and murdering leading Tutsi and moderate Hutu politicians, and evacuating MRND officials and their families to a camp where they would be safe. UNAMIR went on red alert at around 9:30 P.M.

That evening Dallaire was invited to Rwandan army headquarters to meet with several high-ranking Rwandan military officials. The group of sixteen was led by Colonel Théoneste Bagosora, who was already known to several in UNAMIR as an extremist sympathetic to the radical CDR. Dallaire was unable to determine whether he was facing a military coup, a return to civil war, or something else. While Bagosora insisted that the military would now take charge of the situation, he denied that there had been a coup d'état, yet refused to acknowledge that the rightful successor was the Rwandan prime minister, Agathe Uwilingiyimana (widely known as

Madame Agathe). Many in UNAMIR feared that Kigali, which was relatively tranquil, was about to become an inferno.

Now Dallaire would face his worst-case scenario: a lightly armed and malnourished force of twenty-five hundred peacekeepers operating under strict
rules of consent while confronting a wave of violence. UNAMIR's immediate efforts were focused on preserving the cease-fire and some semblance of
the Arusha process. Toward that end, it called for calm and respect for the
cease-fire, offered its negotiating services at this perilous moment, and had
its soldiers make rounds in Kigali in order to assess the situation and to project an appearance of resolve. Yet there was hardly a pretense that at this
point in time and in its current state, UNAMIR could act as a credible deterrent force, even if it wanted to. UNAMIR was stretched thin and quar-
tered in different parts of a hilly Kigali, complicating its already difficult logistical situation. And months of impartiality, and of capitulation to
assassinations, civilian killings, and known violations of the weapons ban,
meant that UNAMIR had little credibility as a deterrent force. To make
matters worse, the putsch and the presumed end of the Arusha Accords
meant that civil war would soon reignite, probably in the next day or two
(as expected, the RPF began a military campaign on April 8).

UNAMIR struggled to preserve the cease-fire and the Arusha agreement. One of Dallaire's first actions in this regard was to hurriedly dispatch
peacekeepers to protect moderate Rwandan politicians. In recent months
UNAMIR had played bodyguard for politicians who were rumored to be
marked for assassination. In these new circumstances Dallaire quickly expanded this service; there was a humanitarian imperative, and whatever remained of the peace process depended on keeping these politicians alive. In
the early hours of April 7, Dallaire sent some peacekeepers to Radio
Rwanda to secure the premises. He also sent ten Belgian soldiers to
Madame Agathe's house, with instructions to escort her to the radio station
in the morning where she could address the nation and call for calm. The
soldiers arrived at dawn only to find themselves quickly surrounded by
Rwandan soldiers. Madame Agathe escaped out the back, accompanied by
her husband, while her five children scrambled off in another direction
searching for safety. The Belgian soldiers then radioed back to headquarters
with disturbing news: they were surrounded by the Rwandans and were
being told to surrender their weapons. Acting on the belief that the soldiers
were exaggerating their fear that they were about to be lynched, the Belgian lieutenant colonel in charge at headquarters ordered the Belgian soldiers who still held their weapons to do as they were told. They did as he
advised. The Rwandan soldiers then took the Belgians to Camp Kigali,
where they tortured and mutilated them, and then left them in a pile in the

Kigali hospital. Such brutality was calculated to intimidate UNAMIR into fleeing Kigali, thereby leaving a clear killing field for the genocidaires.

UNAMIR understood the design of the message and prudently assumed that the Belgian peacekeepers had been singled out because of Belgium's colonial legacy and because it was part of the "West" that the genocidaires wanted to chase away. Accordingly, while the Belgians were presumed to be marked, not so the other peacekeepers. This did not mean, however, that they were safe. The entire mission was in jeopardy because it was running dangerously low on fuel, water, and food, a direct consequence of the fact that their constant pleading for essentials had gone unanswered by officials at UN headquarters. Even worse, there was little prospect of being resupplied in the immediate future. The airport was hardly secure, raising the specter that any approaching aircraft might suffer the same fate as Habyarimana's. UN troops were torn between two, increasingly untenable tasks: carrying out what remained of their mandate and defending themselves.

After having just voted at the beginning of the week to give UNAMIR a four-month lease on life, the Security Council did not expect Rwanda to return to the council's agenda a few days later. But this was a transfigured Rwanda. On April 5, the Security Council observed a Rwanda that was in trouble but still committed to a peace process, respectful of a cease-fire, and making halting progress toward the transitional government. By April 7, the portrait of Rwanda had been inverted: there was no cease-fire; the peace process was in tatters; ten peacekeepers had been brutally murdered and an entire force was in immediate danger; and politicians and civilians were being killed in Kigali and elsewhere.

The council now had to decide UNAMIR's future in this dangerous and radically deteriorating environment. The death of the Rwandan president, the subsequent violence and chaos, and the dead peacekeepers: the danger to UNAMIR meant that the council had to act with speed. UNAMIR had been established to oversee the Arusha Accords and to monitor a cease-fire, but the accords and the cease-fire had now vanished into thin air. For all practical purposes, UNAMIR's mandate was over, as virtually everyone immediately concluded at the time. The only option the council quickly eliminated was the status quo. This threadbare force could not function either safely or effectively under these new circumstances. It also would be grossly irresponsible for the council to permit UNAMIR to languish in this condition; UNAMIR was no good to anyone and a danger to itself. Eliminating the status quo left the Security Council with a choice between one of two broad options: the operation's withdrawal, or its reinforcement with a new mandate to replace the one that had just been extinguished.

During the first days after the president's death, the council's attention was diverted to the evacuation of foreign nationals from Rwanda. Because of the deteriorating situation and the growing violence, governments concentrated on removing their nationals from danger. Planes from several European countries, including France and Italy, descended on Kigali and ferried away their citizens and other European nationals. A U.S. military contingent waited on the other side of the Rwandan border in Burundi for the American convoy, preferring to have the Americans come to safety rather than deliver safety to the Americans. Even though UNAMIR was overwhelmed by the crushing demands on its meager resources, the Secretariat asked UNAMIR to assist and help coordinate this evacuation effort.

Dallaire found the entire episode obscene.[1] At the same moment DPKO was telling him that the international community did not want to intervene in Rwanda to protect civilians, he was being directed to skim from his scarce resource base to coordinate the rescue efforts of several powerful Western states. Even more disheartening was that these foreign troops were evacuating their citizens while abandoning many Tutsis who had worked in their homes, embassies, and offices. The U.S. embassy fled but had no room for the Tutsi staff that were at risk. As the French escorted home their citizens, they also found room for various members of the *akazu*, and even the embassy dog, but apparently no room for the Tutsis who worked in the embassy. And DPKO explicitly told Dallaire that he could use the very ROEs that were off limits for the protection of Rwandans. In an April 9 cable, Riza ordered Dallaire to help with the evacuation and then issued the following reminder: "You should make every effort not to compromise your impartiality or to act beyond your mandate. But you may exercise your discretion to do [*sic*] should this be essential for the evacuation of foreign nationals."[2]

When UNAMIR peacekeepers were not busy directing traffic in Kigali, various member states asked them to locate and rescue one or another Rwandan who was fortunate enough to be remembered by a powerful person or organization in the West. Reluctantly obeying these individual requests, peacekeepers scoured the landscape at considerable risk to their own lives to pluck that lucky individual from among hundreds if not thousands who also were marked for death. While these states were asking a lot of UNAMIR, they showed little interest in returning the favor. Running out of ammunition, gas, food, water, and other basic supplies, UNAMIR watched one cargo plane after another arrive empty and without provisions and leave with foreigners.[3]

Meanwhile in New York, the council formed two camps regarding UNAMIR's future: those favoring intervention, guided by Nigeria, New Zealand, and the Czech Republic; and those insisting on withdrawal, led by the United States and the United Kingdom and joined by the muted voices of France, Russia, and China. The council's discussions were guided by the rules of peacekeeping that had been legitimated in recent months. Beginning in late 1993, it had been gradually and authoritatively referring to a set of criteria to determine whether a peacekeeping operation should be authorized or maintained. Although these criteria were not formalized until a month later, on May 3, they had been largely accepted by the time of the April debate.[4] These criteria included the following: there must be a genuine threat to peace and security; there must be a cease-fire and the parties themselves must be committed to a peace process; a precise mandate must be formulated; there must be sufficient political will on the part of the international community; and the safety of UN personnel must be reasonably assured. These criteria emerged because of lessons learned and the desire to save the UN from excessive deployment of peacekeeping forces in inappropriate circumstances. These rules helped to rationalize the council's decisions and determine when peacekeeping was the right tool for the job. They forced the council to think with its head and not its heart. They helped to preserve the very future of the UN because they reduced the possibility of overexposure and any more self-inflicted wounds.

Those opposing intervention in Rwanda had the upper hand during the entire debate, as the most powerful states wielded muscular rules to argue their case. From the very moment Habyarimana's plane went down, the United States argued forcefully and loudly in favor of withdrawal. Although it appealed to the collectively recognized criteria, it argued the case as strongly as it did because of domestic politics. For several months the Clinton administration's tough love strategy, which was designed to keep congressional critics of the UN and the administration at bay, had been on display. Above all else, this meant limiting the peacekeeping bill and shrinking the number and expense of those operations that did not involve American national interests. This strategy was in full force in its policy toward Rwanda.

During the initial debate on the authorization of UNAMIR in October 1993, the United States had proposed that for budgetary reasons, the peacekeeping contingent comprise no more than five hundred troops. Only the week before, during the discussions regarding extension of UNAMIR's mandate in early April 1994, the United States favored closing the operation because the transitional government still had not been established; the policy was partly motivated by a desire to show Congress that the Clinton administration could be tough on failing operations. And now the administration was ready to make Rwanda a sacrificial lamb if that might keep Congress quiet. The United States could almost recycle the talking points from the previous week's renewal debate, but could now add greater urgency and more evidence behind its claims. Indeed, there was scant debate in Washington over how to proceed. The bad aftertaste of Somalia and Rwanda's absence of strategic relevance meant that there was virtually no interest in intervention. Rwanda did not even merit high-level attention.[5] In the absence of any high-ranking official ready to sponsor a debate on Rwanda, the few isolated voices that were willing to consider an intervention were drowned out by those of more skilled and powerful policymakers.

Wielding the rules of peacekeeping like a chisel to whittle away at the cause of intervention, the United States and others in the Security Council insisted that by the council's own criteria the UN had no business being in Rwanda. Rwanda was surely a humanitarian nightmare but it was not a genuine threat to international peace and security. Although the council had authorized several operations on humanitarian grounds, in recent months it had become more insistent that peacekeeping is best applied when there is stability on the ground. Rwanda hardly passed the test.

A cease-fire did not exist. Not only could UNAMIR not impose a cease-fire, but also the RPF had warned the UN that it might treat any intervention as a hostile force—it feared that France would use the UN as a cloak to intervene on behalf of its Rwandan allies. The Security Council, therefore, had to worry that the UN would become an unwitting and outgunned combatant. The fact that this discussion was taking place against the backdrop of what was happening in Goražde, Bosnia, only served to reinforce the view that putting peacekeepers into conflict situations was irresponsible. The Security Council had established a series of safe havens in Bosnia, notifying the Bosnian Serbs that any offensive action directed against these enclaves would trigger a severe response by the UN. The Bosnian Serbs tested and found hollow the UN threats. As a result, the council was left embarrassed and in no mood to pledge enforcement action in another part of the world, especially where the most powerful members of the council did not have strategic interests, such as in Rwanda.

The mandate in Rwanda, furthermore, was over. The Arusha Accords might be formally on the books, but the parties had demonstrated little commitment to the peace process over the last several months and certainly not over the past few days. Now that UNAMIR's mandate had been shattered by the violence, the council had to consider what might be UNAMIR's new raison d'être.

The answer to this question depended on how Rwanda was defined. And on this critical point there was general unanimity that Rwanda was a civil war. This consensus was due to both the current reality and how the past became projected into the present. There was the plain fact that the RPF and the government had resumed war. But the tendency to treat all violence as related to the civil war derived from a prior understanding of the nature of the Rwandan conflict and the assumption that this presumed past could be mapped directly onto current circumstances. The accepted script was that UNAMIR was to oversee a cease-fire and resolve a civil war between contending ethnic groups. During the preceding months all fears regarding a possible return to violence imagined a renewed civil war. When the violence did return, all eyes in New York assumed that they were seeing a civil war. The council was well aware of the obscenely high civilian death toll and the gruesome conditions on the ground. But because they predicted that sustained violence would be connected to a civil war, that is what they saw. Moreover, the council's focus on the civil war elevated the necessity of a cease-fire. But a cease-fire presumes a civil war, and not a genocide or ethnic cleansing.[6] And the focus on the cease-fire enhanced the prominence of the civil war. The discourse of civil war reinforced the urgency of the cease-fire, and vice versa.

The council generally saw the situation in Rwanda as a "civil war," "ethnic conflict," and a "failed state" all rolled into one, terms that seemed as naturally connected as "peacekeeping" and "consent." In retrospect it is possible to see the civil war and the coming genocide as running along in two semi-independent streams. At the time, however, the council could only see a civil war. In retrospect it is known that Rwanda was not a failed state. To carry out this level of killing in such a short time requires a tight chain of command, discipline, and an organization that is hardly reflective of a failed state. But the discursive inferno of the civil war consumed the oxygen for all other possibilities.

The claim that Rwanda was a civil war gave force to the argument that the UN's sole function under the circumstances was to try to negotiate a cease-fire. If the RPF and the Rwandan forces were determined to settle their differences on the battlefield, then there was little that the UN could do beyond trying to get the parties to hold their fire. And if that was UNAMIR's chief task, then a handful of UN personnel could do the job.

Most damaging to the cause of intervention was the absence of troops to brace a UNAMIR in dire straits. The operation was in grave danger. Ten peacekeepers had been brutally murdered. The Secretariat was providing graphic depictions of a UNAMIR consumed by self-protection tasks, situated in relatively isolated and fairly exposed encampments, and fearful that the airport, which was its only lifeline and had become a battleground, would soon be unavailable for any rescue or resupply operation.

There were no troops ready to march into Rwanda—and the troops that were there were preparing to leave, whether the council liked it or not. In the first few days of the crisis, the Secretariat canvassed member states to ascertain whether any troop contributions might be available. There were no takers. With seventy thousand peacekeepers already stretched across the globe, nearly an all-time high, member states were not ready to dig deeper into their reserves and contribute soldiers to an ill-defined operation that was to engage in undefined action in the midst of a bloodbath.

The prospects of an intervention dwindled further after April 10, when officials in Brussels indicated that in the next few days they were likely to vote to withdraw their troops in the immediate future, a decision that was justified as warranted given the recent deaths and continuing risks to their troops. Not publicly known, however, was that the Belgian policy was doing a quick about-face. Belgium's initial reaction to the death of Habyarimana and the first accounts of civilian killings was to call for reinforcements. For several months it had been arguing for a stronger force that would be unbridled from a stifling policy of consent. Now that the worst was upon UNAMIR, Belgian Foreign Minister Willy Claes argued that public opinion would not understand a UNAMIR that remained passive in the face of massacres.[7] On April 8, the day after learning that it had lost ten soldiers, the Belgian cabinet decided that it would withdraw its contingent unless the mandate was widened and UNAMIR was reinforced by non-Belgian troops. This information was communicated immediately to Boutros-Ghali, who promptly replied that the Security Council had no stomach for intervention.

Unwilling to either leave its troops in an isolated and exposed position or field a multilateral force of one, on April 12 Belgium formally notified Boutros-Ghali that it would be withdrawing its forces in the very near future.[8] But Belgium wanted to avoid the perception that it was the cause of UNAMIR's demise, so it sought the moral cover provided by the complete closure of the operation. Belgium now began lobbying the United States to end UNAMIR's mandate and was pleasantly surprised to find that it was pushing on an open door.[9]

Belgium's decision represented more than bad news piling up. It was a potential deathblow to the operation. Belgium was UNAMIR's backbone. No other government volunteered to reinforce UNAMIR when Belgium was a fixture on the ground, and none were now rushing to take its place. Without the Belgian troops, UNAMIR would be even more exposed and vulnerable. Belgium's departure, moreover, would soon trigger Bangladesh's retreat (though the exit of this hapless force, from the force commander's perspective, was probably a blessing in disguise).[10] There was the real prospect that the troops might vote with their feet before the council took a formal vote.

Acting like the lead counsel that was expected to provide the opening and closing arguments for the anti-intervention camp, the United States strenuously argued that the council should end the operation. The events of the past few days proved, it insinuated, that the prior American position had been correct: the parties lacked a basic commitment to the Arusha Accords. It was sheer lunacy, the American representative hinted in diplomatic nomenclature, for the council to consider an intervention when there was a civil war with deadly overtones, no peace process, dead peacekeepers on the ground, a UN operation in self-protection mode, and no volunteers for an intervention. UNAMIR should be withdrawn immediately, and any delays only increased the risk to UN personnel.

As tragic as it was, there was very little that the international community could do when ethnic groups were determined to kill each other. The difference between responsible and irresponsible humanitarian statecraft was knowing when to let the head rule the heart. There also was the future of peacekeeping to consider. Peacekeeping depends on the willingness of member states to provide troops. If member states believed that the council was unable to take reasonable measures to protect their soldiers, then they would be reluctant to provide such forces in the future. Peacekeepers, unprotected and exposed, could do little good for those on the ground and much harm to the UN's reputation and longevity. The United States and others were able to argue persuasively that by the council's own criteria, which were intended to rationalize its decisions, the peacekeepers must be withdrawn.

Those proposing an intervention were expected to address how Rwanda, at this moment, fulfilled the minimal conditions for a peacekeeping operation—and their inability to do so crippled their cause. They could point to the massacres that were occurring alongside a civil war, but they could not credibly claim that this was an international threat to peace and security. They could not point to troops lining up to interject themselves into the middle of a civil war. They were not offering their services. Eloquent statements were no substitute for soldiers. They could not point to a cease-fire either in place or on the immediate horizon. They could not point to a viable peace process. They could not point to the essentials. The rules of peacekeeping were an impregnable barrier to action.

By the beginning of the second week of the debate, the council ceased to consider intervention. The last gasp from the intervention camp came on April 13 when Nigeria circulated a nonpaper on intervention among the nonpermanent members on the Security Council. The nonpaper was a textual record of its oral presentations, now given semiofficial standing and designed to become the focus for a strategy for intervention. In the end, Nigeria opted not to distribute the paper to the entire council, a decision

Ambassador Ibrahim Gambari later recalled was due to the tremendous pressure to achieve consensus.[11] By letting the nonpaper fall to the floor, the proponents of intervention conceded defeat.

The council's debate now turned to the question of whether UNAMIR should be reduced or completely closed. The United States was still holding firm to its position that UNAMIR should be dismantled. On April 15, in a rare moment when Rwanda did receive high-level attention, Secretary of State Warren Christopher cabled instructions to Madeleine Albright making clear Washington's reasoning. He said that while he had taken into consideration the humanitarian situation, there was still "insufficient justification" for UNAMIR's continued presence and that "[o]ur opposition to retaining a UNAMIR presence is firm. It is based on our conviction that the Security Council has an obligation to ensure that peacekeeping operations are viable, that they are capable of fulfilling their mandates, and that the UN peacekeeping personnel are not placed or retained, knowingly, in an untenable situation."[12] The United States did not want itself or the UN near Rwanda and was able to use these rules of peacekeeping as a thruway for withdrawal.

Those who had favored intervention now were working behind the scenes to maintain at least a semblance of a force in order to protect the thousands in UNAMIR's care and provide the platform for a future intervention. Colin Keating, who was the UN ambassador from New Zealand and president of the council during the month of April, and DPKO worked closely together toward this end.[13] The United States, at this point, was the least of their worries. More ominous was that a huge chunk of the remaining troops presented a problem and not a solution, and they were threatening to vote with their feet to leave Rwanda. As Keating later wrote:

> The Secretariat was telling me that there was indeed a serious problem with the troops in the field. We were reaping what we had sown by putting in a force with inadequate equipment, inadequate training, and lack of firepower. The force was only suitable for the most benign environment and minus the Belgians, who had pulled out, they were in deep trouble. Desertion was already occurring. It was only a matter of days before some troop contributing countries unilaterally withdrew their troops. At that point UNAMIR would have been dead. For UNAMIR to have collapsed in that way would have been an ignominious failure for the UN.[14]

Dallaire, too, was insisting that while he would never abandon Rwanda, if there were no available reinforcements, then it was preferable to remove the mediocre troops and save the remaining provisions for those troops that could perform their mission.[15] Under such circumstances it would have been pointless if not reckless to keep the troops in the field.

By the end of the second week of debate the council decided to maintain a presence. Even a nay-saying United States finally conceded, unwilling to suffer the costs associated with its position and swayed by the merits of the argument. If there was a slim chance that Dallaire might be able to arrange a cease-fire, then keeping several hundred troops on the ground was worth the risk. It also wanted to maintain appearances and not be viewed as heartless and abandoning "Africa" in its hour of need. Several council members made thinly veiled charges of a double standard, that the powerful were willing to expend unlimited resources on "losing propositions" in Europe but ready to fold at the first hint of trouble in Africa. Indeed, at the very moment the council was also considering what to do about the situation in Goražde; several members dryly noted that no Western state had argued that UNPROFOR should be closed down because there was "no peace to keep." For those who had opposed intervention, there were compelling reasons for maintaining a token force, reasons having to do with principled objectives and keeping in character. For those who had advocated intervention, this was the best they could hope for given what they were hearing from the Secretariat about what was occurring in the field, the absence of forces, and a determined, rule-carrying opposition in the council.

On April 20, a fairly restrained secretary-general delivered his long anticipated and inexplicably delayed report on Rwanda. Largely mimicking the logic behind the council's recent discussions, the report contained no new information. It gave only a brief and vague description of the killings as it highlighted the civil war and the need for a cease-fire. It made clear that of three different alternatives, the least bad was to reduce UNAMIR to 270 troops, which would be given the task of attempting to negotiate a cease-fire. The Secretariat's first formal words signaled to the council that it was time to vote.

———————

THE Secretariat had been remarkably quiet between April 6 and the delivery of its report. Although the council was involved in a highly intense debate over Rwanda, brief, vague, and indecisive were the defining qualities of the Secretariat's formal statements and informal presentations to the council. Its reports dwelled on unfolding chaos, the renewed civil war between the

RPF and the interim Rwandan government, Dallaire's unsuccessful efforts to arrange a cease-fire, and the increasing risks to a UNAMIR that was consumed by a self-protection stance. These factors, it consistently suggested, made it nearly impossible to get more detailed information or concrete recommendations from the field. When repeatedly asked by the council when it might be prepared to present contingency plans or to recommend options, the Secretariat apologetically responded that UNAMIR was unable to present recommendations at this time, though it hoped to do so in the very near future. The council was visibly frustrated by the Secretariat's incomplete presentations. To proceed without the Secretariat's input would be highly unusual and undesirable, particularly so in this situation where UNAMIR was a critical source of information since the diplomatic community had fled Rwanda.

Boutros-Ghali's own indirect and plodding contributions captured and defined the Secretariat's generally reserved and not very helpful stance during this critical period. In Europe at the time of the downing of the plane, he chose to stay abroad rather than return to New York and oversee the crisis. The result was that his vague and not very informative statements were always delivered and mediated by proxy. He always straggled one or two steps behind the debate in the Security Council and almost always mimicked its recent conclusions. His first full statement came almost a week after the downing of the plane and long after the basic terms of the debate and next steps had been identified. At this moment he offered little support for the idea of intervention and noted that withdrawal might be unavoidable in order to protect UN personnel. Hardly insightful contributions. When he finally delivered his report on April 20, the council had all but voted on UNAMIR's fate.[16] The Secretariat seemed to be in top bureaucratic and diplomatic form throughout the debate, minimally performing its roles and responsibilities and following the trade winds coming from the council.

The Secretariat's unusually low-key demeanor and passivity were the subject of much speculation outside the council's chambers at the time. One possibility was that the Secretariat was simply overtaken by events. Although its recent involvement in several high-wire operations had made it quite accustomed to being in a perpetual state of crisis, what occurred in Rwanda was highly unusual. This situation was rare for an international organization that still measured time in lengthy and leisurely plenary sessions and not in rapid-fire battlefield hours, and that had only recently established a situation room that was open twenty-four hours a day, seven days a week. Another distinct possibility was that the Secretariat was not receiving anything of value from the field. Because there was no apparent reason why it would not pass on to the council everything it knew, its lackluster behavior probably reflected a paucity of information. In either case, the Secretariat's refractory presentations and languid posture hardly reassured the council, increasing its anxiety and reinforcing the view that UNAMIR should be withdrawn before it was too late.

It has since come to light that there was a gap between what Dallaire was communicating to the Secretariat and what the Secretariat, in turn, was reporting to the council. UNAMIR's situation reports and Dallaire's twice-daily phone calls provided meticulous and graphic accounts of the violence, a diagnosis of the source of the violence, and a prescription for ending the violence. Specifically, these communiqués contained two critical pieces of information that the Secretariat inexplicably failed to bring to the council's attention.

The first critical piece of information was a characterization of the violence as ethnic cleansing in its most sinister form.[17] In the first few days the violence was directed at the elite and politicians supportive of the Arusha agreement, which led Dallaire to label the violence as an attack on the peace process and a prelude to civil war. By April 8, however, he came to realize that the violence was rapidly transmuting into something grander and more gruesome. In one telephone call during this first week, Dallaire provided methodical detail about what was happening. Hutu extremists at road blocks would stop all cars and demand identity papers and examine the physical characteristics of the occupants. They would then separate Tutsis from Hutus, marching the Tutsis to nearby but secluded locations where they would be murdered. This scene was repeated at checkpoints around the Kigali area. The very fact that the Hutu militias, the Interahamwe, and elements of the Rwandan army were taking away those whose identity cards were marked Tutsi and murdering them in another location was all UNAMIR needed to know. Within five days, Dallaire clearly understood that Hutu extremists were carrying out ethnic cleansing in Kigali and elsewhere; he emphasized to headquarters the magnitude and scale of the crimes and that civilians were being targeted for no reason other than ethnic identity.[18]

The second essential piece of information was Dallaire's pleading for reinforcements, but not in order to impose a cease-fire. Instead, his view was that the Interahamwe and the Presidential Guard could be induced to return to the barracks and halt their plans if they believed that they confronted strong opposition from the international community. This would require the threat but, hopefully, not the actual use of force. He envisioned a strategic chain reaction: a symbolic demonstration of the international community's resolve through the deployment of reinforcements, in addition to some determined saber rattling, would re-establish the cease-fire, which in turn would halt the killings.[19]

Dallaire's analysis and prescription were not new. Ever since the events of January, he had urged that DPKO permit "deterrent" action in order to convince the extremists that there would be a price to be paid for their actions. Thus, when the fighting broke out, Dallaire knew exactly how to answer the challenge. Hours after the plane crash, Dallaire sent a message to New York saying, "Give me the means and I can do more."[20] DPKO's immediate reply was that "nobody is interested in that." On April 10, he appealed for five thousand troops. Headquarters delivered the same reply.

Over the next several weeks Dallaire continued to plead for reinforcements. To prove his point that even the mere presence of reinforcements would stop the bloodbath, he noted that Kigali had become calm by the mere presence of the foreign forces that were on the ground to evacuate their nationals. This was not mere coincidence, Dallaire asserted. Officials at UN headquarters were not buying.[21]

There is an extraordinary chasm between what Dallaire told UN headquarters and what headquarters told the Security Council. Dallaire told DPKO that there was a well-organized plan for ethnic cleansing. The Secretariat's reports to the council highlighted the "chaos" and conveyed an image of violence that was spontaneous, erupting from long-standing tensions and hatreds. Dallaire told DPKO that there were two dimensions to the crisis, humanitarian and political, and that the most efficient way to control the humanitarian crisis was to re-establish the cease-fire. The Secretariat's reports honed in on the civil war and the political crisis to the neglect of the humanitarian crisis. Dallaire pleaded for reinforcements as a show of the international community's resolve and as the only chance of containing the extremists. The Secretariat reported to the council that it had not received any concrete recommendations from the field, and that UNAMIR was so consumed by self-protection tasks that it was unable to develop any.

UN staff now concede that they possessed critical information and details that they failed to pass on to the Security Council. A sheepish Iqbal Riza confessed that "[p]ossibly we did not give all the details. . . . And if we did not, I really can't tell you what happened then to prevent us from giving those details."[22] What accounts for the gap between what Dallaire reported to the Secretariat and what the Secretariat communicated to the Security Council? Two broad classes of explanations—sincere accidents and strategic omission—are likely candidates. Both explanations acknowledge that the Secretariat possessed information that it failed to transmit to the Security Council, but point to radically different reasons for that failure.

Accidents might result from any number of situational or structural factors. Crises produce stress, and stress can be the enemy of rational decision making and cause individuals to see what they want to see and deny the unusual or the uncomfortable. Organizations like the UN frame information in subtle ways that have profound effects. Regardless of the identified factors, the suggestion is that for some reason UN staff had unfortunate lapses of judgment, diminished capacity, if you will. Strategic omission raises the possibility that UN officials accurately heard Dallaire but manipulated the information they presented to the council in order to increase the likelihood that there would not be an intervention. The explanation found to be the most plausible has profound consequences for how the responsibility and culpability of UN officials are assessed.

What follows are two alternative scenarios built around the themes of sincere accidents and strategic omission. I find myself forced to provide not one but two plausible accounts because presently there is simply not enough evidence, in my judgment, to reject one or to favor the other. When I attempted to make sense of the Secretariat's shortcomings at the time of these events, I presumed that it was simply not up to the job and was overwhelmed by the need to make life-saving and-ending decisions with incomplete information and on such short notice. When I later learned that it possessed critical information that it failed to transmit to the Security Council, I instinctually concluded that the Secretariat probably had made honest mistakes as it struggled to find the least bad of alternatives under very difficult circumstances. After all, like everyone around me, I too focused on the civil war to the exclusion of all other ways of seeing Rwanda. I also found it difficult to imagine an intervention that might possibly halt the violence given the understanding of the conflict. My sympathies were more than academic. They were lived.

But upon further reflection, after learning the extent to which UN officials probably knew about the goings on in Rwanda, after considering the alternative explanations, and after contemplating the possible motives that might have led them to act duplicitously, I became more open to the possibility that what occurred were not "misreadings" or "misinterpretations" but rather good old-fashioned politics. There were plausible reasons why the Secretariat might have preferred the reduction of UNAMIR over its reinforcement, reasons that revolved around the exigencies of the situation and the possible long-term damage to the organization caused by a possible failure in the field. It might conclude that this was politics in the service of principles.

"Mistakes were made," confessed Riza in a flattened bureaucratic tone.[23] These mistakes, he continued, occurred because of a misinterpretation of the situation. If only the Secretariat had known then what it knows now, then it would have transmitted the critical information to the Security Council. But claims to having "misread" the situation are tautologies, and nothing more. We still need to know how and why the Secretariat "misread" the situation. What distracted its attention, causing it to overlook the crimes against humanity and the coming of genocide?

Statements by UN officials signal that these mistakes had an organizational basis. When Riza confessed that "we" misinterpreted the situation, he was not speaking in a royal idiom or deftly attempting to shift blame from himself to the group, but rather was speaking as a member of a corporate body. He was not referring to the aggregation of discrete personalities but rather to a collective mentality. There is something about the UN culture. Like all modern organizations, the UN is attentive only to certain features of the environment and ignores others; establishes routines for reducing uncertainty; contains rules that tell it what sort of action is appropriate given the situation; and generates schema and frames that individuals use to interpret and filter information, making it quite likely that new information reinforces previously held views. The Secretariat's mentality, how it was organized to think, and the social optics it donned, shaped how it saw and acted upon Rwanda, making it difficult for it to see the warning signs of genocide and leading it to interpret the violence against civilians as nothing other than an awful feature of civil war.

UN officials could only see a civil war because that was what they were prompted to expect. Ever since the UN became involved in Rwanda, it had a particular way of understanding the nature of the conflict and the violence it generated. This understanding derived from the categories the Secretariat employed to interpret many of the post–Cold War domestic conflicts. Specifically, the peace between the superpowers had encouraged war between various ethnonational groups, providing the opportunity and motive for many long-simmering ethnic conflicts to transmute into civil wars. The perceived fix for ethnic conflicts and civil wars included power-sharing agreements and democratic practices that preserved individual security and ethnic autonomy and produced some semblance of mutual tolerance. The UN's role was to help craft a cease-fire agreement and negotiation process between the combatants, and once accomplished, to establish a peacekeeping operation that would give the parties the confidence to follow through on their commitments.

The UN's view of the Rwandan conflict corresponded to this script. Ethnic conflict had been a troubled part of Rwandan history, observed Riza, especially since 1960. "Look, since the 1960s there have been cycles of violence—Tutsi against Hutu, Hutu against Tutsi. I'm sorry to put it so cynically. It was nothing new. This had continued from the 60s through the 70s and into the 80s, and here it was in the 90s."[24] Coinciding with the end of the Cold War, the RPF came into existence and the civil war began. Ethnic violence, therefore, was a two-way street. Although the Hutu government was undoubtedly responsible for much of the recent violence, both sides had bloody hands. The only way to end the civil war and break the cycle of ethnic violence was to establish a political process that secured a cease-fire and led to a multiethnic government that enshrined democratic practices. This was the raison d'être of the Arusha Accords. As an impartial and neutral executor, UNAMIR was created to employ consensual means to monitor the cease-fire and facilitate the implementation of those accords.

The violence that continued in Rwanda was typical of many euphemistically and optimistically titled "post-conflict" operations that were overseeing transitions from civil war to civil peace. The violence only seemed to be worsening because of the political paralysis and the failure to establish the transitional institutions. The longer they took to establish, the more violence there would be. This was a primary reason why the council and UN staff were so insistent on the immediate establishment of the new government. Consider the following statement, again by Riza, to explain how he and other staff mistakenly viewed the ethnic killings as an unfortunate manifestation of a political process:

> [E]verybody was concentrating on the political aspects [meaning the Arusha Accords and the transition government]. Everyone was preoccupied with a political solution. A transitional government should have been established by the 31st of December. Here we were going through January, February, and March without this government. This was the first priority, and [we] had the conviction . . . that if they had a political solution, then the violence would subside. In other words, *the violence was not connected to a planning of a genocide, nobody saw it like that. It was seen as a result of a political deadlock.*[25]

Ethnic violence was expected, it was part of a political process, and the only solution to the ethnic violence was the fulfillment of the political process.

Because UN officials tended to see the pre-April violence as part of a political process that was designed to end a civil war, the April violence was logically and instinctually connected to the resurrected civil war. They certainly knew, like everyone else, of the mounting death toll. But they tended to see these killings as an unfortunate consequence of the civil war. As Riza understandably contended, everyone was prepared to imagine a return to civil war and could entertain the possibility of ethnic conflict. But not a genocide.[26] "Our mandate was not to anticipate and prevent genocide," Riza explained.[27] The UN's mandate was to anticipate and help prevent the return of civil war, so that was all it could see.[28]

Because the Secretariat was primed and predisposed to associate all violence with the civil war, it was likely to overlook potentially contradictory information. Organizational and sociopsychological theories suggest why it might have been insensitive to new information. The crisis environment and high degree of uncertainty would have encouraged staff to rely on decisional shortcuts that were based on their personal experiences from recent events and broader organizational ways of knowing.

If the Secretariat was going to completely alter its understanding of the nature of the conflict, it would have to simultaneously revise its established heuristics and receive unadulterated and undiluted information that pointed away from civil war and toward crimes against humanity. But there were several reasons why that did not happen. In addition to the fairly rigid ways of framing Rwanda, there also existed contradictory information. The force commander and the special representative provided alternative interpretations of the same events. An April 8 cable is representative of this discordant presentation. Special Representative to the Secretary-General Booh-Booh wrote the opening parts of the cable. He reported that the security situation was worsening, but linked that development to the fighting between the government and the RPF. The rest of the country was "calm, although tense." Booh-Booh's inflection conveyed little urgency, gave no thorough assessment, and provided no concrete guidance.

Dallaire's contribution to this cable is striking in its contrast. He emphatically and excitedly wrote, in uppercase letters:

THE APPEARANCE OF A VERY WELL PLANNED, ORGANIZED, DELIBERATE AND CONDUCTED CAMPAIGN OF TERROR INITIATED PRINCIPALLY BY THE PRESIDENTIAL GUARD SINCE THE MORNING AFTER THE DEATH OF THE HEAD OF STATE HAS COMPLETELY REORIENTED THE SITUATION IN KIGALI. AGGRESSIVE ACTIONS HAVE BEEN TAKEN NOT ONLY AGAINST THE OPPOSITION LEADERSHIP BUT AGAINST THE RPF, AGAINST PARTICULAR ETHNIC GROUPS (MASSACRE OF CIVILIANS IN REMERA), AGAINST THE GENERAL CIVILIAN POPULATION (BANDITRY) AND AGAINST UNAMIR. DIRECT AND INDIRECT FIRE ON U.N. INSTALLATIONS, VEHICLES, PERSONNEL AND AFFILIATED AGENCIES (I.E. UNDP) WHICH HAS RESULTED IN FATAL AND NONFATAL CASUALTIES. THE PARTICULARLY BARBAROUS MURDER OF THE 10 CAPTURED BELGIAN SOLDIERS EMPHASIZES THIS SITUATION. . . . [29]

Booh-Booh and Dallaire's presentations were nearly *Rashomon*-like. Given the Secretariat's preconceived notions of the source of the violence, it would be understandable if it elevated the civil war to the neglect of the ethnic cleansing. The bits and pieces of "evidence" of the ethnic cleansing and the coming genocide, therefore, were obscured by the din of contradictory information. A visibly irritated and highly defensive UN spokesperson chided, "No one, no one did enough to stop this, but it is a sure lot easier . . . to say what we should have done two and a half, almost three years ago with the knowledge we have today—than with the very scant information that we had then."[30]

The Secretariat's spokesperson raised an important point. There is a tendency of otherwise excellent studies to impose a reading on cables that might or might not be warranted but are clearly influenced by retrospective reasoning. For instance, in support of its claim that the Secretariat overlooked the painfully obvious signs of ethnic cleansing, Human Rights Watch quoted from the aforementioned passage from the April 8 cable. But by extracting and placing under a microscope one small section located in the middle of an eight-page cable, it essentially inverted the passage's rank, making central what arguably was secondary. The cable did not use key concepts like ethnic cleansing to discuss the killing. Nor did it request troop reinforcements for the purpose of protecting civilians. Instead, most of the cable dwelled on the deteriorating security environment, the threat to peacekeepers, and the desperate attempt to establish a cease-fire. In fact, the parts of the cable that conveyed the greatest urgency concerned UNAMIR's desperate straits:

> UNAMIR WILL DEVOTE MUCH STAFF EFFORT AND RESOURCES TO IMPROVING OUR SUSTAINMENT CAPABILITY BUT IT MUST BE EMPHASIZED THAT WE FACE CRITICAL SHORTAGES THAT WILL REDUCE THE ABILITIES OF AND ENDANGER THE FORCE WITHIN A MATTER OF DAYS.[31]

The most important parts of any cable are the opening and closing paragraphs, and here is how that April 8 cable closed:

> UNAMIR REMAINS COMMITTED TO ITS MANDATE EVEN THOUGH THE PRESENT SITUATION IS NOT ENABLING THIS MISSION TO FULFILL OUR ASSIGNED AND DESIGNED FOR TASKS. HOWEVER, THERE IS NO DOUBT THAT KIGALI WOULD HAVE BEEN IN A WORSE SITUATION WITHOUT UNAMIR. ALL PRESENT EFFORTS ARE AIMED AT SELF-PROTECTION, SUSTAINMENT, SECURITY OF KEY PEACE PROCESS INDIVIDUALS, LIMITED HUMANITARIAN SUPPORT AND EMPLOYING EVERY SKILL WE POSSESS TO GET THE PARTIES TO A CEASE-FIRE AND NEGOTIATE BACK TO THE POLITICAL PROCESS.

Headquarters could be certain of mass violence, the immediate need for a cease-fire and return to the political process, and the peril facing UNAMIR. Retrospective reports that isolate bits of information with the advantage of hindsight distort how decision makers proceed in real time, how they must sort out contradictory information as they balance competing priorities, and how contradictions are resolved by reference to established categories and decisional shortcuts.

Once the UN staff categorized the conflict in Rwanda as a civil war, then its range of responses narrowed considerably and trained on consent-based alternatives. Bureaucracies are organized around rules, routines, and standard operating procedures designed to trigger a standard and predictable response to environmental stimuli. This kind of routinization is, after all, precisely what bureaucracies are *supposed* to exhibit—it is what makes them effective and highly valued. Although the UN would never be mistaken for a prototypical Weberian bureaucracy, it had developed some fairly standard rules concerning when peacekeeping was appropriate and how peacekeepers should operate in the field, rules that derived from the constitutional principles of neutrality, impartiality, and consent.

The recent experiences in Somalia and Bosnia had shaken the confidence of even the most forceful advocates of enforcement operations. In an interview given just three days before the April 6 plane crash, Boutros-Ghali referred to the new "U.N. mentality" and how "our whole philosophy is based on talk—negotiate—and then talk again. To use force is an expression of failure. Our job is diplomacy, the peaceful resolution of disputes. The peaceful resolution of problems. The possibility of using force is only as a dissuasion. If you read the U.N. Charter . . . the whole philosophy of the charter is to avoid military force."[32] Although this mentality might have been "new" to the architect of forced disarmament in Somalia, it was as old as peacekeeping to everyone else. The rules of consent, impartiality, and neutrality returned to their hegemonic standing.

With an understanding that the situation in Rwanda was a civil war and that any use of military force was tantamount to enforcement, headquarters immediately argued that UNAMIR could do little more than help negotiate a cease-fire, and demonstrated tremendous difficulty imagining the use of military force for anything but an enforcement operation designed to impose a cease-fire. This stance was well grounded in the reality of the situation. UNAMIR was hardly fit to defend others and could barely defend itself. UNAMIR's situation reports dwelled on the threat to the operation. A force that was barely competent during peace time now was barely afloat. It was likely to run out of food within two weeks, the drinking water in some posts would last only one or two days at the most, and it had fuel for about three days. Its ammunition and medical supplies were in a similar dismal state. The APCs were few in number and in disrepair—sometimes only one or two were in working condition at a time. UNAMIR had no ambulance. The force's precariousness became nearly unendurable once the Belgians announced their departure. The several-hundred-strong Ghanaian force could pick up some of the slack, but UNAMIR's fortunes become bleak after that. The Bangladeshis were of little value. They had proved unreliable over the past several months and had scampered the moment the shooting began. Indeed, on April 7, Bangladeshi peacekeepers even refused to open the gates of the compound to Belgian soldiers who were being chased and cornered by a mob, ostensibly because they believed that the Belgians were marked and thought that the best way to protect themselves was to keep the Belgians outside the compound. This was not the warrior culture in its purest form. UNAMIR was coming apart at the seams.

Yet when the Secretariat proceeded to reject the possibility of intervention at the outset of the crisis, it cited not only pragmatics but also principles and the need to use peacekeepers only when there was a workable cease-fire. In its view, the rupture of the cease-fire meant that the UN's responsibility was diminished. This was made clear to UNAMIR throughout these difficult days.[33] Days before the April 21 vote, DPKO explained to Security Council President Keating that peacekeeping only worked in benign environments, and therefore UNAMIR should limit its role to the attempt to negotiate a cease-fire.[34] Nor could DPKO imagine military options that straddled peacekeeping and enforcement, including the possibility that military force might be used to protect civilians. As one study observed, "[O]ptions to reinforce UNAMIR were always put by the Secretariat in terms of an enforcement operation, suggesting intervention between the two armies, rather than maintaining or increasing troop strength to protect civilians."[35] Military force could only be tied to the enforcement of a cease-fire, nothing else.

The Secretariat also instructed Dallaire to follow more restricted ROEs than were available to him, essentially ordering him not to protect civilians.[36] Partly informed by headquarters' assessment that UNAMIR was not militarily equipped to undertake a protective mission, DPKO "insisted that UNAMIR must remain 'neutral.' To permit any apparent deviation from this position could result in military action against UNAMIR, a weak and lightly armed force unable to defend itself. . . . They also feared creating a precedent (i.e., having another failure) that would have repercussions on other peacekeeping operations. They recalled the unfortunate consequences of a too assertive policy in Somalia. Rather than intervene to protect the population, all that the troops could do was to patrol and be visible in the city."[37] UN staff drew an immediate line between the resumption of the civil war, the principle of consent, and the operation in the field.

Well-meaning individuals made regrettable choices, owing to a UN culture that restricted their field of vision and a crisis environment that made it doubly difficult for them to imagine alternative ways of seeing, knowing, and acting. The Secretariat's representation of Rwanda as a civil war, and its insistence that the nature of the violence meant that UNAMIR should avoid all enforcement operations and restrict its activities to the attempt to arrange a cease-fire, flowed from a UN culture that tended both to see conflicts such as Rwanda as civil wars and to place great stock in consent-based exercises.

The shift from an unstable peace to the spasm of violence did not cause the Secretariat to alter its diagnosis that this was a political process that led to civil war and ethnic violence which could only be addressed through a cease-fire. Its initial analysis of the Rwandan conflict and its possible remedies did not go through a single modification during the entire April period. Moreover, the threat to peacekeepers on the ground and the unlikelihood of reinforcements meant that the Secretariat would have difficulty recommending anything more than it did. Its handling of the information, however tragic and consequential, was understandable and excusable. These were awful but not indictable mistakes committed by decent individuals.

An alternative scenario, however, speculates that the Secretariat heard Dallaire just fine but decided to embargo that critical information because it did not want to encourage an intervention. This possibility is suggested by three factors: the sheer distance between what Dallaire told the Secretariat and what the Secretariat communicated to the council, a wealth of circumstantial evidence indicating that the Secretariat opposed intervention, and a motive for why it opposed intervention that is directly related to its desire to make sure that the UN would not go down with Rwanda.

Even giving UN officials some benefit of the doubt because of the very uncertain and cloudy situation, there did exist a trove of information from the field that was supposed to be delivered to the Security Council but was not. Asked to consider the possibility that DPKO might have simply misinterpreted what he was saying, Dallaire insisted, "I say no. The information was there." Within a matter of days after the plane crash, he was telling headquarters about the Hutu-led ethnic cleansing campaign and giving DPKO a concept of operations for intervention.[38] Dallaire, moreover, asked DPKO about the mood of the council and whether the council understood what was happening. DPKO, which routinely praised him for his exhaustive and thorough analysis, assured him that it conveyed in detail his observations and recommendation for reinforcements, but that there was "no will in the international community."[39] Yet the Secretariat told the council that it was not receiving much concrete information or recommendations from the field. Simply put, at this time DPKO was telling Dallaire that the Secretariat was communicating to the council all of the information that the Secretariat would later claim it did not have.

Most of the Secretariat's statements and actions provided subtle but important support for reducing UNAMIR's exposure. As early as April 8, Boutros-Ghali's office told the council that evacuation might become unavoidable. According to the notes taken from the April 12 meeting of the Secretary-General's Task Force on Peacekeeping Operations, on April 9 Boutros-Ghali communicated that UNAMIR should be withdrawn if the situation became "sufficiently dangerous."[40] DPKO and Boutros-Ghali consistently told Dallaire that UNAMIR would not be reinforced and that he should prepare to evacuate. On April 10, Boutros-Ghali's Special Political Adviser Chinmaya Gharekhan called UNAMIR and strongly hinted that UNAMIR would probably be closed. At that time "Dallaire refused on the grounds that for him it was 'a matter of moral concern,'" and then proceeded to ask for five thousand troops.[41] The secretary-general's representative in the council consistently and persuasively argued that the council should reduce or withdraw UNAMIR if there was no change on the ground. The failure to forward to the council a concept of operations alongside its many statements in favor of protecting UNAMIR through its evacuation certainly projected the image that withdrawal was, at the very least, the secretary-general's default option.

If Boutros-Ghali preferred intervention prior to April 21, then he acted very oddly. Past calls for intervention highlighted that it was doable and justifiable, underscored the strategic necessity, and elevated the humanitarian consequences. Yet the Secretariat failed to provide even the most rudimentary military and logistical foundations for such an operation or undertake any contingency planning.

Nor did the Secretariat provide a moral imperative for intervention or invoke a duty to aid. In the case of Somalia, Boutros-Ghali passionately and persistently demanded an intervention on the grounds that only concerted international involvement could avert a famine, a famine that could claim upwards of a million people, which in turn could destabilize the region. For good measure, he accused the council of caring for the rich man's war in Bosnia but abandoning indigent Africa. No single statement by Boutros-Ghali on Rwanda came close to his appeal for Somalia. And, finally, why did the Secretariat sit in silence as the interventionist camp struggled to make its case? At any point it could have provided the council with information that supported the arguments advanced by this camp, but it never did. This is hardly the expected behavior of an advocate for intervention.

Yet the grammar for intervention was certainly available. If Boutros-Ghali had wanted an intervention, he could have portrayed the mounting deaths as due to ethnic killings and referred specifically to the Tutsis as the primary targets. Instead, he and his staff consistently portrayed the violence as "chaotic" and spontaneous, projecting an image of killing that was reciprocal and multisided. Indeed, DPKO's own notes from the Security Council meetings record that the secretary-general's representative consistently referred to the "civilians" in the broadest and most generic sense.[42] Even as late as April 29, even though Dallaire had been arguing for weeks that the Hutus were responsible for the ethnic cleansing, and even after Dallaire had discovered the word "genocide" and begun using it instead of "ethnic cleansing" in his communiqués with headquarters, Boutros-Ghali still claimed that Hutus were killing Tutsis and Tutsis were killing Hutus.[43] Even if the Secretariat believed that the nature of the killing remained somewhat ambiguous, there was enough room to portray the violence as crimes against humanity—if it wanted to.

The Secretariat's focus on the civil war and portrayal of spasmodic violence chilled the intervention impulse. To frame the events in Rwanda as a civil war implied that the long-suffering Arusha Accords collapsed because of the failure of both parties to carry out their obligations. Under such circumstances, the UN would have an obligation to try to negotiate a ceasefire, but the burden of responsibility would be on the parties to the accord. To frame the killing in Rwanda as ethnic cleansing implied that there was an armed and deliberate campaign against civilian populations. Under such circumstances the UN would feel a greater moral burden to intervene. The discourse of "ethnic cleansing" is much more likely to compel action than is the discourse of "civil war." The Secretariat adopted a vocabulary that bodychecked the intervention camp.

The Secretariat surely knew all this. From previous actions in similar circumstances, these experienced international civil servants knew the language that was likely to make the best case for different options. The implication is that it knowingly deprived the intervention camp of the ammunition it required to make a compelling case. If the Secretariat had communicated Dallaire's recommendations, then those pushing for intervention could have pointed to the force commander's assessment as realistic, credible, and authoritative. Instead, the intervention camp was crippled by the Secretariat's failure to provide a realistic military option and buried by its suggestion that an overwhelmed UNAMIR was unable to provide any contingency planning. If the Secretariat's own military advisers, the experts on ground, were unable to recommend intervention, then how could officials who were thousands of miles away? If the Secretariat did not want an intervention, then there is imaginably no more effective way to stop it than to fail to provide a methodology for it. It would not be the first time that bureaucrats resorted to such tactics to halt action they opposed.

Before I suggest why the Secretariat might have decided independently against intervention, it is important to consider the possibility that its actions came at the behest of the Security Council or powerful member states. The "mood of the council" explanation falls short in several respects. The Secretariat previously had presented options that it fully expected the council to reject and lived to tell about the experience. Nor does the Secretariat always tell the council what it thinks it wants to hear. Furthermore, there *were* council members arguing for intervention, so if the Secretariat claims that it was merely following the council's wishes, then it must have either selective memory or selective vision concerning who was sitting on the council. The council was still quite divided and had not ruled out an intervention until the beginning of the second week of the debate—influenced, as I will argue, by the Secretariat's silence on this very option. Therefore, it is factually incorrect to argue that the Secretariat was merely reflecting or anticipating the council's already firm determination to reject an expanded operation.

There is the possibility that the Secretariat's perjury was suborned by permanent members. Stories of behind-the-scenes machinations and full-blown conspiracies have circulated in various forms since it has become known that the Secretariat knew much but did little. There might be a French connection: France played patron to the Rwandan government and was close to the Francophile secretary-general. Although France supported the Arusha Accords, it refused Belgium's early request to field an intervention force (on the grounds that it would be targeted by the RPF) and in the council attempted to project an air of impartiality (all the while ferrying out Habyarimana's entourage and various Hutu elite associated with the genocide).[44] France and Boutros-Ghali were quite chummy; if the secretary-general was going to listen to a permanent member, it probably would be France (and not the United States, which he bitterly resented). Moreover, there is some evidence that France coached Boutros-Ghali's presentations to the council in order to elicit a verdict against intervention. Specifically, France is rumored to have given Boutros-Ghali the vocabulary to describe the killings—"chaos," "indiscriminate violence," "a people who have fallen into calamitous circumstances"—in order to mask the true nature of the violence and to decrease the probability of an intervention.[45] Boutros-Ghali might not even have been a difficult person to convince to play along. As

Egypt's minister of foreign affairs, in 1990 he received several Rwandan officials and personally approved the transfer of Egyptian military equipment to Rwanda.[46] Even if France had a compact with a coquettish Boutros-Ghali, however, there is no evidence that it worked its magic on DPKO.

There is little evidence, either, that the United States imposed its views on an unwilling Secretariat.[47] Belgium initially pressed the Secretariat to recommend intervention but was told that the council would not agree, and only then did Belgium shift its policy and lobby for UNAMIR's mass evacuation. So far there is no compelling evidence that the Secretariat was in the pocket of the West.

The Secretariat had its own reasons to oppose intervention, even though it knew about ethnic cleansing. It was certainly concerned about the threat to peacekeepers. From the very beginning of the crisis, the Secretariat was well aware that UNAMIR was hardly ready for battle. With few capable troops, a quick reaction force that was neither quick, able to react, nor a force, and a shortage of necessary logistical supplies and equipment, UNAMIR could barely protect itself, not to mention Rwandans. Ten peacekeepers were already dead and the prevailing circumstances meant that more might meet a similar fate. The deaths of the peacekeepers understandably caused DPKO to fear for the safety of its personnel, certainly influencing the secretary-general's April 9 letter outlining the possibly unavoidable need to evacuate UN personnel and foreign nationals.[48] Knowing that the council was in no mood to authorize reinforcements, the Secretariat might have concluded that the only way to protect the peacekeepers was to remove them from danger.

The situation worsened for UNAMIR as the council's debate continued into the second week. The massacres were accumulating at a furious pace, the Belgians were exiting, supplies were dwindling, and the risk to UNAMIR was increasing. Dallaire was quite anxious about UNAMIR's state. A situation report written on April 17 acknowledged that it was highly unlikely he would be able to negotiate a cease-fire, devoted only one paragraph to the continuing existence and likely acceleration of ethnic cleansing, and spent the remaining four pages on UNAMIR's current status. The final two paragraphs of the cable are worth reproducing in full:

THE FC [force commander] ASSESSES THE SITUATION AS BEING VERY DIF-FICULT, DANGEROUS, AND EXPLOSIVE ONCE ONE SIDE OR THE OTHER ACTUALLY START TO SMELL VICTORY. THE FORCE SIMPLY CANNOT CON-TINUE TO SIT ON THE FENCE IN THE FACE OF ALL THESE MORALLY LE-GITIMATE DEMANDS FOR ASSISTANCE/PROTECTION, NOR CAN IT SIMPLY

LAUNCH INTO CHAPTER 7 TYPE OF OPERATIONS WITHOUT THE PROPER AUTHORITY, PERSONNEL AND EQUIPMENT. IT IS THUS ANTICIPATED THAT OVER THE NEXT 24 HOURS OR SO, THE FC WILL EITHER RECOMMEND A THINNING OUT OF THE FORCE DOWN TO A RESPONSIBLE LEVEL NEEDED TO ENSURE THE SECURITY OF THE AIRFIELD FOR HUMANITARIAN RELIEF EFFORTS, THE POLITICAL/MILITARY PROCESS AND THE HUMANITARIAN SUPPORT TASKS. THUS A FORCE OF ABOUT 1300 ALL RANKS BASED ON THE PREFERRED OPTION OF ONE LARGE BATTALION OF 800 MEN (INSTEAD OF TWO SMALL 450 MEN BATTALIONS WITH ALL THEIR OVER HEAD) OR THE FC WILL RECOMMEND OPTION B, IE THE 250 MEN FORCE JUST TO KEEP THE FILES GOING IN A SECURE SITUATION.

MAINTAINING THE STATUS QUO ON MANPOWER UNDER THESE SEVERE AND ADVERSE CONDITIONS IS WASTEFUL, DANGEROUSLY CASUALTY-CAUSING AND DEMORALIZING TO THE TROOPS. EITHER UNAMIR GETS CHANGES IN ITS PARAMETER OF WORKS IN ORDER TO GET INTO THE THICK OF THINGS (WITH MORE RESOURCES), OR IT STARTS TO THIN OUT IN ORDER TO AVOID UNNECESSARY LOSSES AND REDUCE THE OVERHEAD AND ADMINISTRATIVE BURDEN TO THE NEGOTIATION PROCESS FOR A CEASEFIRE AND PEACE.[49]

At this point, UN staff knew that the council had decided against an intervention and that UNAMIR needed immediate protection, which could be provided either by the reinforcement or by the reduction of UNAMIR. Because there was no prospect for the former, the only option was the latter. By April 19, even Dallaire, a relentless advocate for intervention, conceded that it was better for everyone concerned if UNAMIR was reduced to a few fit troops. Baril, DPKO's military adviser and a comrade of Dallaire in the Canadian military, told the Security Council that "there was not a military commander in the world that would leave a force exposed" under those conditions.[50]

The Secretariat also was probably concerned that another failure might translate into the further diminution of the UN. UN officials were on tenterhooks, anxious that any more debacles would only give more evidence to the prosecution. Operations were judged in terms of whether they were good or bad for the UN. Although UN staff did not allow this calculation to determine their decisions, it did shape them. "Most of the staff at the UN were fixated on averting another failure in peacekeeping operations, even at the cost of Rwandan lives."[51] The possibility of failure was heightened not only because of the risks associated with an intervention but perhaps also because of the fear that the council would repeat its established pattern of authorizing a half-hearted involvement, using peacekeepers as a token of the international community's concern, and then failing to provide for them an adequate resource base or solid political support. And when events turned against the UN, member states could be counted on to provide little assistance but lots of criticism. Once bitten, twice shy.

Such criticism was not merely difficult to suffer. It also would increase the ongoing diplomatic offensive against the UN. The UN initially had envisioned that this "easy" operation would help inflate its sagging reputation. Now this easy operation had turned into its worst nightmare. If the UN's intervention was labeled a "failure," then the predictable result was that the UN would be thanked through censure. UNOSOM saved hundreds of thousands of lives, but all anyone cared to remember was the eighteen dead Americans in Mogadishu. In these precarious times, the UN had to worry that its next step might be its last. The Secretariat came to view Rwanda as a threat, and the best way to dispose of the threat was to decouple the two.

But not a complete severing of ties. At no time did the Secretariat advocate abandoning Rwanda. Throughout it lobbied for a reduced presence that would enable UNAMIR to defend the thousands of civilians in strategically protected positions across the city, to act as a base of future operations, and to continue to work for a cease-fire. A stripped-down presence represented a middle ground and pragmatic response to, on the one hand, an intervention that was both unlikely to succeed and potentially fatal to peacekeepers and the organization, and, on the other hand, a complete withdrawal that violated its lingering responsibilities. And, it gladly went along with the decision by Dallaire and Ghana to allow additional Ghanaian troops to remain in Rwanda over the authorized troop limit of 270 (bringing the total number of troops to around 450).

In this strategic scenario the Secretariat gave a calculated and staged performance that was designed to discourage intervention. Its preferences were born not from cynical, immoral, or purely instrumental reasons. It rank-ordered its responsibilities and calculated the risks associated with different types of actions. There were peacekeepers to protect. Also to consider was an organization that might not survive another failure. Protecting the organization from further harm or exploitation was, from the Secretariat's view, ethical, legitimate, and desirable.

WHAT if the Secretariat had come forward with the critical information it withheld and advocated intervention? Could it have changed the outcome? There is that distinct possibility—and the very fact that the Secretariat did not do what it could suggests that it was aware of that possibility. The Secretariat certainly has the opportunity to alter the council's debate because of its agenda-setting capacity and authoritative voice. The Secretariat is expected to write a report and deliver informal observations and recommendations prior to the council's debate. Its observations frequently serve to outline the parameters of the council's discussions, shaping which options are given serious or slight consideration. Its observations carry weight because of its knowledge of the situation on the ground and its credibility, which derives from the presumption that it is impartial and unbiased. By no means does the council accept the Secretariat's word as gospel or always agree with its observations. But its influence at these moments helps to explain why even permanent members are anxious about the Secretariat's reports and recommendations.

All these factors were in play the week following April 6. The council was looking to the Secretariat for information and recommendations. It had the best eyes and ears on the ground because the diplomatic corps was evacuating Rwanda. The future of UNAMIR was still an open question. The initiative, in short, lay with a Secretariat that had a "window of opportunity" to define UN policy toward Rwanda, because there were an array of options on the table, Belgium was still on the ground, and the council was actively seeking information and recommendations from the Secretariat.[52]

A different presentation by the Secretariat might have altered the council's decision. Of course, no definitive conclusion can be drawn in this counterfactual world. But there is good reason to speculate that a more forthcoming and forceful argument by the Secretariat in favor of intervention might have done the trick. Imagine the following hypothetical statement made to the Security Council by a Boutros-Ghali who immediately returned to New York from Europe and took personal control over the crisis:

> We are facing a grave crisis in Rwanda that is not simply about the breakdown of a cease-fire but is fundamentally about what the international community is prepared to do when it confronts crimes against humanity. What is taking place today in Rwanda represents one of the most heinous examples of crimes against humanity that this decade has confronted, and perhaps one of the worst in the twentieth century. Although the situation is quite fluid and our understanding is still in its formative stages, our analysis suggests the following. Tens of thousands of individuals, because of their ethnicity, are being slaughtered at a fearsome rate. We see little indication that the killing will abate. We have good information to conclude that the same parties that are involved in this terror campaign are also the ones who have blocked the Arusha process.

We do not know if an international intervention will dampen this fury, but we do know that if we do nothing then the killing will likely continue. Based on the observations and recommendations of the UNAMIR Force Commander, we conclude that a relatively modest force is likely to cause the architects of these crimes to think twice and halt their killings. Therefore, we recommend a battalion to reinforce UNAMIR's position. Again, this intervention force will not be asked to impose a cease-fire on the parties who are now involved in a civil war. Instead, the purpose will be to signal that we are determined to stand by Rwanda and its population in its hour of need. Also, UNAMIR is presently able to use a mere handful of troops to protect thousands of terrified Rwandans in various parts of Kigali, who would surely be dead if not for UNAMIR's presence. We can reinforce their efforts and save thousands more. There are risks to UN forces, but the risks to hundreds of thousands of Rwandans are greater. We have the moral imperative to intervene, now we must find the courage and the means to do so.

A demarche like this one would have given considerable support to the case for intervention. No longer would the situation be characterized as "chaotic" or would it be insinuated that the violence was uncontrollable and being manufactured by all sides and at all levels. Now it would be known that this was ethnic cleansing. No longer would the situation be characterized as wanton bloodletting from the ground on up. Now it would be forcefully understood that the interim government and its associates were orchestrating a premeditated campaign of ethnic cleansing against civilians. No longer would the focus be only on the civil war or could the council easily pass on responsibility from itself to the parties. Now the council would be forced to confront the ethnic cleansing and the moral imperative it presented. No longer would those arguing for intervention be undercut by the Secretariat's silence on the issue. Now the Secretariat's forceful and impartial statements would be available. No longer would the council or potential troop contributors believe that they were being asked to hand their national armies to a peacekeeping operation that did not have a concept of operations or a just cause. Now it would be understood that there was a moral imperative and a workable military plan.

A different presentation by the Secretariat would have altered the debate, given muscle to the arguments for intervention, and shaken the case for withdrawal. The entire parameters would have shifted, and such a shift might very well have led to a different outcome. *It might have changed the outcome.* Wistfully reflecting on what might have happened had Boutros-Ghali shared Dallaire's cables with and made a pitch for intervention to the Security Council, Ambassador Gambari said that it might have changed the council's decision. "If the Secretary-General had made a pitch [for intervention] then it would have given us moral backing, it might have really changed things. Yes, it would have highlighted the double standard [lots for Europe and nothing for Africa]."[53]

The Secretariat did make a significant impression on the Security Council. By reporting the ongoing violence and "chaos," by conveying the impression that it was overwhelmed by events, and by failing to forward concrete recommendations, it played directly into the hands of those arguing against intervention. If those arguing in favor of intervention were to succeed, then they would require the Secretariat to recommend an expanded operation and to provide a reasoned basis for it. But the Secretariat did not.

By the end of the second week of debate, the Secretariat and the council were on the same page, in favor of a stripped-down operation and mandate. At long last, on April 20, the secretary-general delivered his report on Rwanda, which was better characterized as minutes of the council's discussions than as independent advice and observations.[54] The report concluded by reminding everyone that it is the "[g]overnment of Rwanda (or its successor) and RPF, who must bear responsibility for deciding whether their country and people find peace or continue to suffer violence." Because there was little new in the report that the council had not already heard, the vote was overdue, and the security situation was becoming even more precarious, the council spent little time discussing the report's contents and quickly moved to take a vote.

On April 21 the council unanimously decided to reduce UNAMIR to 270 troops and restrict the mandate to the core task of trying to negotiate a cease-fire. Most in the council had not arrived easily or casually at this decision, agonizing every step of the way. Those who had strenuously argued for intervention were resigned to the fact that with no troops on the horizon, a civil war raging, and a UN operation coming apart at the seams, the second-best and only available option was a stripped-down UNAMIR. Those who opposed intervention had the rules on their side. Although not everyone was as certain as was a very confident United States that this was the best and most desirable action, the rules acted like warning lights and seemed to flash only more brightly with each passing day.

With this vote the council effectively decided that the "international community" would not disturb the killers. This was not an unintended consequence. At this point the council members did not recognize the genocide. Still, they knew that tens if not hundreds of thousands had either been or were about to be killed. No council member could feign ignorance or argue after the fact that it was unaware of the implications of its decision. This action was premeditated.

Yet the vote was informed by reasons and rules that were connected to a higher purpose, and thus served to give the decision an ethical foundation. As those around the table discussed what they should do and why they should do it, I cannot recall a single member state uttering the language of national interests. Such language would have been heretical, virtually obscene, at a moment when the Security Council, the representative of the international community, had the fate of an entire country in its hands. Instead, the rules and reasons of peacekeeping towered over and guided the discussions, rules and reasons that were drawn from recent lessons learned from the field and connected to a transcendental purpose. The resurrection of the UN after the Cold War was driven by the desire not only to resharpen a forgotten tool for peace and security but also to recapture an ideal. Because of a combination of exuberance, naiveté, and expedience, the council had deployed peacekeepers to places where there was no peace to keep, and with inadequate resources and unrealistic mandates. The short-term consequences were failures in the field, but the more lasting and long-term consequence seemed to be the eclipse of a transcendental ideal. To make peacekeeping work effectively and to preserve an ideal required that the council find rules and reasons to judge between competing responsibilities and obligations.

To intervene in Rwanda in this post-Somalia moment and under these circumstances, therefore, risked not simply another failure but the exhaustion of a much-hoped-for ideal. Although remaining indifferent to the killings might be a sin if judged in isolation, once balanced against the (higher) commitment to the international community's cathedral there emerged mitigating circumstances that made the council's actions part of a record of "self-defense" of the organization. The reasons the council forwarded were connected to a moral compass that pointed away from Rwanda, not toward it, thus legitimating a stance that onlookers at the time and critics at later moments assumed was amoral and devoid of legitimation principles. But principles and reasons proved to be a spiritual guide and moral comfort to those at the UN, instilling confidence in the belief that their actions were necessary and proper. To let the killings be at this moment was not a sign of their shallow commitment to the international community. Instead, it was evidence of it.

UNAMIR was now a shell of a peacekeeping operation. It was able to protect the lucky few who found sanctuary in Kigali and was forced to bear witness to a genocide that was at the very early stages and being carried out with unbelievable cruelty and brutality. Booh-Booh's parting words as he departed from the genocidal scene were that if the "warring parties do not reach an agreement on a cease-fire, it must be very clear we shall not stay here. We came to assist Rwanda but we cannot impose any solution on the Rwandan people, who have to help us to help them."[55]

5

Diplomatic Games

The Security Council's vote on April 21, 1994, could be reasonably defended as long as the violence in Rwanda was understood to be a civil war and the latest and bloodiest installment of a centuries-long cycle of ethnic violence. Although the scale and speed of the killings were shocking, the conclusion was that there was little the UN could or should do beyond trying to broker a cease-fire between the combatants. Anything more was unrealistic because of the absence of troops and inappropriate because of the ineffectiveness of peacekeeping under these violent circumstances. Soon after the vote, however, the signs of genocide became unmistakable and undeniable, subverting the alibi for inaction and quickly transforming what once passed as prudence and reasoned self-control into complacency and gross indifference.

The knowledge of the genocide produced a collective anxiety born from a generalized sense of helplessness and a desire to do something, if only, at the very least, to play the part of representative of the international community. The easier it was for those in New York to see the genocide and distinguish it from the civil war, the harder it became to imagine how anything short of a Gulf War–like invasion would make much of a difference. The sheer scale and manner of the killings had a numbing and chilling effect. Mass murder was carried out in the most immediate, direct, personal, and physically demanding manner imaginable. An entire country appeared to be possessed by some maniacal death wish. By the end of April, the number of dead was estimated conservatively at around two hundred thousand, and then a few weeks later the number routinely cited was a half million. Although those at headquarters were not statistically inclined, it was quickly deduced that between five and ten thousand people were being killed each day. As Boutros-Ghali's spokesperson understatedly confessed, "I think everyone has a sense of being overwhelmed by the numbers and wondering what to do."[1] The very scale and technology of the killings that drove an impulse to do something also produced the opposite conclusion that very little could be done. The killing defied the imagination. Even less imaginable was what realistically might be done to stop it. Shock created a generalized sense of impotence.

The numbness was generated not only by apparitions but also by the material reality that it was highly doubtful the UN would be able to assemble a force for intervention. The private calculations that led states to decline the secretary-general's invitation to join a reinforced peacekeeping operation in April continued over the entire period. Once the genocide became known, it certainly produced the moral wellspring for action, something that was generally absent when the killings were swept under the rug of "civil war." But it was undoubtedly difficult for most states to imagine sending their troops into a demonic space where killings were accumulating in record numbers. Yes, later on a few African countries volunteered for duty, but these volunteers were not combat ready and expected to be compensated for their role as assuager of international shame. The only countries with the resources, organization, and acumen to possibly make a difference were the ones that were performing miserably in Bosnia and were hardly keen to act in an unfamiliar part of the world where the circumstances were even less hospitable. The genocide had the physical property of both repelling and compelling action.

Yet the horrors of Rwanda meant that even the most indifferent among them could not look away. The UN remained "actively seized of the matter," a fixation produced by a mixture of motives. Many were genuinely pained by the tremendous human suffering and believed that the UN had an obligation to act. There were members who came to lament their previous vote to reduce UNAMIR, a vote taken under the influence of incomplete information and increasingly regretted in the face of the genocide, and who were now determined to reverse history if possible. And then there was most everyone else, who remained involved and engaged not so much because they believed that doing so would magically produce an end to the genocide but rather because they were keenly aware that this was the role they were expected to perform in this situation.

This emotional brew of duty, remorse, and face-saving led to a period between the April 21 vote and the end of the genocide, which came three months later with the RPF's military victory on July 19, that can be cynically described as the attempt to construct a Potemkin village of engagement and caring. The UN was caught between the force of moral obligation and the reality that it was not going to deliver a rescue operation.

The central truth that there was not going to be an intervention clashed with the fundamental expectation that as the representative of the international community, the UN was expected to deliver precisely that. This conflict created its own anxiety because officials in New York knew that they were not living up to expectations. They saw themselves as they imagined others saw them: as dithering and spineless politicians and bureaucrats who answered the crime of genocide with silence and shibboleths of concern. Some certainly tried to live up to expectations and to deliver a rescue party. But others in the diplomatic class tried to minimize the moral censure without delivering concrete action by miming the act of engagement. Hollow resolutions, shallow statements of concern, and false promises of action were born from a combination of cynicism, despair, self-deception, and wishful thinking.

The cold gap between expectations and reality became even more frigid because of the tendency of nearly everyone at the UN to follow procedures and routines in these extraordinary times. The reasonable expectation that the lives on the line and the genocide on the ground might cause those in New York to dispense with the diplomatic courtesies and bureaucratic procedures soon yielded to the reality that the manners and rules of the club would be scrupulously followed. There were occasional outbursts. But these flashes of anger were few and far between and almost always took place behind closed doors where their full effect was muted. Those in New York represented the well-mannered and civilized set, and so there existed a strong inclination to act appropriately at all times. The result was that any outrage or disgust anyone might have felt was routinely censored and channeled into acceptable diplomatic discourse. At times their behavior became a near parody of the UN's culture and style, and the outcome would have been laughable if the stakes had not been so high. The sum total of their actions, behavior, and mannerisms reinforced a singular truth: the genocidaires had bet correctly that the international community would not lift a finger to stop their murderous plan.

While the genocidaires in Rwanda took the April 21 vote as a signal to accelerate the genocide—after all, now they knew that the UN would do nothing—the Security Council used the vote to take a breather from the intensely fought and felt debate about Rwanda.[2] Having just voted to reduce UNAMIR, there was little for them to do but wait and see if Dallaire could arrange a cease-fire. Rwanda's rapid descent into genocide, however, generated considerable pressure on the Security Council not only to remain "seized of the matter" but also to redefine what the "matter" was. There was no mistaking the civil war, but there also was a gnawing sense and growing evidence that the situation in Rwanda was more than a civil war and that the UN's recent vote was not the final answer to the question of what was to be done.

Boutros-Ghali inaugurated the new round on Rwanda. On April 22, the day after the Security Council voted to reduce UNAMIR with his silent blessing, the nearly inconspicuous secretary-general announced through his spokesman that he regretted the council's decision and wished that it had found the backbone to authorize a humanitarian intervention. A week later he informed the Security Council of the further "deterioration" of the "situation," reminding the council of the tens of thousands who had already died and warning of more massacres. The cause of this violence, he concluded, was the "incident of April 6" and the resumption of the civil war, which "reawakened deep-rooted ethnic hatreds, which have plagued Rwanda in the past and which have again led to massacres of innocent civilians on a massive scale." He urged the council to answer the massacres with an intervention.[3]

Boutros-Ghali was wasting little time attempting to cover up his great disappearing act of the past few weeks. That his most forceful statement to date on the Rwandan massacres came the day after the April 21 vote can be interpreted as more than just ironic coincidence but as a cynical attempt to camouflage his previous silences. And while he was no longer keeping quiet, what he had to say simply recycled the mischaracterization of Rwanda as a site of massacres being mutually visited on two ethnic groups by each other, the inevitable result of age-old "ethnic hatreds."

What makes Boutros-Ghali's observations highly curious if not shameful is that by the end of April Dallaire had abandoned the language of ethnic cleansing in favor of the more legally correct and morally propulsive concept of genocide.[4] And Dallaire had been giving the perpetrators of the genocide a name and an address. Yet Boutros-Ghali continued to speak of a civil war and ethnic conflict in vague terms, avoiding the language of genocide and failing to pin the violence on a single party. Boutros-Ghali's observations reinforced the existing narrative that he surely knew would coddle complacency. It was not until a May 4, 1994, broadcast of *Nightline* that Boutros-Ghali uttered the word *genocide* in a public forum, nearly a full week after the council had begun to suspect that Rwanda was no mere ethnic conflict. Boutros-Ghali might have affected a public persona of leadership, but in fact he remained steps behind the Security Council.

In the Security Council the assumption that this was a civil war with strong shades of ethnic killing was coming unhinged by the growing evidence of genocide. The need for action also was reinforced by a wave of 250,000 refugees streaming over the Rwandan border into Tanzania on May 1, drawing attention away from the killings and toward a refugee crisis that threatened regional stability. Although there is no definitive date for when the possibility of genocide was mentioned in the Security Council's private sessions, my personal recollection is that soon after the April 21 vote, several representatives, including the Czech and New Zealand ambassadors, began publicly entertaining the possibility of genocide. They reached this conclusion not with the help of the Secretariat but rather with the assistance of human rights organizations and independent reports.

Other members of the council were not receptive to the initial insertions of "genocide" into the council's conversation as an important observation that bore weighty consideration. Instead, the very word was nearly treated as a moral pollutant. This attitude became apparent on April 29 when Ambassador Keating, in his final act as president of the Security Council, attempted to push through a presidential statement that acknowledged Rwanda as a genocide.[5] An ally, Czech Ambassador Karel Kovanda, lambasted the council for spending 80 percent of its time discussing the withdrawal of the peacekeepers and 20 percent of its time trying to broker a cease-fire. He pointedly observed that "it was like wanting Hitler to reach a cease-fire with the Jews."[6] The draft statement included the following paragraph:

[T]he horrors of Rwanda's killing fields have few precedents in the recent history of the world. The Security Council reaffirms that the systematic killing of any ethnic group, with the intent to destroy it in whole or in part constitutes an act of genocide as defined by relevant provisions of international law. . . . [T]he council further points out that an important body of international law exists that deals with perpetrators of genocide.[7]

Unable to get agreement in the council, Keating decided to circulate a draft resolution for the last day of the month. The effect would be to force those who were blocking the presidential statement to "explain their position before the media."[8] The result of many hours of intense debate was a presidential statement that elliptically referred to genocide, a major development given the context. That statement "recalls that the killing of members of an ethnic group with the intention of destroying such a group in whole or in part constitutes a crime punishable under international law."[9] The United States took the lead position in arguing against the use of such inflammatory language, a position that received considerable backing from other members for a variety of reasons. Although the Genocide Convention does not require a military response to genocide, the council did not expect a literal reading from the international public, who it imagined would treat anything less than military action as a whitewash. Sir David Hannay, the British ambassador, warned that the council would be a "laughing stock" if it called Rwanda a genocide and then failed to act.[10] And it was not exactly certain, others noted, that this was genocide. According to the legal definition in the convention, there had to be a premeditated attempt to eliminate another group because of its identity. There was considerable evidence that Tutsis were being targeted because of their ethnicity, but there was no reliable information concerning premeditation; after all, this could very well be a spontaneous eruption of age-old ethnic hatreds, as it was often portrayed as being.

Moreover, even if the council decided then and there that the killing in Rwanda was a genocide, it would not alter the central fact that there were no troops lining up to storm Kigali. The insinuation was that to make this discursive move would only expand the gap between the moral imperative and the lack of action. Finally, to accuse the interim government of complicity in genocide would certainly undermine both the UN's stated position of impartiality and its effectiveness as a facilitator for a cease-fire. The Djibouti ambassador pragmatically cautioned, "You have to be prudent. We don't want to divide the people by talking about genocide before we bring them together in a cease-fire," a position supported by other African countries, including Nigeria.[11] Even though the council now acknowledged that Rwanda was a genocide, these arguments encouraged it to slowly converge on the implicit policy to shelve the explicit usage of the concept of genocide and to categorically prohibit such incendiary language outside the chambers.

But elsewhere many world leaders and many human rights organizations were calling the killing in Rwanda a genocide. The first newspaper accounts of the genocide taking place behind the lines of the Rwandan military were published, and the media was beginning to juxtapose the mass killings with the Security Council's recent vote to reduce UNAMIR. The result was that the council increasingly looked either cowardly, cautious, or callous in its failure to call the killing in Rwanda by its rightful name. Ugandan President Museveni diplomatically captured the sentiment of many when he accused the UN of simply wanting to "smother the problems—to put a canvas over rotten eggs. And as long as the smell in the room is suppressed then the problem is solved."[12] Others were less diplomatic, wondering aloud what sort of Security Council this was that could close its eyes, ears, and mouth to the genocide.

The evidence of genocide coupled with the growing embarrassment it felt because of its inaction caused the Security Council to put its shoulders behind the idea of an intervention. In the lead were those members who had initially advocated intervention, using the very arguments that were not available to them in the first weeks. As Human Rights Watch sorrowfully speculated, "Had they [those in the intervention camp] been more accurately informed about the slaughter during the first week of April, they might have taken their responsible stand earlier and shamed other members and staff into joining them."[13] In tow were those who had initially argued against intervention but could no longer reasonably do so given the enormity of the crisis and the power of the arguments.

With a growing consensus in favor of some sort of intervention, the council formally requested the secretary-general to prepare contingency plans for humanitarian assistance. In fact, at this moment several draft proposals were already in the works. The range of possibilities was great: a peace enforcement action with "all necessary means" provisions that called for actively combing the country and protecting civilians, though not necessarily imposing a cease-fire; a "Bosnia-style" operation that would construct safe havens in the heart of Rwanda;[14] and an American-sponsored proposal that envisioned the UN stationing forces on the border to establish "safe havens" to receive and protect civilians who managed to crawl to safety.

A week later the secretary-general delivered his report and plan of action. UNAMIR would become UNAMIR II and would provide "safe conditions" for displaced peoples; would assist and protect the relief efforts of humanitarian organizations; and would provide protection sites for displaced peoples throughout Rwanda, but most importantly in and around Kigali. These tasks would require fifty-five hundred personnel, including five battalions, a helicopter squadron, a military police force, a military observer group, and UN civilian police.

UNAMIR II would be deployed in three stages. The first stage would begin the week after the Security Council passed the authorizing resolution and involve the immediate deployment of Ghanaian troops (currently holed up in Nairobi) to secure the airport and other sites in Kigali. The next stage would begin the following week and would involve the deployment of two battalions to areas of "greatest concern." Then two weeks later, the third stage would kick in and UNAMIR II would be at full strength and be sent to various parts of Rwanda. The resolution imagined, then, a fully equipped force of over five thousand assembled in a few weeks. Ideally, the forces would land at the Kigali airport, but because it was an occasional battleground, other ports of entry might have to be entertained.

UNAMIR would not be an enforcement operation, but it would use "deterrence" and employ force to defend itself, civilians in the protected sites, and humanitarian convoys. This was the very force Dallaire had been requesting since the first days of the crisis.

The report subtly noted several critical holes in the plan. It envisioned a rapid deployment. But peacekeeping operations often took months to move from the drawing board to the field. The only way that UNAMIR II might defy history was if the countries that volunteered forces also provided fully outfitted units and if a country like the United States was willing to provide strategic lift support. Yet it was not exactly clear what troops were available. Although a few African countries volunteered, they made their participation contingent on being outfitted with the latest Western military equipment, which they would be allowed to keep as peacekeeping booty. Even if the UN was willing to pay the price (and, more specifically, Western governments were willing to pay the price), it was highly doubtful that these forces were up to the job. As diplomatically put by U.S. Ambassador Madeleine Albright, it remained unclear whether African countries were ready or able to send forces for a dangerous and complex operation at the "epicenter of a civil war."[15] The result was that the UN could look forward to lengthy bilateral negotiations, an interminable process that could take several weeks, only to find first-rate equipment being handed to third-rate forces.

The report also strongly suggested that the rescue party's ability to get into the field was highly dependent on the "cooperation and support of the Rwandan parties," if not a cease-fire. But the RPF looked warily on any UN intervention and warned the UN to keep its distance and stick to its humanitarian mandate, or else. Its reasons were well understood. It now had a decisive military upper hand, the remnants of the Rwandan army were on the run, and it was determined to finish off the Rwandan government. Calls for a cease-fire and repair of the Arusha Accords ostensibly meant that the RPF would be forced into a compact with the very individuals who had destroyed the accords and planned the genocide. It found such a possibility repugnant. The UN had abandoned the Tutsis to the genocide, the RPF was the only fighting force capable of and willing to stop the killing, and the RPF was not about to stand in place in order to permit UN "action." The RPF also feared that any UN intervention would be a cover for France, once again, to aid its Rwandan allies. Therefore, the RPF warned the UN to do nothing that impeded its advance. The improbability of a cease-fire meant that a UN force would be plunged into the middle of a civil war.

Still, most on the Security Council asked few questions as they quickly embraced the plan. There certainly existed a "build it and they will come" attitude. Also prevalent was a desire to be able to show the world an intervention plan to reduce some of the public heat. After weeks that seemed like years of inactivity and passivity, the council was relieved to be able to release news of an intervention plan and not the same tiresome statement concerning the council's grave concern and determination to remain "seized of the matter." Now the UN had something to show the international community and to answer the accusations of indifference.

A complication, however, was that the United States would not go along with what it perceived as little more than a public relations stunt, and it was willing to open itself up to a barrage of criticism in order to expose what it viewed as a Potemkin operation. The United States' willingness to present itself as the poster child for indifference can only be understood as a warped blend of political and principled logic saturated with tremendous apathy.

The United States argued that its position was the logical one, following from established rules and an understanding of how to best protect the UN from further abuse. For some time the United States had suggested that the UN had no business being in Rwanda because of the breakdown of the peace agreement, the chaos on the ground, and the return of civil war. The United States refused to concede what everyone knew at that point—that Rwanda was a civil war *and* a genocide. In early May administration officials were willing to give testimony to Congress acknowledging that the massacres were being directed by Hutu forces against Tutsis, and they did not correct the members of Congress who referred to the killing in Rwanda as a genocide. But they were not going to let the word *genocide* pass their lips. The official line was that there was no genocide. When that position looked foolish, administration officials retreated to phrases such as "acts of genocide." In response to a query about whether the killing in Rwanda constituted a genocide, on April 28 the State Department spokesperson clumsily observed:

> The use of the term genocide has a very precise legal meaning, although it's not strictly a legal determination. There are other factors in there as well. . . . When in looking at a situation to make a determination about that, before we begin to use that term we have to know as much as possible about the facts of the situation. . . . This is a more complicated issue to address, and we're certainly looking into this extremely carefully right now. But I'm not able to look at all at those criteria at this moment.[16]

The statement might have been written by Joseph Heller. And then when Secretary of State Warren Christopher finally conceded on June 10 that

Rwanda was a genocide, the United States looked like the dullest and most callous kid in the class.

The United States' official line that the conflict in Rwanda was a civil war formed the basis of its argument that there were no grounds for peacekeeping. To bolster its case, the United States (and Russia) approvingly cited the Security Council statement of May 3 that established the conditions under which the council would establish an operation. According to the council's own rules, the United States reminded the body, it had no choice but to say no to the plan. In private, representatives from the Departments of State and Defense warned their UN counterparts that pushing ahead with the plan invited a Somali-like disaster. Such an occurrence, they continued, would only result in further discrediting of the UN and peacekeeping and in risking what little credibility it retained.[17] In her May 17 testimony to the House Foreign Affairs Committee, Albright insisted that it would have been "folly" for the UN to rush into the "maelstrom" in Central Africa, and that "we want to be confident that when we do turn to the UN, the UN will be able to do the job." This was, she added, the first test of PDD-25.[18]

On May 4, President Clinton had signed PDD-25, the United States' review of multilateral operations, which contained a set of criteria intended to guide the United States' decision making on peacekeeping operations. The document had been in the works for several months, and during that period it had been used as an informal guide for American policy toward peacekeeping. But the signing and publication of the document at the very moment that the situation in Rwanda was being discussed at the UN meant that it was impossible for the United States not to apply its criteria. A casual review of the criteria made it clear that in the United States' opinion it had no business being in Rwanda, and neither did the UN. This did not mean that by those same criteria the United States should be in Bosnia, or many other places for that matter. But the issue at hand was Rwanda.

The hypocrisy contained in what the Americans said and did was joyfully exposed by UN officials during a private briefing the U.S. Mission gave to top-ranking UN officials soon after the document was signed. The U.S. deputy ambassador to the UN, Karl Inderfurth, attempted to explain how PDD-25 was not a policy shift but was, in fact, an attempt to drum up more domestic support for the UN. A normally respectful UN crowd turned positively raucous, challenging the Americans to explain how interventions were justified by the American criteria in places like Haiti and Bosnia but not places like Rwanda, where the human rights calamity was far greater.

While the UN crowd might see hypocrisy in the United States' behavior, the Clinton administration viewed it as politically prudent and mindful of national interests. For much of April, a Clinton administration that saw Somalia lurking around every corner never even debated the merits of intervention. But now that the Security Council was actively considering an intervention plan, the United States feared that any such authorized measure would invariably require its participation. This fear was not unreasonable given that those in the press who were arguing for intervention understood that there were few countries with the ability to execute an emergency operation, the United States being one of them.

The result was that American officials like National Security Adviser Tony Lake were wont to argue in public that it was not the American people's responsibility to respond to every humanitarian emergency, and bureaucratically powerful Pentagon officials were fearful that any approved authorization would lead down a slippery slope to American participation.[19] Those in Congress who cared enough to comment on the situation counseled the administration not to repeat the mistake of Somalia. When the Clinton administration explained to Congress why it was not going to be sending troops or why it opposed the secretary-general's latest scheme, only a handful objected. Also, Clinton had to fear a domestic backlash if he sanctioned another African operation that was not connected to American interests. There were few letters or phone calls to the U.S. Mission to the UN or to the White House to urge that something be done, and these few signs of compassion were overwhelmed by the sheer number that urged the administration to resist the intervention temptation. If Somalia was any indication, this administration had little to gain from an intervention and much to lose—especially at a time when it was actively contemplating a military operation in Haiti.

The United States also pointed to perceived holes in the Secretariat's plan. It was not exactly clear what the force would do once it arrived in Kigali. There was terrific language in the secretary-general's report about how UNAMIR II was going to help with displaced peoples and protect the humanitarian operation. But the operation was supposed to avoid the civil war and not confront either army. The problem was that the killings were reported to be occurring behind Rwandan military lines and near the sites of the civil war, which meant that if UNAMIR was going to protect civilians in any numbers it might find itself not only near the war but also embroiled in it. There was the possibility, in short, that UNAMIR would confront the Rwandan military, transforming the UN troops into combatants and creating an informal alliance with the RPF, which was not the role of impartial, humanitarian operations. There also was the enormous task of translating the generic political language of the resolution into a workable military document. This plan, the United States further argued, could not satisfy basic military requirements. The United States concluded that the UN was about to send an inferior force into a battle zone with no real guidance.

In the Security Council Albright and other American officials argued that the UN was not doing the Rwandans or itself any favors by adopting a plan of action that was hopelessly unrealistic and possibly dangerous on at least three counts. One, by the secretary-general's own admission, while the plan called for peacekeepers to be on the ground within two weeks, it was unimaginable that they would be there within two months. Two, the UN began getting into trouble when it rushed prematurely into dangerous situations, resulting in the failure to execute the mandate and placing peacekeepers in harm's way. Had it not learned anything from recent events? Three, the UN's fixation on this unrealistic and half-baked scheme was squandering precious time that was better spent on more realistic and modest scenarios.

The United States proposed, instead, to deploy forces on the periphery of Rwanda, just on the other side of the border, to provide relief to the Rwandans who could make it that far. Granted, such a force would do little to help the Tutsis who were being exterminated far from the border. True, the U.S. proposal was designed to solve a different problem. But at least this plan was workable. American officials argued that the very modesty of the plan was its virtue: only a modest plan had any chance of being implemented. While others found such measures immoral given the circumstances, the Clinton administration implicitly argued that it was unethical to waste time on proposals that would never be implemented.

Most on the council stood behind the Secretariat's proposal, leaving the United States and Russia as powerful backbenchers who favored a more circumscribed plan. The American proposal never stood a chance. At the very least it would not represent the public relations coup desperately desired by a UN that was increasingly embarrassed by its inaction. In fact, the secretary-general's proposal already represented something of a compromise between the American plan and those who wanted a more forceful intervention. And most on the council had tired of the United States' stonewalling, nay-saying, and cynical denial of the genocide. Still, the United States was relentlessly determined to halt the Secretariat's plan, threatening to veto the resolution as presently written. At this point some UN aides conceded that the Secretariat's plan was probably overly ambitious.

A compromise solution that envisioned a two-stage solution soon emerged. In the first stage, the 850-strong Ghanaian peacekeepers with APCs would be deployed immediately. Their principal task would be to help UNAMIR protect civilians in Kigali and at the airport (with additional military observers sent to other parts of the country). The deployment of the remaining troops would be contingent on receiving satisfactory answers to some basic issues, including the "cooperation of the parties, progress towards a cease-fire, availability of resources and the proposed duration of the mandate for further review and action."[20] While many in the council believed that this represented an unwarranted restriction and unnecessary hoop, there was no getting around the veto-wielding United States.

On May 17, the Security Council authorized Resolution 918, with three parts designed to address three pressing issues. The first part authorized the expansion of the original UNAMIR mandate and the number of troops to fifty-five hundred in a two-stage formula. Operating under Chapter VI, UNAMIR II's mandate would be to help protect displaced peoples and civilians at risk through the establishment of secure humanitarian areas (the language of safe havens was purposefully avoided), and to protect and assist international relief operations. Deployment and implementation largely depended on a cease-fire in the civil war. Yet there was little prospect of a cease-fire because the RPF had quickly gained military advantage and was not stopping until victory, had little faith in the UN, and had little interest in concluding a cease-fire with the very extremists who were enacting the genocide and had scuttled the accords. The second part of the resolution established an arms embargo on Rwanda and the parties; this part passed on a vote of fourteen to one. Rwanda voted against the proposal on the grounds that Uganda and not Rwanda should be the target of the arms embargo. The third part requested the secretary-general to report on serious violations of human rights. With the adoption of UNAMIR II, the only obstacles to intervention were a workable cease-fire and the transfer of military equipment from Western to African countries. It was only a matter of time.

The next month was an extended waiting period created by the absence of both a cease-fire and troops. Although it was increasingly common to call the killing in Rwanda a genocide, the civil war remained front and center during most discussions. In the council's view, the civil war was responsible for creating the conditions for the genocide, and a cease-fire was required before UNAMIR II could be deployed. Most officials recognized that short of an immediate cease-fire and a radical reversal in the interim government's policies, the only hope for an end to the genocide resided with an RPF victory. But that did not mean that the UN was suddenly going to side with the "rebels" in the civil war. The only thing that the UN could do was search for a cease-fire.

The secretary-general sent Riza and Baril to Rwanda in late May—the first time high-ranking UN officials had visited Rwanda since the operation was established—to see whether the conditions on the ground might be altered to facilitate the rapid deployment of UNAMIR II, that is, a cease-fire. Based on their observations and recommendations, the secretary-general wrote a lengthy report that called the killings genocide and placed the burden of blame on the Presidential Guard, the Interahamwe, and the interim government.[21] These were important observations and conclusions given the amount of misdirection that had occurred over the preceding six weeks. But most of the report dwelled on the political situation and the elusive quest for a cease-fire, thereby reiterating what was already known and reinforcing any brake to action.

Various African states volunteered to send troops but on the condition that they be completely and sometimes lavishly equipped with the latest technology, which would be theirs to keep. Western states were then encouraged to "adopt a peacekeeping force." These extended negotiations were standard fare for peacekeeping operations. But this circumstance was not ordinary, and any promise of assistance was almost always received as bringing the UN one step closer to an intervention, which was, as already stated, the desired impression. But the most immediate result of these negotiations was to send the disappointment downstream, ensuring that blame and recrimination settled on someone else.

This was the context for the infamous APC incident involving the United States. Under UNAMIR II Ghana was to provide peacekeepers for the first stage of the operation, but its deployment was contingent on receiving APCs, a military necessity and by no means a luxury. The United States agreed to sponsor the Ghanaians and provide fifty APCs. But soon the American pledge got waylaid by bureaucratic procedures of Kafkaesque proportions. The United States refused to donate the APCs. After all, Congress had been scrutinizing and criticizing nearly all monetary and in-kind contributions to peacekeeping operations, and the Clinton administration was not about to donate the equipment only to find itself skewered by the likes of Bob Dole and Jesse Helms.

Then the issue became whether the United States would sell the equipment outright to the UN, how much transport costs were, what sort of insurance coverage was to be provided in case the vehicles were damaged, and so on. The image of Pentagon bureaucrats holding endless meetings with their UN counterparts while the genocide was raging appeared stunningly callous to nearly all. But the United States insisted that there were bureaucratic procedures to follow, and while Tony Lake, the national security adviser, got personally involved and attempted to expedite the process, the only American official who possessed the laser-like ability to cut through the red tape was Bill Clinton, and he remained aloof. Nor was the United

States willing to begin preparing the vehicles until all the paperwork was complete, a restriction it said was imposed by law. The UN could easily match the United States rule for rule. The United States would deliver its conditions, and then the UN bureaucrats would take their time returning with an answer and would invariably deliver their own conditions.

After weeks of attempting a bureaucratic meeting of the minds, an agreement was finally reached, and the APCs were shipped from Uganda, where they arrived at the end of June. But the vehicles were not immediately routed to Kigali. Proceeding on UN time, the first APCs did not arrive in Kigali until early August, long after the genocide was over and the RPF controlled the country.[22]

Passing resolutions that did not stand a chance of being implemented, and sending emissaries into the field to try to produce a cease-fire when it was clear that none would be had—these and other diplomatic undertakings can be reasonably and rightly justified on the grounds that attempts had to be made. In response to those who criticize the UN for mechanically going through the motions, those in New York can rightly say that they are damned if they do, and damned if they don't. Certainly many were persistent in their efforts, even knowing that it was an uphill struggle and that they would have little to show for it. It is too easy to be critical and cynical, especially when the results of such concentrated and tireless efforts are so minimal.

But these activities also served another function: they helped to hide the UN's reluctance to act. Consider the council's endless meetings. Although their ostensible purpose was to try to achieve collective action, they also served to hide collective inaction. Many of these meetings arguably served no conceivable function because there was no proposal on the table and the information communicated could just as easily have been delivered through another mechanism. But keeping Rwanda on the Security Council's agenda certainly provided evidence that the UN was "seized of the matter." These meetings also gave all the members the opportunity to express their moral outrage and furnished a cost-free way to show that they cared. At the end of each day's debate, the president of the Security Council would announce to the press that the council was disturbed by the violence and would continue to follow events closely. Indeed, there was a nearly rhythmic quality to the deliberations during these first weeks. On one day, hours would be spent exchanging information and exhorting the need for concrete action. Satisfied that now the council had demonstrated sufficient concern, the following day's meeting would be highly abbreviated. The rhythm and swings flattened considerably after May 17, and for the next month all that occurred were updates on the situation on the ground and on the failure to assemble the force. By filling the halls of the UN, remaining in constant session, and generating a flood of documents and statements, the council could present a facade of action when in fact there was little chance of it. The UN provided a shield behind which member states could hide their individual apathy and indifference.

But the tendency to do what was appropriate for the circumstance could also generate conduct that attempted to maintain decorum and civility in the face of outrage and villainy. On April 5, José Ayala-Lasso became the first UN high commissioner for human rights, a post created to bring greater attention to human rights violations and to permit speedier and more flexible responses to humanitarian crises. The assumption of the post on the very eve of the genocide provided an opportunity for him to make his mark, to use his position to call attention to the crimes, and to demand forceful action. But the high commissioner turned opportunity into almost a parody of the UN. Although he wrote to the secretary-general on April 15 to offer his assistance, by and large the high commissioner was absent for much of the month. He undertook a surgical visit to Rwanda on May 11–12 to appeal to "both parties to stop the human rights violations immediately and to work for a negotiated settlement of the conflict."[23] Although at this point the secretary-general was calling the killing in Rwanda a genocide, Ayala-Lasso could do no more than to observe that "the situation in Rwanda can be characterized as a human rights tragedy," to describe in abstract terms the mass killings, and to threaten the ultimate bureaucratic sanction: the possibility that the Commission on Human Rights might consider investigating human rights violations.

The genocide was physically in the Security Council's midst. Rwanda had become a member of the council in January 1994. During the pre-April period, this could be convenient because the council's growing impatience with the delays in the Arusha Accords could be communicated directly to the Rwandan government. During the April debates, however, it meant that the council housed a representative of a government that was increasingly suspected of genocide (and also knew firsthand that nothing was going to be done and could, and probably did, communicate that information to his government). It also allowed Rwanda to interject its own views and introduce its own version of events. For much of the time the Rwandan representative had little to contribute, and his presence was tolerated.

There were occasional moments when Rwanda's insistence on contributing its own version of events invited a reaction, and only a few members of the council used these moments to deliver a diplomatic slight. In mid-May Rwanda's Foreign Minister Jerome Bicamumpaka came to New York to defend his government and to accuse the RPF and the Tutsis of launching a genocidal campaign against the Hutus. Most received him as a representative of an accredited state and extended to him the same courtesies extended to any representative of a state. For a few this charade was too much, and some refused to meet with him.

Before the May 17 vote authorizing the UN's intervention, Bicamumpaka addressed the council. He delivered a lengthy address that managed to reproduce nearly every single racist myth of Africa and the ethnic origins of the conflict and, essentially, to exonerate the bloodletting. Denying that the interim government of the army bore any responsibility for the killings, he argued that the "actual reality . . . is deeply rooted in the subconscious of every Rwandese and in the collective memory of an entire people . . . [and that] the hatred that is erupting now was forged over four centuries of cruel and ruthless domination of the Hutu majority by the haughty and domineering Tutsi minority."²⁴ After essentially justifying why the Hutus were seized by the desire to kill and seek revenge because of centuries of domination, he then proceeded to claim that the killings were being delivered by the RPF who had shot down Habyarimana's plane and started the civil war. One falsehood after another was delivered with a straight face.

Most representatives let the remarks go unchallenged or without comment. A few did not. Ambassador Keating of New Zealand referred to the speaker as "merely a mouthpiece of a faction" that does not represent a state and has no legitimacy, and accused him of delivering a "shameful distortion of the truth." The Czech ambassador argued that while the situation in Rwanda was routinely referred to as a "humanitarian crisis as though it were a famine or perhaps some natural disaster," in his view "the proper description is genocide." The members could easily reveal their outrage in abstract terms, but most would not challenge the genocide's representative.

Whatever outrage might have been felt by his presence became increasingly overtaken by the question of what legal right he had to be there. He represented a Rwandan government that no longer existed. The "interim government" was established on April 9, and it had promptly fled Kigali and taken up residence elsewhere. But its claim to be the new government was based solely on its asserting as much. It certainly was not based on constitutional procedures or on being recognized by other states. The implication was that this individual sitting in the Rwandan chair had no legal right to be present. But if not him, then who? The problem was that Rwanda existed, but an accredited government did not. So it was unclear who would replace him. Never before had the Security Council been forced to address such an odd situation, and instead of doing so it allowed the status quo to continue into the future. So, as the genocide proceeded and the RPF controlled more and more Rwandan territory, this individual who represented a government that no longer existed and was accused of genocide simply took his seat at the table, day in and day out.

This situation continued until the Security Council was forced to act because the representative for Rwanda was scheduled to become the president of the council in September. The position of president is rotated on a monthly basis and according to alphabetical order, and now it was Rwanda's turn. The next president of the Security Council might be the last representative of a genocidal government. Perhaps this was apropos for a council that removed itself from the genocide, but the council certainly did not relish the idea of the face of genocide being its representative to the media and the organizer of its agenda. To compound the strangeness of the situation, the RPF had controlled the country by July 19 and had quickly formed a national unity government. Meanwhile, the RPF representative at the UN had been pacing the hallways outside the Security Council for months, increasingly treated as the de facto Rwandan ambassador to the UN. The council decided to suspend the rules governing the rotation of the presidency; it skipped Rwanda and gave the office to Spain. By the end of August a new Rwandan representative presented his credentials to the secretary-general. Rwanda got its chance to be president in December 1994.

By the middle of June almost an entire month had passed since the May 17 resolution—and the UN had little to show for its efforts, except a stream of documents and statements concerning the failure of member states to provide the barest of resources and material support to implement the mandate. During this period Boutros-Ghali was continuously urging the international community to act, occasionally juxtaposing the genocide against the international silence. He even proposed alternative deployment schedules in an attempt to hasten the peacekeeping force. Still, there was no progress.

On June 19, a visibly frustrated Boutros-Ghali publicly acknowledged what had been widely known for some time: UNAMIR II probably would not be anything more than a paper force for several months. This was hardly news. The plan never had a chance. The United States was not the only culprit. Other states deserve credit as well. Boutros-Ghali ascribed the delay to peacekeeping fatigue, the consuming presence of seventeen other operations, and the unwillingness to jump into another war—genocide or no genocide—after watching events in Bosnia and Somalia.[25] This was a collective effort.

After almost two months of talk with no action, on June 15 France offered to lead a multinational operation into Rwanda. The reasons had little to do with a desire to save Rwandan lives and more to do with scoring political points back home and protecting foreign policy interests in the region.[26] The government of François Mitterrand was beginning to feel the pressure that comes from being so dismissive of a genocide being committed by its close allies, and began to worry that if the "Anglo-Saxon" world did actually intervene, then France would lose some control over the situation and even more face. Also present, at least among some within the French government, was the desire to protect its retreating Rwandan allies from the victorious RPF.

Regardless of the mixture of motives, in its statements France loyally held to the line that it was acting out its humanitarian instincts, that its policy shift was due to the gravity of the humanitarian nightmare and the impotence of the international community, and that it would provide some relief until the arrival of, and would provide the eventual beachhead for, UNAMIR II. In order to implicate others in its pretense that it was acting on behalf of the international community, France was determined to enlist other African states in its operation and receive the UN's blessing. Even though several African armies had stated their readiness to contribute contingents to UNAMIR II once they were outfitted with the requisite equipment, only Senegal immediately agreed to ride with France into Rwanda.

Few on the Security Council believed that France was motivated by strictly humanitarian concerns. And with good reason. This was the same France that only the year before had intervened in Rwanda to save its allies, the very same individuals who were now closely associated with the genocide. Therefore, the council's general opinion was that it was virtually unimaginable that France had had a crisis of conscience and much more believable that it was about to use the cover of the UN's seal of approval to rescue its Rwandan allies and perhaps even to confront the RPF. If so, then the council might very well be providing support to the genocidaires.

To complicate matters, the RPF announced that it opposed the French intervention, and warned France to keep its distance lest it become part of a wider war. If this came to pass, then the council might very well discover that it had authorized a resolution giving a permanent member of the council the opportunity to join with the genocidaires to wage war on the only military organization that might stop the genocide. At the very least, the Security Council had to worry that France's entry into Rwanda might very well jeopardize UNAMIR's safety because the RPF might conclude that these two separate international forces were a combined threat. The overall fear, then, was that France might be using the UN as a Trojan horse, and the UN might wind up aiding the genocidaires and jeopardizing its peacekeepers.[27]

But it was hardly imaginable that the Security Council would reject the first offer to provide humanitarian assistance to come its way in over two months of empty searching. So, the Security Council delivered sharply worded statements that it would closely monitor France's conduct in the field, and then inserted into the authorizing resolution the cautionary clause that "the strictly humanitarian character of this operation . . . shall be conducted in an impartial and neutral fashion, and shall not constitute an interposition force between the parties."[28] In other words, no monkey business and stay away from the fighting and the RPF. With these strong reservations and cautionary warnings, the council reluctantly approved Resolution 929 on June 22. The vote was ten in favor, none opposed, and five abstentions. The tally accurately reflected the palpable fears, made all the more evident by the very fact that five countries, including New Zealand and Nigeria, which had been early advocates of intervention, abstained. The Security Council held its breath and hoped for the best.

Much to its public embarrassment, France's arrival was greeted with enthusiastic cheers by many Hutus and the Rwandan army, who believed that France was not on a mission of mercy but rather on a mission of strategic assistance. Within days of its landing, a change in the military situation on the ground expanded and shifted the French role. In early July the RPF's steady advance toward southwestern Rwanda triggered the flight of roughly 1.2 million people, most heading toward that part of Rwanda and the border of Zaire (now the Democratic Republic of the Congo). In response and with the UN's authorization, on July 9 France established a safe humanitarian zone, a protectorate of sorts, in that region. The general concern was that France's "humanitarian safe zone" was intended as a military protectorate for the retreating genocidaires and Rwandan forces, and only as a second thought was it to provide relief to the displaced peoples.[29]

France quickly welcomed the displaced peoples and provided emergency relief and some protection, a courtesy it also extended to the Rwandan troops and known genocidaires. At no time did France ever try to disarm the Rwandan army or the genocidaires as they fled into the area. At no time did it ever arrest a single suspected war criminal. France's assistance went beyond mere passive relief. France did not release to UNAMIR the information it gathered on the perpetrators, and when local officials turned over two suspected war criminals, the French gave them military protection to Zaire. France also enabled the resupplying of the genocidaires.[30] Still, anywhere from fifteen to twenty-five thousand Tutsis found sanctuary in the French zone.

The nearing RPF victory triggered a new humanitarian nightmare in early July. Waves of Hutu refugees came tumbling through narrow entry points and into neighboring Zaire, Tanzania, and Burundi. Almost two million people in all, they settled in overcrowded camps the size of large cities but without shelter, water, or medical assistance. These unhygienic and cholera-infested encampments would eventually claim around thirty thousand lives in Goma, Zaire, and thousands more elsewhere.

The refugee crisis mobilized the first sustained visual coverage of the horrors of Rwanda. The media had been relatively slow to cover the events in Rwanda. During the entire month of April, most of its attention was focused on the South African election and the military assaults on the Bosnian safe havens. Once the media turned its gaze toward Rwanda, it had to stand at a distance because the security situation precluded any immediate reporting. The result was that the genocide was a private affair, occurring behind closed doors. The cameras had to wait until the consequences of the genocide came to them. So when the refugees spilled over the border and into the camera lens, the media swarmed on the awful spectacle and gave sustained coverage to the plight of the refugees.

This coverage generated an outpouring of sympathy and assistance. It almost seemed as if the guilt that had been amassing and the compassion that had been suppressed during the genocide now exploded and were transferred to these displaced peoples. Somewhat uncharitably put, the almsgiving was slightly misplaced because it focused almost all attention on the plight of many of the same people who had committed genocide and neglected those still in Rwanda who were its real victims. In short, the popular media and various public figures confused these two events—the genocide and the refugee flight—treating them as a singular moment. "Victims" became an omnibus category that could easily obscure important differences.

The result was that while the media tended to describe everyone coming out of Rwanda as a refugee, that was hardly accurate. Many Rwandans fleeing the country were implicated in the genocide or were part of the Rwandan army and were looking for a sanctuary where they could either be protected from the victorious RPF or recoup the energy and resources to attack the new Tutsi-backed Rwandan government. "Through this confusion," observed Alain Destexhe, the secretary-general of Doctors Without Borders, "the original, singular and exemplary nature of the genocide is denied and the guilt of the perpetrators becomes diluted in the general misery."[31]

The camps were quickly controlled by the genocidaires and the remnants of the Rwandan army. This was not the first time that relief operations had fed not only the destitute but also the martial, providing shelter not only for the needy but also for combatants. A way out of this situation would have been for member states to provide a security force in the camps that could separate the refugees from the renegades. But they were no more willing to confront the genocidaires now than they had been during the genocide itself. In lieu of a protection force in the camps, the relief operations, accustomed to paying kickbacks and allowing part of their supplies to be skimmed off by those with guns and power as the price of doing business in similar situations, continued to operate as best they could. Those delivering aid were often racked with a guilt that came from knowing they were delivering relief not only to bona fide refugees but also to the perpetrators of the genocide. The paradox of international assistance stretched from the UN peacekeeping operation to the UN relief efforts.

For those who recognized that the killers lurked among the refugees, and for those who sometimes insinuated that all Hutus bore collective responsibility, watching the disease-ridden camps slowly kill off thousands of refugees was a near biblical event. Justice was being delivered. This was "divine retribution," as the perpetrators of the genocide were now being slowly killed and forced to suffer a fate of their own making.[32] One journalist wrote, "The slaughter in Rwanda may have been an expression of the bestiality of man, what is happening in Zaire today is surely the wrath of God. Epidemics of biblical proportions sweep the land. Water is poison. . . . The dead are everywhere. . . . It is as if Mother Earth did not want to accept the remains of the Hutu refugees from Rwanda."[33]

By mid-July the RPF had conquered most of Rwanda. On July 18 it declared a unilateral cease-fire and immediately announced the establishment of a broad-based government of national unity. The government was to include all the major political parties that had participated in the Arusha Accords but would understandably exclude the MRND and the CDR, the two racist, anti-Tutsi political parties. Meanwhile, UNAMIR still had fewer than five hundred troops on the ground, with offers of forty-four hundred from eight African countries waiting in the wings, most still needing equipment. With the French departure from the safe humanitarian zone increasingly imminent, the UN adjusted UNAMIR II's deployment schedule at Dallaire's insistence and sent the first troops to the zone to hasten the departure of the French forces.

On August 10 the first troops from UNAMIR II began arriving in the area, and it assumed full responsibility within two weeks. By early October over four thousand troops were in Rwanda, and by the end of October UNAMIR II was nearly at full strength. With the RPF in power and the genocide over, Rwanda was now safe for the UN. But full strength did not mean fully capable, for the troops arrived in the same bedraggled shape the first UNAMIR troops had arrived in during late fall of 1993. Upon seeing the force he had long begged for come several months late and in disrepair, a crestfallen Dallaire could only bow his head in disbelief.

6

The Hunt for
Moral Responsibility

Since 1995 Rwanda has played host to an intermittent stream of public officials who come to pay their respects and to acknowledge the failures of the international community. Roughly a year after the end of the genocide, Boutros-Ghali descended on Rwanda for a whirlwind eighteen-hour visit. If the Rwandan people or the Tutsi-led government were expecting remorse or contrition—a secretary-general coming to apologize for the UN's failure during the genocide—they were sorely disappointed. In his address to the National Assembly, Boutros-Ghali reminded the Rwandans "that I was the first to use the word genocide in the international assemblies in order to secure and mobilize and sensitize international public opinion. I did not succeed. I encountered far greater difficulties than in other situations which were not so serious but which called for assistance."[1] The message was unmistakable: he had done more on their behalf than anyone else, all that was humanly possible, so don't expect him to apologize; if you want an apology, look to others. He also advised Rwanda to get past the genocide and get serious about its contemporary problems, for an impatient international community was about to abandon Rwanda for a second time. He was trying to be their advocate, he said, but Rwanda was not making his difficult job any easier. In Kigali, a stunned National Assembly caught Boutros-Ghali at his haughty best.

In March 1998 President Bill Clinton stood on the tarmac of the Kigali airport and told the Rwandans that the international community had failed them. He and others had not quite understood what was happening in

Rwanda until it was too late. "The international community, together with nations in Africa, must bear its share of responsibility for this tragedy. We did not act quickly enough after the killing began. . . . We did not immediately call these crimes by their rightful name: genocide."[2] Five weeks later Secretary-General Kofi Annan came to "acknowledge that the world failed Rwanda at the time of evil. The international community and the United Nations could not muster the political will to confront it."[3] Several weeks later he rhetorically asked, "Why did no one intervene?" His answer: "The question should not be addressed only to the United Nations, or even to its Member States. Each of us as an individual has to take his or her share of responsibility."[4]

There are several reasons why we should be disquieted by confessions of these sorts. The very individuals who had made the momentous decisions were now relocating responsibility by "democratizing" blame. Although they were the ones who came to Rwanda, they presented themselves as emissaries of other publics that, they insinuated, also shared responsibility. This democratization of blame, in effect, reduced their own particular culpability to a meaningless fraction. The public apologies rarely detailed their shortcomings, providing merely generic references to ignorance or the lack of political will and avoiding specifics about what they did during the war. The same individuals who were ready to establish a war crimes tribunal to prosecute those who carried out the killing were unwilling to come clean regarding why they had not tried to stop the killers. No wonder many Rwandans were unmoved by the apologies offered by the principal bystanders to the genocide.

My own response to these public accounts has been by turns sympathetic and incensed. On the one hand, it has been virtually impossible for participants to get a fair hearing. The harsh glare of the genocide has made it all too easy to dismiss their claims of ignorance. Military operations that at the time seemed excessively risky now look like a small price to pay. Officials in New York have insinuated that the very same rules they had been advised to construct in order to save peacekeeping from excessive use had misled them—but they could hardly say so without sounding heartlessly bureaucratic. At these moments they have beseeched critics to see how the world looked to them at the time, and not to judge them with twenty-twenty historical hindsight. Yet I also have been dismayed by public apologies predicated on generic excuses, buck passing, and obfuscation concerning their personal involvement. This ethical history has re-created the moral universe that made ethical the UN's decision not to intervene, but in this concluding chapter I explore whether the UN bears some moral responsibility for the destruction of a country.

It does. The UN bears some moral responsibility if its actions or omissions can be causally linked to the genocide and it does not have a compelling excuse for its behavior. Like many previous inquirers, I am concerned with whether the UN's actions or omissions can be linked to the outcome; whether the UN had an obligation to act; and whether the UN has a reasonable excuse for why its actions fell short. The UN can be accused of many things in the period before April 1994. It was short-sighted. It was overly cautious. It was too rule-bound. It was, in short, so fixed on the convenient and the familiar that it refused to acknowledge dire possibilities. Its consent-based policies proved to be dysfunctional and cleared a path for the genocidaires. But because it could not have predicted genocide and reasonably fixed its energies on the revival of civil war, it cannot be held morally responsible for actions during this period.

The events of April present another matter, however. The initial shock of the crisis and return to civil war quickly yielded to recognition of the bloodbath. High-ranking UN staff and some council members either knew of, or had good reason to suspect, crimes against humanity. They had an obligation to urge UN action. They did not. At that time there was still a chance that a modest intervention might have either halted or narrowed the scope of the genocide. There are good reasons why they feel that they have been unfairly accused. There are also good reasons why the expression etched on their faces is not the look of helplessness but rather of responsibility.

Excuses

When they offer excuses, the UN staff and representatives on the Security Council attempt to explain that their conduct was, objectively speaking, wrong but that they were not responsible moral agents. They are saying, in other words, that extenuating circumstances interfered with their ability to act responsibly. Properly speaking, excuses are different from justifications. Excuses involve an attempt to identify extenuating circumstances for an action that violates moral expectations. Justifications are provided when individuals own up to an action but claim that the action was not morally reprehensible under the circumstances—that is, no social norm or moral stricture was violated. I have not found a single attempt by participants to justify their actions, but many at the UN and powerful governments frequently offer excuses that revolve around claims of ignorance or duress. They did not know and they could not have known about the situation. Or, there were forces that made it virtually impossible to act in any other way.

[margin note: Important for Ethics?]

Whether or not we find these excuses credible takes us some distance in sorting out the UN's moral responsibility.

UN and government officials offered ignorance as their dominant excuse. They had no way of predicting genocide and tremendous difficulty diagnosing it until late April. Boutros-Ghali insists that given his limited knowledge, he acted properly. During his March 1998 visit to Rwanda, President Clinton confessed, "It may seem strange to you here, especially the many of you who lost members of your family, but all over the world there were people like me sitting in offices, day after day after day, who did not fully appreciate the depth and the speed with which you were being engulfed by unimaginable terror." Others in the council and the Secretariat uniformly assert that they did not recognize the genocide until it was too late. Should we accept the excuse of ignorance? The answer depends on whether we find credible the claim that these officials could not have predicted the genocide or distinguished it from civil war until late April.

[margin mark] For several reasons I find the claim utterly believable. Few dared to imagine the apocalyptic possibility of genocide. Genocide is not simply a low-probability form of violence that ranks at the bottom of any list of violent alternatives. It resides outside the realm of human imagination. Few Rwandans openly speculated about the possibility of genocide, and presumably their intimate knowledge of the situation made their prognosticating skills superior to those of the officials in far-off New York. It seems unfair to ask people in New York to be more clairvoyant than the local population.

The warning signs that in retrospect presaged genocide were almost instinctively connected at the time to a possible return of civil war. The infamous January 11 "genocide cable" is an exemplar of the tendency in some postmortems to transform cloudy speculations about the future into nearly undeniable revelations. The "genocide cable" is, in fact, a misnomer. Nowhere in this so-called genocide cable does the word *genocide* appear. Certainly the descriptions of planned killings were horrific and alarming. But at the time UNAMIR and New York officials had good reason to connect them to a stalled political transition and to imagine that the collapse of the Arusha Accords would explode into civil war with a heavy loss of life. Everyone feared a return of civil war, and the fear proved well founded.

Throughout much of April 1994 the council and the Secretariat had a difficult time distinguishing civil war from genocide. They folded the latter into the former and treated civilian casualties as a grisly by-product of the civil war. The blurring of the two had several sources. There *was* a civil war. Although some historical accounts focus exclusively on genocide, the simple truth is that the RPF and the Rwandan government had smashed the cease-fire and were back at war. Civilian deaths were accumulating at a heinous pace, but it was reasonable to tie these deaths to civil war and not to a premeditated campaign of extermination. Also, the genocidaires did not completely unleash the dogs of genocide until after April 21, when they could be certain that there would be no international intervention. Several prominent nongovernmental organizations, including Human Rights Watch, presumably those most likely to sound the alarm, did not call the killings in Rwanda a genocide until around this time. The council was slow to recognize genocide and then disgraced itself by its refusal to call it by its proper name, but the high degree of uncertainty coupled with the assumption that all violence could be attributed to the civil war makes a plausible case for ignorance.

New York's reaction suggests that ignorance was rooted not simply in objective uncertainty or the absence of telltale indicators of genocide but also in the UN's culture. This culture provided the social optics that brought the ethnic conflict into sharp focus and placed the crimes against humanity in deep background. The UN had a particular way of understanding both the nature of conflict in ethnically divided societies and the mechanisms that would facilitate the transition from civil war to civil society. Rwanda fit comfortably into that template, in part because the template shaped how the UN came to know about Rwanda. In Rwanda two ethnic groups had been waging a civil war. The solution was political institutions and power-sharing agreements that would give each side the confidence that its interests would be protected. In the UN's view, the Arusha Accords contained all the ingredients (demilitarization, refugee repatriation, power sharing, and democratic elections) required for a successful transition process. By 1994 some peacekeeping operations had begun to include a small human rights component, but not UNAMIR, underscoring the UN's conception of conflict and the perceived centrality of political solutions to civil war.

When in January 1994 the security situation had begun to deteriorate, officials at UN headquarters insisted that UNAMIR honor the sacrosanct principles of neutrality, impartiality, and consent. Following such guidelines was both prudent and principled: prudent because this was an emaciated force and principled because it related to the very identity of peacekeeping. Almost all violence at the start of the year was associated with the transition process, and the antidote was the immediate establishment of the transitional government. There was no other way out or forward. The return of violence in early April was instinctually associated with the civil war. UN officials could see only civil war because that was what they were prompted to expect. The power of suggestion was enormous. Once the situation in

Rwanda was defined as a civil war, then the rules of peacekeeping demanded the withdrawal of peacekeepers. The UN's established categories cramped the Secretariat's understanding of and policies toward Rwanda.

This observation is consistent with the observed effects of organizational culture more generally and the UN's policies more broadly. Scholars note that human reasoning is limited not only by imperfect information and innate intellectual capacities but also by the broader culture that subsequently shapes the very optics that individuals use to categorize the world. The consequence of the UN's culture, moreover, can be seen not only in Rwanda but also in the other site of moral transgression at this time, Srebrenica in Bosnia. Responding to a commission of inquiry that found the UN's conduct wanting, Annan wrote of an "institutional ideology of impartiality even when confronted with attempted genocide."[5] That ideology caused errors of judgment that created a situation where massacres could happen under the neutral eyes of the UN. Annan, in effect, acknowledged that the UN, the very body established to help alleviate suffering, can come to categorize violence—even crimes against humanity—in such a way that makes it reasonable to be a bystander.

I am reluctant to leave ignorance at the doorstep of organizational culture, and I am reluctant for three main reasons. One, it too easily shifts responsibility. The organization is to blame, not specific individuals. Two, it too quickly accepts the claim that organizational culture transforms individuals into cultural dupes, incapable of expressing independent judgments. Three, evidence suggests that UN staff knew much more than they let on.

There are reasons to doubt Boutros-Ghali's claims that he advocated intervention from the very outset of the crisis and that any lapses on his part resulted from the sparse reports he received from DPKO. Boutros-Ghali puts forward flimsy evidence in support of the assertion that he championed intervention. As proof of his good intentions he cites his April 12 demarche to the Security Council, in which he asked it to consider withdrawing the operation if it could not be reinforced. He insists this was a subtle attempt to cajole the council into authorizing intervention, a tactic he had used previously in Bosnia.[6] But the tactic seems queer on two counts. These were completely different contexts, and a strategy that might work in one context was inappropriate for another. The West had already stated that it had strategic interests in Bosnia, had already committed troops and prestige, and had involved the UN in part because it wanted to distribute the burden. Boutros-Ghali's strategic gambit, recommending withdrawal in order to extract more resources, worked because the West had strategic interests in Bosnia and calculated that a reduced role for the UN would mean an increased role for the West. But none of these factors were present in the

Rwandan case. Furthermore, Boutros-Ghali did not provide a logistical blueprint or moral imperative for intervention as he was "challenging" the council to authorize an intervention. Without specifics regarding the whys and hows of intervention, his challenge played directly into the hands of the withdrawal camp. If he truly wanted intervention, he surely could have found more transparent signals. He could have simply said so, authoritatively and simply, and backed the statement with a moral imperative and a military plan.

What of Boutros-Ghali's claim of ignorance? He insists that he simply did not know what was happening on the ground and labored under the misconception that it was a civil war and a requited bloodbath. He depended for information on DPKO, and DPKO's ignorance became his ignorance. Yet when asked to respond to Dallaire's charge that DPKO did in fact possess the information, Boutros-Ghali hypothesized that DPKO deliberately kept him in the dark.[7] Why would DPKO withhold information? Boutros-Ghali insinuated that DPKO opposed intervention because it wanted to placate the United States. His argument devolves to this: because DPKO wanted withdrawal and knew that the secretary-general favored intervention, it decided to withhold the ammunition he needed to make the case.

There are several reasons to dispute this version of events. DPKO was more than a sycophant of the United States and quite capable of opposing intervention for its own reasons. DPKO might have opposed intervention, but it certainly exhibited enough independence from the United States to work covertly against the superpower's desire for complete withdrawal. Boutros-Ghali provides no evidence that DPKO and Washington were in cahoots, citing only a structural imbalance that he hypothesizes co-opted UN officials (including Annan, who was later rewarded for his servitude with the plum position of secretary-general).[8] More significantly, according to a highly reliable source, DPKO gave the secretary-general everything it had. If the secretary-general had cause for concern, he certainly did not express it at the time.[9]

But let us give the former secretary-general the benefit of the doubt. Let us assume that he truly did not comprehend what was taking place on the ground, because he was kept in the dark by duplicitous subordinates. Even this scenario does not exonerate him. It may seem unfair to expect the head of a large, complex organization to be aware of everything that goes on under its roof. Exculpation, however, depends not only on what he knew but also on what he could have been expected to know. On this score Boutros-Ghali's leadership leaves much to be desired. He did not cut short his tour of Europe to return and preside over the crisis. He did not educate himself in even the most rudimentary way. At the very least he could have picked up the phone and spoken personally with his force commander, to hear in his own words what he was seeing. He did have one very brief exchange with Dallaire, but that was to prepare him for the decision to withdraw, not to be briefed or to debate the military options.[10] His detachment under the circumstances is astonishing—doubly so in a situation where peacekeepers were dead and UN troops continued to be at risk, yet more so for a secretary-general who claims to be a friend of Africa and an advocate for intervention.

Under these circumstances ignorance is no excuse. *If* he was ignorant, I conclude, it was because he wanted to be. As one knowledgeable UNAMIR official emotionally asserted, "[F]rom the field and reinforced from subsequent information it is impossible that he was not aware. But he might have been uninterested in Rwanda."[11]

I also believe there is good reason to conclude that DPKO staff understood the nature of the killing. There was no denying the civil war. But there was also no denying the mounting civilian death toll, which clearly was ethnically specific. The situation reports that I have seen are somewhat vague regarding, or at least do not emphasize, the form of the violence, but Dallaire and others in UNAMIR insist that their oral reports emphatically clarified that Hutu militias were carrying out a campaign of killing against civilians, a campaign they routinely framed as ethnic cleansing. Riza, who was the assistant secretary-general for peacekeeping operations, later acknowledged that UNAMIR did call the violence ethnic killings and cleansing, but, he continued, "ethnic cleansing does not necessarily mean genocide, it means terror to drive people away."[12] This strikes me as a convenient interpretation. It cannot be sustained by even a superficial knowledge of the untold number of massacres in Rwanda, or even a knowledge of Bosnia. Any remaining doubts could have been answered with follow-up queries to the field, but there were few, which led Dallaire to believe that DPKO was well aware of the extraordinary events taking place.[13] All this information, moreover, could have been fused with the earlier situation reports that warned of ethnic cleansing. DPKO was probably not as ignorant as it later claimed to be.

Some member states are better able than others to use an excuse of ignorance. The nonpermanent members of the council probably had little awareness of the volcano that was Rwanda. The modus operandi for all members is to rely on the Secretariat for critical information and updates; this dependence is particularly acute for nonpermanent members because they are less likely to have independent sources of information. But the secretary-general kept most of the council in the dark and so arrogated to himself the authority to make important political decisions, a point a former New Zealand ambassador to the UN emphasized.[14]

A cloud of suspicion, however, hangs over the permanent members. A prevailing argument holds that the most powerful member states must have known at a fairly early stage, an argument based less on evidence than on the assumption that powerful states have immense resources and intelligence networks at their disposal. As Dallaire later commented, "A lot of the world's powers were all there with their embassies and their military attaches. And you can't tell me those bastards didn't have a lot of information. They would never pass that information on to me, ever."[15]

Belgium, though not on the council, and especially France certainly knew more than they revealed at the time. Belgium's intelligence network was extensive. Its contacts were responsible for locating the person who provided the information contained in the January 11 cable, and until its troops pulled out in mid-April, they religiously relayed information back to Brussels (keeping Brussels better informed than Dallaire). The Belgian Commission of Inquiry concluded that while Brussels was caught off guard by the ferocity of the violence, it fully understood the explosiveness of the situation.[16] France was up to its neck in Rwanda, providing not only military assistance but also training to those who committed genocide. It is unknown whether it was forewarned about the genocide, but there is little doubt that France had good reason to suspect something much more than civil war.

The United States' claim that it could not have predicted the genocide is credible. It had little interest in predicting the future of a country that was far outside its strategic interests. Perhaps one day we will learn that the United States knew more than it let on, but for the time being, interviews, cables, and circumstantial evidence corroborate the claim that it was no smarter than anyone else because it had little interest in becoming so. The events of April did not cause Rwanda to leap to the top of the foreign policy agenda in Washington because Rwanda did not magically become important. For much of this month Rwanda received scant attention at the highest levels, and it was not until the refugee crisis in July that Washington finally gave Rwanda top billing. American officials knew by the latter part of April that the killings were the product of not simply a civil war but rather a genocidal campaign.[17] Clinton's claim that he was not fully aware is implausible at best—or admits a callousness that cannot pass any reasonable test of benign ignorance. The bedrock position is clear: the United States did not care to get involved. It did not matter if the killing in Rwanda was due to a civil war or genocide. The United States was going to respond in the same anemic way—a point callously underlined in May when the genocide was well known but the United States refused to acknowledge its existence and opposed the plan to intervene. The United States cannot use the ignorance excuse.

The viability of the ignorance excuse is highly dependent on whether individuals had any reason or opportunity to learn more. Ignorance can have many sources. It was virtually impossible to predict the genocide. The situation on the ground during April was caked with uncertainty and so those in New York were more likely to see what they expected to see. Claims of ignorance, however, weaken once we ask not what these officials did know but what they might be expected to have known, what they could have known, what they probably did know. Each day in the month of April brought fresh evidence that should have led them to become smarter or encouraged them to gather more information. In either case the ignorance excuse wears out as April unfolds.

While many government officials advance ignorance as the principal reason for their failure to act, those in the Secretariat and their sympathetic critics also have hinted of compulsion or duress. Over the years I have spoken with officials from the United States and elsewhere, staff from human rights organizations, journalists, and scholars who were shocked by the Secretariat's behavior. These observers nevertheless offer an account that essentially excuses its actions because of pressures from the United States and the council.[18]

Excuses involving compulsion or duress invariably include a highly moralized account of what makes a choice just too hard and when it becomes unfair to ask a person to do otherwise.[19] In the context of bureaucratic compulsion, the issue is "rarely the extreme physical and psychological kind that philosophers and lawyers usually discuss" but the organizational context in which individuals make decisions.[20] Two broad scenarios are typically forwarded: when a superior issues an explicit order or when "no explicit order has been given but a subordinate believes that a superior expects him or her to pursue what is seen as a morally dubious course of action."[21]

Those who excuse the behavior of UN staff highlight not only immediate constraints but also their state of mind. The story combines the long-term impact of being subjected to powerful and unforgiving patrons and the immediate pressures emanating from the council. It goes as follows: Those working for the UN are highly committed to global peace and justice. The end of the Cold War allowed them to turn halted dreams into action. By mid-1993, however, these realized dreams were producing their own complications. Failures in the field were discrediting the UN and soiling its reputation. To compound matters and heighten anxieties, the United States and other powerful states were openly questioning the UN's role in world politics. And then came Somalia. Not only was it scored a failure, but the UN's unbridled ambitions were viewed as a proximate cause of the deaths of American soldiers. The United States scapegoated the UN for its own policy failures. Relations between the United States and the UN became positively poisonous, and the mood at headquarters turned despondent. Traumatized and terrorized, UN staff feared that the United States was about to eviscerate the organization. The Security Council contributed to this high anxiety. Authorizing one operation after another but not supplying the necessary resources, the council left the UN overstretched, underresourced, and overexposed. Failures were beginning to mount and so too were the criticisms. By early October 1993 many in the building began to fear that the next misstep might be their last.[22]

It was in this context that the Secretariat confronted a souring situation in Rwanda. DPKO certainly was disturbed by the growing number of reports of threats to the operation. But it was reluctant either to authorize a robust response, for fear that Kigali might become another Mogadishu, or to fully inform the council of the gravity of the situation, for fear that it might give more ammunition to council members keen to close troubled operations. By withholding information from the council and denying Dallaire's requests, the Secretariat was protecting the operation and the organization.

Then came the events of April. A spooked Secretariat opposed intervention and concealed Dallaire's reports. The most powerful member states, with the United States in the lead, opposed intervention, so no intervention was going to happen. An equally grave concern was that the council might actually authorize an intervention. If the past was a good prophet, it would dispatch a token force without the requisite means; this failure in the making would be of no help to the Rwandans and might be fatal to the UN. So a catatonic Secretariat, fearing that any move might prove disastrous, quietly closed its eyes.

We are being asked to imagine a "UN syndrome." In medical terminology a syndrome is a "collection or configuration of objective signs and subjective symptoms that together constitute the description of a recognizable pathological condition."[23] Individuals suffering syndromes are claimed to exhibit various psychological traits, including low self-esteem and psychological paralysis. Women suffering from battered wife syndrome, for instance, are particularly astute observers of cues and signals that indicate imminent violence. An established pattern of violence, typically beginning with specific rituals and erupting into life-threatening violence, can cause the abused to take preemptive action to deter the threat. Key here are an established pattern of abuse that has played havoc with the abused's state of mind and a trigger that is a legitimate cause for concern. If under such circumstances a woman kills her abuser, a plea of self-defense or diminished capacity is reasonable, and the claim of diminished responsibility is tenable.

The form of the legal argument resembles the compulsion thesis raised by defenders of the Secretariat. UN officials were abused and battered bureaucrats. They were forced to suffer a series of indignities and injustices at the hands of Great Powers that left them in a constant state of terror and panicked about their future. Living in constant anxiety, feeling at the mercy of moody, impulsive, and capricious patrons, could shatter even the healthiest egos and compromise their judgment. Then along came Rwanda. Fearing yet another blow from the council, the Secretariat relied on its survival instinct and it enfeebled the cause of intervention. The Secretariat's behavior during the Rwanda episode was lamentable but understandable; fear and abuse manufacture a case for diminished responsibility.

By writing of a "UN syndrome" and "battered bureaucrats," I am intending not to mock the compulsion argument but rather to highlight its implications for thinking about responsibility. Compulsion arguments depend not simply on the presence of constraints but rather on evidence of environmental pressures that are extraordinary or traumatic. Are we prepared to accept that such pressures affected the state of mind of UN staffers to the point that they had a diminished capacity?

Recognize that the believability of this claim depends on prior typing of these actors. American officials have suggested that their Rwanda policy was affected by pressure coming from congressional critics of the UN; they hoped that if they were tough on laggard UN operations, Congress might show greater mercy toward the global organization. We might accept this as important background for understanding the reasons behind American policies, but most would probably reject this information as credible evidence of diminished responsibility and would conclude that officials had acted out of self-interest, not virtue. Conversely, the ability of UN officials to make a credible case for abuse depends on the belief that they are usually virtuous individuals whose momentary lapse must have been caused by extraordinary pressures. More broadly, the abuse argument is parasitic on a moral division of labor where the UN is ethical but Washington is not. I certainly accept the claim that the Secretariat was more likely than the White House to be concerned about Rwandans. But I also recognize that such claims are based not only on evidence but also on stereotyping.

More consequential for the plausibility of a UN syndrome is the claim that the Secretariat had no choice but to embargo information and muzzle the case for intervention. Certainly the permanent members of the council would have opposed a proposal to intervene. As one DPKO official put it, "If we had gone to the council at the beginning to ask for reinforcements we would have been laughed out of the chamber."[24] But what grave harm would have occurred if the Secretariat had forwarded the information, raised concerns, and outlined possible responses? Rejection or censure hardly counts as compulsion. Nor does American pique. What of the fear that the council would authorize a token intervention that would proceed to save a few Rwandans but lead to another UN failure? This question turns Rwanda into a possible threat to the organization. It was either Rwanda or the UN. This is akin to a self-defense argument like the classic philosophical scenario of being forced to permit the taking of a life in order to save one's own. But the situation hardly rises to the level of self-defense.

The willingness to accept the "state of mind" of UN staff as a part of a duress excuse raises two deeply troubling issues. The first is an uncomfortable parallel with a familiar argument about the banality of evil. In *Eichmann in Jerusalem*, Hannah Arendt too noted that bureaucrats do not see themselves as being in charge or as having any real autonomy. She too hinted that the psychological effect may relieve bureaucrats of the sense of responsibility for their actions and allow them to act in an unreflexive way. She too argued that bureaucrats can come to treat the morality of the bureaucracy as superior to their private morality. She too observed that action once judged as morally wrong may become behavior that is merely difficult to bear. She too seemed ready to advance the argument that a bureaucratic mentality immediately qualifies for diminished responsibility. The banality of evil bears an uncomfortable resemblance to the banality of bureaucratic indifference. A bureaucratic mentality inspires ordinary individuals to tolerate evil. Bureaucratic virtue is now found in tolerating the existence of immoral acts. Note that we are no longer speaking of unrelenting pressures but rather of the predispositions of all bureaucracies. Organizational culture is a veritable petri dish for moral amnesia and the distortion of ethical principles.

Note also that this state-of-mind argument transforms the Secretariat from perpetrator to victim. Several investigations begin with an attempt to understand how UN officials could have behaved in a morally questionable way and conclude by extending sympathy to them. The lines separating victim from assailant are redrawn. UN officials edge closer to the Rwandans; we recognize that their fates were distinctively different, but we nevertheless now hold an image of the Secretariat in many ways as a victim. It seems hardly fair to ask victims whether they have fulfilled their moral responsibilities.

Before we dismiss the plausibility of institutional duress, I should explore one scenario that is more compelling but typically is overshadowed by the interactions between the United States–dominated Security Council and an undifferentiated Secretariat. This case builds on more traditional arguments of bureaucratic compulsion concerning the relationship between superiors and subordinates, and it recognizes evidence that Boutros-Ghali compelled DPKO to toe a particular line. Several clues point in this direction.

Boutros-Ghali had been involved in a heated turf battle with the council, jealously protecting his autonomy and sometimes failing to give the council full disclosure. He was also an early advocate of withdrawal. One council member suggested that Boutros-Ghali prohibited DPKO officials from having uncensored conversations with the council.[25] DPKO may have had distinct views and preferences, but it was not permitted to express them. Finally, DPKO worked closely with Colin Keating during mid-April to ensure that UNAMIR was not completely withdrawn. Couple heavy pressure from above with a heavy-handed push from the United States and it becomes imaginable that DPKO officials might have felt compelled to sequester information that they knew was critical to the council's deliberations. Even if this is an accurate scenario, I am not sure that it completely excuses their actions; after all, they still could have leaked the relevant information. But this scenario leaves Boutros-Ghali more exposed to moral censure.

I am sympathetic to the Secretariat's predicament, but I worry that some inquiries are too forgiving—they too easily accept an argument that rests on the presumed state of mind of UN staff. I suspect that this excuse finds favor because it taps into the belief that they are naturally disposed toward intervention for the needy whereas member states are not. I share such a belief. But I worry that some allow this belief to affect their assessment of the staff's responsibility. The state of mind argument countenances the claim that overpowering pressures led to diminished judgment and thus to diminished responsibility. Should the bar for compulsion be placed at this level? If it is, what will be the implications for the future?

Responsibility

Investigations of the genocide invariably want to know not only what happened but also who was responsible for it. Yet precisely how might the UN be responsible for the genocide? The concept of responsibility has properties like the Cheshire cat. Some inquiries draw on the view that moral responsibility is contingent on causal responsibility. The UN is responsible only if its actions or omissions can be credibly linked to the genocide itself.

Other observers suggest that moral responsibility is contingent on role responsibility. They train their attention on the UN's violations of basic expectations regarding how it should have acted. In my view, it is the absence of a reasonable excuse and the presence of both causal and role responsibility that indict the UN.

Did the UN contribute to the genocide? It is important to begin with the obvious: the individuals who imagined, planned, and executed the genocide bear ultimate blame. This point needs belaboring if only because my focus on the UN may somehow make it seem that the UN's culpability equals that of the genocidaires. Those who perpetrated the genocide bear ultimate responsibility. Yet Colonel Luc Marchal of the Belgian contingent in Rwanda is right to ask, "When people rightly point a finger at certain individuals presumed responsible for the genocide, I wonder if after all there is not another category of those responsible . . . by omission."[26] There is. The failure to prevent harm can be tantamount to causing that harm. Still, can the UN's omissions be linked to the outcome?

Ever since the genocide, countless thought experiments have replayed history, altering a single decision that leads to the disappearance of the genocide. The underlying premise of these "for want of a nail" counterfactual exercises is that by failing to undertake reasonable actions, the UN contributed to genocide. Three moments loom large. One is the insistence by UN headquarters that UNAMIR avoid provocative security operations, even if that decision meant relying on the same parties who were violating key security agreements. The result was that the genocidaires concluded that UNAMIR was a paper tiger and that their actions would go unpunished. If headquarters had allowed Dallaire to implement his plan, it is speculated, the genocidaires might have concluded that there was too high a price to be paid. Indeed, Dallaire made this argument to support his repeated requests to seize arms caches.

The Secretariat's failure to turn over critical information to Security Council and argue for intervention bolstered the case for withdrawal and is the second such moment. Had the Secretariat provided the logistical and moral backing, then intervention would have stood a much better chance of being authorized. Ambassadors Keating and Ibrahim Gambari raised this very possibility. They argued that this information would have significantly strengthened their hand, perhaps enough to win. Indeed, this information proved decisive in persuading the council to authorize intervention a few weeks later.

And, ultimately, the Security Council refused to authorize an intervention in April. During the first part of that month Dallaire had been insisting that an intervention, even a modest one that did not directly confront the combatants, might reclaim stability and protect civilians.[27] Might an intervention have succeeded? We do not know. But we do know that with the council's refusal, nothing stood between the genocidaires and the Tutsi population.

Could the UN have acted? Those who argued at the time (and since) that such an intervention was impossible or excessively risky were generally talking not about technical obstacles but rather about political constructs, "lack of political will" and the "mood" of the council. I do not deny the presence of technical constraints. The initial decision by the Security Council to authorize a threadbare force, the willingness of many member states to contribute unfit soldiers to UNAMIR, a "constipated" UN bureaucracy that sputtered and then delivered rusted equipment, and the difficulty of quickly assembling a military intervention once the killing began condemned UNAMIR to impotence when the violence erupted. These technical constraints were the products of short-sighted political decisions made by tight-fisted states. States, in effect, inverted the Weinberger doctrine—it is no longer "go in with a overwhelming force" but instead is now "provide minimal force structure and assume a best-case scenario." And while there were risks—risks compounded by UNAMIR's reputation for spinelessness and amplified by the return of war—these risks were almost always defined in terms of what threatened the UN and not the Rwandans.

This moral distribution of risk was partly generated by the UN's self-conception and definition of the situation. By claiming that it is impartial and neutral, the UN by definition has to avoid actions that appear to play favorites or can be viewed as overly aggressive. It excludes such military operations as seizing weapons caches. The return of civil war, moreover, proved that "Rwanda" was not committed to peace and thereby reduced the UN's obligations. Political and not technical considerations underwrote the failure to act.

The UN bears some causal responsibility because it refrained from actions that might have either stopped the genocide or at least reduced its scope. Of course, we cannot simply affirm that if UNAMIR had seized arms caches, if the Secretariat had transmitted information to the council, or if the council had authorized an intervention, then there would not have been a genocide. But the participants themselves attempt to explain how ignorance or duress caused them to eschew policies that might have made a difference: their own words betray how they remain haunted by the possibility that their hands are blood-stained. As several have confessed, there were "mistakes" and misguided policies, and the mistakes probably cost thousands of lives.

Yet our notions of responsibility rest not only on causation but also on the duties that actors are expected to perform. In this important respect, the focus on the UN's omissions highlights our selective vision regarding whose omissions matter. Bystanders were everywhere, yet only some states have been asked to account for their actions. Many states could have come forward, but only a few gave a hesitant and highly qualified "yes." Although they might have felt greater compassion and obligation, African states, including Nelson Mandela's newly formed government in South Africa, remained silent for much of April. Little criticism has been directed at them. The charitable interpretation is not a double standard but rather a prior conception of which actors have special responsibilities. Responsibility, in short, is assigned to actors who are expected to perform specific tasks because of the role they occupy. Only a select few, and not all, will be forever associated with the genocide.

The UN's actions are disturbing because they demonstrate indifference to crimes against humanity. It is not only that negligence proved deadly but the very fact of moral lapses that eats away at us. "While our judgements about causal responsibility, and hence our description of an individual's actions, depend partly on causal evidence," observed Marion Smiley, "they also depend on the expectations that we bring to bear on an individual and his situation."[28]

That it is the UN's indifference that rubs us raw suggests a moral division of labor: human institutions are assigned specific roles that include responsibility for different populations or communities. The division of labor typically is associated with politics and economics and is justified on grounds of efficiency. However, societies also contain and intentionally construct a moral division of labor on the "grounds that it promotes a more efficient pursuit of moral ends."[29] In this view, a moral division of labor allocates responsibilities and duties to specific roles. Not everyone is equally responsible for everyone else. Parents have greater responsibility for their own children than they do for other people's children. Police are supposed to perform specific duties that are not expected of most citizens. States have greater responsibilities for their own citizens than they do for foreigners.

The UN is responsible for the "international community" and has a duty to intervene where states fear to tread. Rising from the ashes of World War II, the UN was created to promote transnational values and protect international peace and security. The passage of the Genocide Convention in December 1948 signaled that the Holocaust informed the purposes of the world body. Immediately thereafter, member states voted for the Universal Declaration of Human Rights. To be sure, they were quite insistent that the UN should not run roughshod over their sovereign prerogatives. Still, they came to treat the UN as a concrete expression of their transcendental values.

After the Cold War the UN pursued a more far-reaching peace and security agenda, an agenda intimately connected to fundamental issues of human rights and human dignity. The UN began to argue that its role included the defense of peoples who were without the protection of a state or were assaulted by the very state that was supposed to safeguard their rights. In essence, it became less apologetic regarding its unique place in the international moral division of labor. As Secretary-General Annan reflected:

> Why was the United Nations established, if not to act as a benign policeman or doctor? Our job is to intervene: to prevent conflict where we can, to put a stop to it when it has broken out, or—when neither of those things is possible—at least to contain it and prevent it from spreading. That is what the world expects of us, even though—alas—the United Nations by no means always lives up to such expectations. It is also what the Charter requires of us, particularly in Chapter VI, which deals with the peaceful settlement of disputes, and Chapter VII, which describes the action the United Nations must take when peace comes under threat, or is actually broken.[30]

The UN's entwinement with the Holocaust, its defense of transnational values such as human rights, its standing in the international community, and its growing involvement in a more expansive conception of international peace and security—all of these factors nourish the expectation that it should take responsibility for the Rwandas of the world.

A moral division of labor that allocated differentiated responsibilities to different actors was a glaring feature of the response to the genocide. The international community purports to view genocide as the ultimate crime, and the response should equal the outrage. All states should feel compelled to act. The Genocide Convention, however, observes the time-honored vagueness regarding what actions states should perform. States agreed to do something but what that something should be was left to their discretion. Simply put, there is no categorical imperative for military action contained in the UN Charter, the Genocide Convention, or any binding resolution. Most states issued urgent calls for dramatic action, but they always imagined others doing the acting. The history of the events in Rwanda betrays the fact that states calculated it was not worth risking their own soldiers in yet another humanitarian nightmare.

Many assumed that because the Great Powers have greater responsibilities, they should organize and lead any collective effort. These powers, however, disagreed. Indeed, there seemed to be an almost inverse relationship between their power and their willingness to help. Initially the permanent members banded together to oppose intervention. In May, and with knowledge of the genocide, they became reluctant interventionists, willing to approve a rescue effort but not to assist. China feared that any intervention based on human rights might invite other states to question its treatment of its own population. Russia teamed with the United States to oppose the idea of intervention until the very end. Britain fought against the initial push for intervention in April and then shifted position in May when it had overwhelming evidence of the genocide. Still, it contributed no real resources.

France's behavior throughout the genocide was scandalous. It failed to use personal contacts to warn leaders of the genocide about the consequences of their actions. In mid-May the French government met with Rwandan officials who had been implicated in the genocide, and there were even reports that French officials helped Colonel Théoneste Bagosora, a leader of the genocide, to escape.[31] During Operation Turquoise, its intervention in late June 1994, France probably gave protection and weapons to individuals who had already been accused of genocide.[32] (If so, it might be charged with aiding and abetting a genocide.) Its own apathy can be ascribed to a perverse mix of racism and warped strategic consequentialism. President François Mitterrand reportedly confided to a colleague that "in countries like that, a genocide is not very important."[33] An obsession with an "Anglo-Saxon" conspiracy presumably was reason enough to become involved with criminal elements; faced with such a dire threat, any means are legitimate.

All eyes fell on the United States, and the Clinton administration found the attention unwarranted and unwanted. At the time of the genocide, Tony Lake, President Clinton's national security adviser, rejected the insinuation that the United States was the world's "911" and was obligated to use its tremendous might for humanitarian causes. Years of reflection have not altered his views. Recently he wrote that with

> heightened perception of military omnipotence . . . may come a sense of ex post facto omniresponsibility. Years after the devastating genocide in Rwanda, scholars and reporters maintain that simply because the United States possessed such power, we had—and reneged on—a moral obligation to stop the slaughter. Our power does indeed require that we consider carefully its use in such circumstances—and there is no doubt that the United States shares the blame for the failure by the international

community in Rwanda. But the possession of such power does not bring with it an automatic responsibility to use it.[34]

Because the United States is a superpower does not mean that it is responsible for all that takes place on the earth. *Can* does not imply *ought*. Most Americans would probably agree.

Lake provides a reasonable counterpoint to those who insist that the United States must be more noble and altruistic than other states. But under close inspection his tightly patrolled conception of American responsibility begins to fray. His formulation rests on the unstated presumption that state sovereignty limits state responsibility. Yet state sovereignty is not a fixed category. It is a changing set of practices and obligations. States are nested in a web of international institutions that place legal and normative limits on their actions and impose various obligations. The practices include how states relate to other states and their citizens. The obligations include how states can carry out their humanitarian commitments through multilateral and unilateral actions. I suspect Lake agrees with this observation. Many of his official statements said as much.

As a permanent member of the Security Council, moreover, the United States accepts a responsibility to defend threats to its national security *and* to international peace and security. The two are not identical, though sometimes the United States acts as though they are. The Cold War largely confined the working definition of international security to interstate war and Great Power stability. After the Cold War the definition expanded considerably, to include intrastate wars and humanitarian ordeals. This expansion occurred with an American blessing. Lake's point is well taken: having the muscle and being on the council does not obligate the United States to risk its troops in alien lands. But it is inappropriate for the United States to demand that the UN's responsibilities be as narrow as its own. As Keating provocatively observed, "[T]he U.S. had a curious identification with the UN. It was almost as if it was so involved with the UN that it could not contemplate the UN doing something it did not want to do itself."[35] In the original biblical story, those traveling with the Samaritan may not have provided assistance, but at least they did not get in the way.

The UN occupied center stage in the moral division of labor. The international public expected not merely action but military action, and it expected the UN to organize and take the helm. Those at the UN were painfully aware of these expectations. For that reason they sidestepped the talk of "genocide" for as long they could—to the point that the UN looked as if it was composed of weak-backed diplomats who lacked moral courage. Boutros-Ghali was the first to speak openly of the killings in Rwanda as a genocide in early May (though behind closed doors, several council members had already insisted that the council should publicly recognize the genocide). From that moment on, the UN began to act more consistently with expectations. By this point, however, heel-dragging states made it a foregone conclusion that any military operation would be too little, too late. Out of excuses, and knowing that the opportunity to make a difference had passed, from late April through July the UN struggled to keep up appearances.

For much of April, however, there was a very different relationship between the perceived duty to act and the possibility that such action might make a difference. Beginning in late April, when the genocide became increasingly undeniable, the UN's duty to aid was assumed but its ability to make a significant difference was rapidly disappearing. Before then, the UN's concentration on the civil war channeled it away from any concerted discussion regarding the difference that intervention might make for the Rwandans because of the presumption that its duties resided elsewhere.

To the extent that states exhibited any sense of duty, it was for their citizens and not for the Rwandans. France and Belgium efficiently evacuated their own nationals from Rwanda, but they showed no concern for Rwandans who were under their protection and who they knew would die immediately after their departure. And they left without resupplying UNAMIR. The United States sat quietly on the other side of the border in Burundi, ready to intervene to save its nationals but unmoved by either the massacres or the perilous state of the peacekeeping operation.

This limited mission now completed, the council turned its attention to the fate of Rwanda and UNAMIR. By this time some of the more powerful council members, most likely France and possibly the United States, either knew or had good reason to speculate that Rwanda was the site of ethnic cleansing. They did not betray such knowledge if they had it, however. In the end, the council determined that the return of civil war and the absence of qualified troops left it no option other than to help the parties come to their senses. It pulled up the only possible lifeline for hundreds of thousands.

The Secretariat looked on in relative silence, delivering perfunctory statements in favor of intervention but vigorous calls to protect the peacekeepers. The Secretariat, however, was not passing along everything it was receiving from the field. Dallaire sent information that was punching holes in the claim that Rwanda was merely a civil war, and he urged reinforcements as a show of force that might reinstate the cease-fire and protect civilians. The Department of Peacekeeping Operations thanked Dallaire for his reports and told him that it had transmitted the information to a Security Council that was unmoved. I cannot definitively conclude that the Secretariat deliberately withheld information. Still, circumstantial evidence suggests that it selectively presented information to the council, opted to avoid the language of ethnic cleansing in favor of the morally neutral language of civil war, and refrained from making the strongest case available for intervention.

At that moment the Secretariat made a choice that violated its duties of office. Its decision might very well have cost thousands of lives. Because Boutros-Ghali did not transmit information, either voluntarily or when the council specifically asked him, he violated his professional responsibilities. Under normal circumstances one might view his actions as part of the normal bureaucratic tug-of-war. But lives were at stake. His professional position gave him the authority to make the case for intervention, and he possessed the information necessary to give ethnic cleansing equal billing with the civil war. His decision to obscure this feature of the killings deprived the intervention camp of moral ammunition. Had he highlighted crimes against humanity, he would have given member states a reason to contribute troops and the council just cause for authorizing an intervention.

The Secretariat bears some moral responsibility for the genocide. If I seem more critical of the Secretariat than I am of member states or the Security Council, it is not because the former had the technical means to stop the killing—after all, member states possessed the military force. It is because the Secretariat made a choice that thoroughly violated its professional obligations and ethical duties.

In Kigali, surrounded by unimaginable acts and a brewing genocide, Dallaire vehemently argued that a demonstration of force was the best chance of reimposing a cease-fire and protecting civilians. The rupture of the peace process and the return of civil war did not dissolve the UN's obligations, he insisted. These obligations lingered. "The Rwandans wanted us there, we had several thousand Rwandans under our protection, we still had communications with both sides, and we could be a foothold for a future operation."[36] Within a few days he recognized that Hutus were engaged in ethnic cleansing. When he heard from Boutros-Ghali for the first and only time, it was as a superior telling a subordinate to prepare for the possibility of evacuating Kigali. Dallaire firmly refused to abandon his post. Innocents depended on the UN for their very lives, and they were vulnerable to the actions of the UN. Their very vulnerability suggested causal responsibility. The UN was present in Rwanda, and it had a duty. Dallaire would not turn his back, he was saying, on his moral responsibilities.

Selective Samaritanism

Ultimately, neither the Secretariat nor the council felt more than a faint duty to aid during the month of April. Two streams of indifference commingled and washed away the moral imperative. There was the sheer weight of national interests. Unable to locate Rwanda on their strategic maps of the world, most states could justify a formulaic engagement but could not envision the loss of blood. The UN's indifference, in short, is the sum of the individual indifferences of member states. The only softening of this despairing conclusion comes from a claim of "compassion fatigue." States and the UN had already given in earlier pledge drives and now were opposed to new requests.

But the UN is more than an aggregation of individual conceits. It is also the bureaucratic arm of the world's transcendental values. The relative indifference of those in the organization has been more unsettling than anything because of our expectations about their professional roles and normative commitments. Why individuals use a different moral yardstick once they are inside an organization is a matter of much empirical debate. Perhaps because one's contribution is relatively small, one cannot relate it to the outcome. Perhaps the sheer physical, psychological, and social distance between office holder and subject makes it more difficult to fully comprehend the effects of one's actions. Perhaps the absence of dissident voices leads to a normalization of complacency, which combines with a normal fear of being ostracized and ridiculed. Perhaps the bureaucratic appeal to broad rules reduces concern for the particular and makes it more difficult to see and to act in extreme and extenuating circumstances. Perhaps Western culture has become governed by rules and legalities to the point that the same rules and legalities become a substitute for private morality. Perhaps blind ambition plays a part, in the belief that one's career prospects are best served by ignoring ethical dilemmas.[37] All of these factors surfaced at various moments during the UN's involvement in Rwanda, shaping the moral terrain and the meaning and practice of duty.

The techniques of moral differentiation were many, but it is difficult to escape the totemic importance of rules. The rules were constructed to determine when peacekeeping would be an efficient instrument of international peace and security. The rules served as channels for arguments and templates for reasons. The rules were connected to the survival of the organization, an organization that is not simply an instrument but also an expression of the international community. These rules created a localized, historicized, and uneven moral landscape that made indifference possible.

Following the end of the Cold War the UN had seemingly begun to invert the maxim that *can* implies *ought;* it assumed that its obligations included helping to resolve conflict and relieve suffering and rarely asked tough questions regarding whether it had the resources to undertake the mission. Accepting the argument that the failure to prevent harm is tantamount to contributing to that very harm committed the organization to an ungodly set of obligations. Drowning in moral demands that material realities could not support, the UN began to revise its understanding of *can* and *ought.* It tightened the rules concerning when peacekeepers should be deployed and how they should conduct themselves. It created benchmarks that could be applied across a range of cases and could be used to help depoliticize and rationalize discussions. No one held the illusion that the mere articulation of these criteria magically expunged power politics, but there was considerable consensus that discussions required greater rigor.

These rules condensed the UN's responsibilities. If the UN was effective only under conditions of stability and a working cease-fire, then it was not obligated to become embroiled in humanitarian nightmares. These rules, in effect, differentiated subjects of concern from subjects of neglect, those whom the UN felt obligated to protect and those whom it did not. This rule-guided development, moreover, dug a moat around the UN. Its overdeveloped sense of responsibility was creating moral overload and proving to be self-destructive. Acting responsibly, the UN concluded, also included a duty to safeguard the organization's health. It was Rwanda's misfortune to be the site of one of the first explicit applications of these rules.

The intensity of the Security Council's debate on Rwanda involved its attempt to choose among competing responsibilities. Ten peacekeepers were dead, and the rest remained in harm's way, in the midst of a full-throttle civil war. Mounting massacres seemed to have no obvious source but grew from the ground itself. There was possible harm to the UN if it remained and failed in Rwanda. Incalculable risks—risks that had to be taken seriously and balanced against the likelihood that positive action might make an appreciable difference—were associated with any decision.

Many on the council used the rules of peacekeeping to prioritize the UN's commitments. Especially robust was a linkage between the civil war and the propriety of withdrawal. The return of civil war fed into a contractual view of responsibility that had begun to take root in the council. An emerging proposition held that the UN was obligated to help those who could help themselves, and that the failure of the parties to fulfill their responsibilities lessened the UN's obligations to them. This shifted the locus of responsibility. It also signaled that the UN's limited resources would be distributed to those who demonstrated a willingness to abide by agreements. The council and the secretary-general had been linking the closing of the operation to the Rwandans' failure to establish transitional institutions, in essence creating a quid pro quo. The United States exploited this contractarian approach in its case against intervention. It argued, in effect, that the Rwanda mandate was an implied contract between voluntary parties, in this case between the UN and the Rwandan signatories to the Arusha Accords. The Rwandan parties had broken the contract, and the mandate was null and void.

This contractual discourse was intertwined with the rules of peacekeeping that arranged the UN's obligations in such a manner that elevated the UN over Rwanda. All were aware of thousands dead and thousands more at risk. But as long as the dead were associated with a civil war, the UN's duties remained limited to trying to find a cease-fire. More caustically, we might say that as long as the number of dead was kept below a certain threshold (say a hundred thousand) and was not convincingly connected to premeditated extermination, then many officials in New York could quickly conclude that the UN's duties should remain limited. This conclusion was not precedent setting but consistent with recent practices. Only months before in neighboring Burundi, upwards of forty thousand people had been killed. There was no public outcry, and the UN had politely refused to intervene on the grounds that its resources were limited and that Burundi did not fulfill part of its job description. Rwanda also was beyond the call of duty given the civil war and the threat to peacekeepers. The rules of peacekeeping functioned as intended, limiting the conditions for a duty to aid and creating an ethic of indifference.

The UN's decision was not merely pragmatic. It was also principled. The rules were a source of guidance. The rules were baptized in both pragmatic and principled waters, bathed in experiences that demonstrated when peacekeeping was prudent and in expectations that reshaped how the UN could better help the international community while limiting its own exposure. Virtue could be found in learning to tolerate the presence of evil and acknowledge one's own limitations. Turning away from the needy was a pragmatism that could become connected to the transcendental. High-ranking officials and diplomats in New York could cushion themselves against any discomfort that came from the unwillingness to act with the knowledge that their actions were born from a commitment to the UN.

Is it possible to build moral institutions? And where would we begin? This has been a prominent theme of many inquiries into the UN's response to the Rwandan genocide. Social autopsies of man-made disasters are replete with remedies to minimize the probability of a recurrence. Inquiries into the UN's actions have tended to connect their diagnosis of the cause of the UN's failure with specific recommendations. Those who find that the UN as an organization was at fault invariably propose institutional reforms. Those who single out errant or unethical decision makers have operated on the implicit premise that the exposure of personal failings might alter future behavior. I fear that each is a false sanctuary.

An impressive number of workshops, reports, and statements from an equally striking array of international organizations, states, nongovernmental organizations, think tanks, research institutions, scholars, and politicians have recommended how to fix the system. Only the most optimistic could see these tremendous efforts as anything more than a ritualistic attempt to find some uplifting message as a substitute for concrete action. Many politicians who showed no courage during the genocide now started preaching the need to honor the dead by creating moral institutions. In his highly abbreviated visit to Kigali, President Clinton echoed these themes but did not specify what he was prepared to contribute (beyond warm thoughts). His subsequent actions suggested not much. He and many other politicians have spun powerful visions of muscular humanitarian organizations but have delivered, instead, emaciated institutions as placeholders for a half-baked humanitarianism.

Why receive such proposals with anything other than cynicism? The UN sponsored a "lessons learned" conference. It delivered sanitized findings that stated the obvious and were crafted to make them least offensive to the very parties that deserved to be offended. Many proposed remedies, moreover, were familiar: they had already been aired in response to previous failures. The more involved and extensive the proposed reform was, the less likely it was to be implemented. States generally preferred feeble institutions to the real thing, for the simple reason that they prefer to stand aside than to get involved. And the UN's attempt to make good on its past failings through the establishment of a war crimes tribunal quickly degenerated into a corrupt and ineffectual exercise that provided a distasteful reminder of the UN's prior failings. When one of its own investigators was charged with genocide, it was tempting to interpret the news not as tragedy but as farce.[38]

Underlying all the various proposals, moreover, was an unspoken faith that the machines of humanitarianism could be improved if only they were more muscular and much less politicized. In essence, they were registering in perfect pitch the bureaucratic ethos. It was hard to argue with the claims that bigger was better and that the humanitarian response should be impartial. But it was also hard to get enthusiastic about proposals that found salvation in technical remedies but overlooked the individuals who staffed these bureaucracies.

The inquiries that focused not on institutions but on individuals were frustrated by a simple fact: the individuals they investigated had little incentive to tell the truth and every reason to democratize blame. Their reluctance to speak had many origins. They had little to gain by coming clean. This was true of government officials and UN staff, who also must have feared additional negative publicity for themselves and their organization. It also is possible that those associated with indifference could not fully accept what they had done and who they had become. Knowledge of the genocide had rotated the moral kaleidoscope, upending whatever faith many might have had in their original decisions. Rwanda, in fact, might not be an isolated mistake on an otherwise spotless record. It conceivably exposed something much more sorrowful. "Perhaps this is why an institution is unlikely to feel or admit to shame; it may be unable to countenance the possibility that at root it is not what it purports, even to itself, to be."[39]

Whatever their reasons, the refusal of participants to speak in the first person deprived the international community of the chance to hold them accountable for their actions and to ensure that such actions would not be repeated. To be responsible is to be accountable. In refusing to make themselves accountable, therefore, the participants violated an elementary aspect of responsibility.

Their refusal to make themselves available had an additional implication. There is a taut connection between morality and publicity, and the ability of public officials to escape such a confessional moment, therefore, allowed them to escape one of the public's ways to keep them honest. As H. L. Mencken observed, conscience is the inner voice that warns us that someone might be looking.

Meanwhile, officials associated with the UN's decision proceeded with their careers. Many experienced a momentary discomfort when they were asked to explain their decisions, but they nearly always sidestepped these questions, refused to go into details, or cut short the interview. There was a nearly inverse relationship between the extent to which UN staff fulfilled their responsibilities and their subsequent professional fortunes. Boutros-Ghali was denied a second term as secretary-general, but not because of his behavior during the genocide. The French handed him a golden parachute as secretary-general of the Francophone, which only increased the suspicion that he had forged an unholy alliance with the French during the month of April. Virtually the entire staff of DPKO rose with Annan to the very top of the UN bureaucracy to occupy the thirty-eighth floor.

Dallaire became a figure worthy of Greek tragedy. He did more than anyone to save as many lives as he could. He remains haunted by what he experienced. The images and smells of the genocide remain powerful and real. He continues to second-guess his decisions, wondering whether he might have acted differently and so altered the outcome. These demons led to his emotional breakdown. Diagnosed with post-traumatic stress disorder, he became one of Rwanda's casualties. In April 2000, no longer able to perform his duties after a long and illustrious career, he resigned his high-ranking commission in the Canadian military.

Many who were responsible for the UN's actions eventually broke their vows of silence, though not because of a crisis of conscience. Instead, they were no longer able to refuse invitations from their national legislatures and from international commissions of inquiry. There was little or no chance that they would be removed from office or find themselves subject to criminal investigations. Instead, the very act of exposure promised to instill nobler action in them and their predecessors. Some have suggested, in fact, that Secretary-General Annan has worked doubly hard to honor his office in his own attempt to make amends for his role in the genocide when he was the head of DPKO. Indeed, his strong stand on humanitarian intervention and his insistence that the council be nondiscriminatory when it determines how to respond to suffering sometimes are attributed to his desire to honor the dead of Rwanda.

The desire to build moral institutions must include an examination of those who staff them. Those who accept responsibility must be held accountable, and at a basic level this means not only to give a public account but also to be removed if their conduct violates expectations. But this personalization of politics may seem to imply that changing the people will change the outcome. If only it were so simple. The UN's involvement in Rwanda is dreadfully disturbing precisely because, in the main, these were highly ethical and decent individuals who believed that they were doing the right thing. Personalization, in effect, may conceal how individuals can become creatures of their institutions.

Rwanda bequeaths no certainties about the shape of the future. Indeed, the historical forces that made possible the international community's response to Rwanda continue almost as if Rwanda never existed. There continues a desire to alleviate suffering. But the administering of comfort and protection continues to be molded by competing interests and responsibilities that can easily impede any humanitarian impulse. States are largely responsible for this stunted samaritanism. And the most powerful states bear most responsibility because they have the capacity to do more and they sit on authoritative councils that profoundly shape the scope of humanitarianism. They are, as well, largely responsible for creating the hollowed-out moral institutions that are supposed to fulfill the community's noblest expressions and obligations.

Humanitarianism, too, can develop its own profanities. We live in an age where our moral expressions are almost always institutionalized and bureaucratized. Proliferating across the landscape are new international and nongovernmental organizations whose very raison d'être is to assuage suffering wherever and however they can. This development should be celebrated. Yet the very institutions that represent progress, liberation, and caring contain the seeds of disappointment. This profanity has many roots. Humanitarian institutions can be run by decent and well-meaning individuals who become timid and fearful as a result both of the soul-breaking demands and of the knowledge that powerful benefactors want only a convenient facade of humanitarianism. The compact between humanitarianism and politics, the mixing of ethics and power, can deliver a pragmatism that bears little resemblance to original intent. The very institutions that we develop to realize our highest humanitarian ends can generate ethical principles that are disconnected from those in whose name they act. The ethical practices of humanitarianism are not singular. They are transfigured as they explore new contexts and environments.

The hope is that the institutionalization of ethics does not lead individuals to substitute bureaucratically laced moralities for private moralities. The wish is that there endures and remains reachable some version of the Nuremberg principle, the belief that individuals are accountable for their actions even if those actions are consistent with the letter of their official responsibilities, if those actions violate a placeless morality.

This possibility reminds me of Dallaire's account of why he refused to leave Rwanda. As his description became less institutional and more personal, it began to bear a strong resemblance to a passage by Max Weber. But not the Weber who wrote of calcified bureaucrats who allow rules to guide their actions and define their ethics. Instead, it was the Weber who wrote of those rare individuals who demonstrate a "calling for politics."

It is immensely moving when a *mature* man—no matter whether old or young in years—is aware of a responsibility for the consequences of his conduct and really feels such responsibility with heart and soul. He then acts by following an ethic of responsibility and somewhere reaches a point where he says: "Here I stand; I can do no other." That is something genuinely human and moving.[40]

Brief Chronology of Rwandan Conflict

1885–1973

1885   Berlin Conference makes Ruanda-Urundi a German colony.

1916   Belgian troops take control of Rwanda.

1923   Rwanda becomes a League of Nations mandate under Belgian control.

1933   Belgian administration conducts census and distributes identity cards.

1945   Rwanda becomes a UN trust territory under Belgian control.

1957   Hutu Manifesto is published.

1959   Thousands of Tutsis flee amid violence.

1960   First municipal elections return rule to overwhelming Hutu majority.

1961   Monarchy is formally abolished; proclamation of republic is issued. There is more anti-Tutsi violence and refugee flight.

1962   Rwanda gains independence.
            Armed attacks by Tutsi refugees are staged from Burundi. Anti-Tutsi violence and flight continues.

1963   There is massive anti-Tutsi violence, and a mass exodus of Tutsis to neighboring countries.

1972	Hutus are massacred in Burundi. There is an anti-Tutsi purge in Rwanda.
1973	Habyarimana becomes president in a coup.

1990

July	Habyarimana concedes the principle of multiparty democracy.
October	RPF invades Rwanda. There is immediate international intervention. A cease-fire agreement is signed at the end of the month and is to be monitored by the Organization of African Unity.

1991

March	After repeated violations, a more comprehensive cease-fire agreement is signed by Rwandan government and RPF.

1992

July	New cease-fire agreement is signed.

1993

February 8	After months of violence, RPF invades Rwanda. The French intervene.
February 21	RPF declares a cease-fire.
February 22	Uganda and Rwanda request UN observation of cease-fire agreement.
March 4–19	Secretary-general sends goodwill mission to Rwanda to examine all aspects of the peace process.
March 7	RPF and Rwandan government renew cease-fire and agree to peace talks, which begin on March 16. Negotiations continue through June.
March 12	Security Council adopts Resolution 812, calling on parties to respect cease-fire and to examine possible military observer mission. Technical mission for a possible military observer post visits from April 2 to 6.
April 8	Secretary-general sends three advisers to Arusha, Tanzania, to assist the negotiations.
April 8–17	Special rapporteur from UN Human Rights Commission visits Rwanda.

May 20	Secretary-general formally recommends the establishment of UNOMUR.

May 20 Secretary-general formally recommends the establishment of UNOMUR.

June 9 RPF and Rwandan government sign agreement on refugee repatriation.

June 14 RPF and Rwandan government send a joint request to Security Council for an international force to oversee anticipated peace agreement.

June 22 Security Council adopts Resolution 846 establishing UNOMUR.

August 4 Arusha peace agreement is signed, envisioning a transitional government within 37 days and an executed peace in 22 months.

August 11 Special rapporteur delivers his findings on human rights and suggests that there is evidence of a genocide.

August 18 UNOMUR advance team arrives.

August 19–31 UN reconnaissance mission visits Rwanda to assess possible UN peacekeeping force to oversee Arusha Accords.

September 10 Parties miss date to establish broad-based transitional government (BBTG).

September 15 Joint RPF-Rwandan delegation visits UN and urges immediate establishment of peacekeeping force.

September 24 Secretary-general proposes a peacekeeping operation to Security Council.

September 30 UNOMUR becomes fully operational.

October 5 Security Council adopts Resolution 872 authorizing UNAMIR.

October 21 Coup in Burundi leaves tens of thousands dead, and hundreds of thousands of refugees flee to Rwanda.

October 22 Force Commander Dallaire arrives in Kigali.

November 23 Special Representative of the Secretary-General Jacques Booh-Booh arrives in Kigali.

December 10 Parties agree to establish BBTG by December 31 (supposed to have been established in mid-September).

December 20 UNOMUR is extended for another 6 months.

December 24 Kigali Weapons-Secure Area agreement signed.

December 31 Parties fail to establish BBTG.

1994

January 1 Rwanda becomes a nonpermanent member of Security Council.

January 5 The current president of Rwanda, Juvénal Habyarimana, is sworn in, satisfying one step in transitional process. Still no transitional government in sight.

January 6   Security Council adopts Resolution 893, which reaffirms Resolution 872.

January 11   DPKO receives cable from Dallaire outlining plan to kill peacekeepers and Tutsis, and denies his plan to seize weapons caches.

February 3   DPKO authorizes seizure of weapons caches if UNAMIR forces are accompanied by Rwandan authorities.

February 7   Special representative to secretary-general holds series of meetings, which lead the parties to accept a new deadline of February 14 for BBTG.

February 14   Parties miss deadline for establishing BBTG.

February 17   Security Council insists that Rwanda immediately establish transitional government.

February 18   Parties announce new target date of February 22 for establishing BBTG.

February 21   Wave of violence occurs in Rwanda.

February 22   Amid violence and assassinations, Rwanda misses another deadline for transitional government.

March 1   Prime minister–designate announces proposed composition of transitional government.

March 22   UNAMIR is now at full strength.

March 30   Secretary-general delivers report to Security Council and recommends renewal of UNAMIR mandate.

April 5   Security Council adopts Resolution 909, conditionally renewing UNAMIR until July 29, 1994.

April 6   President Habyarimana's plane is downed on return from Arusha, Tanzania.

April 7   Ten Belgian peacekeepers are killed.

April 8   Civil war starts.

April 8–19   Dallaire continually urges DPKO to recommend intervention with expanded force that is capable of protecting civilians.

April 9   "Interim" government forms and departs Kigali 3 days later.

April 12   Belgium formally announces that it will leave Rwanda.

April 13   Last intervention proposal is withdrawn from Security Council.

April 20   Secretary-general presents report to Security Council outlining three options and recommending a slimmed-down mandate.

April 21   Security Council adopts Resolution 912 authorizing the reduction of UNAMIR.

April 27   Keating proposes new resolution authorizing intervention and calling Rwanda killings a genocide. Security Council continues to debate future options.

April 29   Boutros-Ghali urges the council to consider intervention but fails to refer to ethnic cleansing or genocide.

May 6   Security Council asks secretary-general to prepare contingency plans.

May 13   Secretary-general recommends expansion of UNAMIR to 5,500 to assist humanitarian intervention.

May 17   Because of objections from the United States, Security Council adopts Resolution 918, which authorizes the creation of UNAMIR II contingent on satisfaction of some conditions.

May 21   RPF, accumulating various military victories, finally takes Kigali airport.

May 31   Secretary-general calls for immediate expansion of UNAMIR II.

June 8   Security Council adopts Resolution 925 extending UNAMIR until December 9, and authorizes the deployment of another battalion.

June 19   Secretary-general recommends that Security Council accept France's offer to lead a multilateral operation.

June 22   Security Council adopts Resolution 929, Operation Turquoise.

Late June   With Rwandan military rapidly disintegrating, RPF steps up offensive and takes control of territory between Kigali and Zaire.

July 1   Security Council authorizes Resolution 935 calling on the secretary-general to establish a commission of experts to examine the possibility of genocide.

July 4   RPF takes full control of Kigali.

Mid-July   In a span of 2 weeks, nearly 2 million Rwandans flee Rwanda.

July 18   In nearly complete control of Rwanda, RPF declares unilateral cease-fire.

Selected Chronology of United Nations' Security Agenda

Events pertaining to Rwanda are enclosed in brackets in order to indicate their peripheral place on the UN's security agenda.

1988

August   UN Iran-Iraq Military Observer Group is established.

1989

January   UN Angola Verification Mission is authorized.
April   UN Transition Assistance Group (Namibia) is established.
November   UN Observer Group in Central America is established.

1990

August   Iraq invades Kuwait.
              Security Council authorizes enforcement action against Iraq.
November   Security Council authorizes "all necessary means" against
              Iraq.

1991

January	U.S.-led forces begin bombing Iraq.
April	Security Council passes Resolution 688 deeming Iraq's repression of Kurdish and Shi'ite population a threat to international peace and security.
	UN Iraq-Kuwait Observation Mission is authorized.
May	UN Operation in El Salvador is established.
June	UN Angola Verification Mission is established.
July	UN Observer Mission in El Salvador is set up.
September	UN Mission in Western Sahara is authorized.
October	UN Advance Mission in Cambodia is established.
December	Boutros-Ghali is sworn in as sixth secretary-general.

1992

March	UN Protection Force (Yugoslavia) is established.
	UN Transitional Authority in Cambodia is established.
April	UN Operation in Somalia is established.
June	*An Agenda for Peace* is published.
December	UN Operation in Mozambique is established.
	United States sends military forces to Somalia under UNITAF.

1993

March	United States hands over Somalia operation to UN.
	{Security Council adopts Resolution 812, calling for parties in Rwanda to respect cease-fire.}
April	Cambodian elections are held.
	First safe haven is established in Yugoslavia; others are added over next 2 months.
May	UN Operation in Somalia II is authorized.
	Volker-Ogata report on the desperate financial straits of the UN is released.
June	{Security Council adopts Resolution 846 establishing UNOMUR.}
	Twenty-four Pakistanis are killed in Mogadishu.
August	UN Observer Mission in Georgia is established.
September	UN Observer Mission in Liberia is established.

UN Observer Mission in Haiti is established.

Clinton delivers address to UN General Assembly and tells the UN to say "no to peacekeeping."

October   Eighteen U.S. Rangers are killed in Somalia.

{Security Council adopts resolution 872 authorizing UNAMIR.}

U.S.S. *Harlan County* is prevented from docking in Haiti.

Security Council reinstates oil and arms embargo on Haiti.

UNOSOM II mandate is extended for 3 months.

November   Security Council issues statement expressing concern regarding deterioration of security situation in Bosnia.

Security Council establishes inquiry into armed attacks against UNOSOM personnel.

1994

January   Security Council condemns continued shelling of Sarajevo.

UN and NATO have further discussions on possible air strikes in Bosnia.

Secretary-general issues paper on the future of UNOSOM.

Secretary-general issues paper on modalities for possible air strikes.

{Security Council adopts Resolution 893, which reaffirms Resolution 872.}

{DPKO receives fax from Dallaire outlining plan to kill peacekeepers and Tutsis, and denies its intent to seize weapons caches.}

February   Fifty-eight civilians are killed in mortar attack on Sarajevo. Intense discussions occur at UN.

Security Council approves extension of UNOSOM.

March   Security Council issues another resolution on Bosnian conflict.

Secretary-general issues report on Angolan operation.

Secretary-general issues report on UNPROFOR mandate.

Bosnian Serbs attack safe haven of Goražde, beginning a month-long crisis.

United States' withdrawal of troops from Somalia is complete.

April   UN sponsors elections in South Africa.

North Atlantic Council authorizes air strikes around Goražde.

{Security Council adopts Resolution 909, conditionally renewing UNAMIR until July 29, 1994.}

{President Habyarimana's plane is downed on return from Arusha.}

{Security Council adopts Resolution 912, authorizing the reduction of UNAMIR.}

May   {Secretary-general recommends expansion of UNAMIR to 5,500 to assist humanitarian intervention.}

{Security Council adopts Resolution 918, authorizing creation of UNAMIR II.}

Acknowledgments

I began incurring debts long before I knew I was going to write this book. I owe much to the Council on Foreign Relations. Its International Affairs Fellowship gave me the opportunity to spend a year at the U.S. Mission to the UN. The serpentine-like evolution in my thinking occurred in fits and starts and through articles, presentations, and conversations. A few months after leaving the mission, I gave my first formal talk on Rwanda, arguing that because the UN could not alleviate all the suffering in the world, including the genocide in Rwanda, it was essential to develop explicit rules regarding the conditions under which it could assist. It was soon thereafter that I began to go beyond surface appearances. My first attempt to understand the UN's decision not to intervene was published in *Cultural Anthropology* ("The Politics of Indifference at the United Nations: The Security Council, Peacekeeping, and Genocide in Rwanda," 12, 1 (1997), pp. 551–78). I am grateful to Michael Herzfeld, Hugh Gustafson, and Dan Segal for encouraging a political scientist to trespass into the world of anthropology. I never quite returned.

This book began to take shape as I was working on a different project. Several years ago Martha Finnemore and I began having conversations about the need of international relations theory to think more broadly about what makes international organizations tick and the various kinds of effects they have on the world. These conversations turned serious and dangerous, developing into a book project on international organizations. It was in this context that I started to dig deeper into various aspects of the

Secretariat's decision-making process on Rwanda. It became fairly obvious fairly early, however, that my concerns were diverging significantly from our framework and were turning into something much larger than either she or I expected or wanted. We agreed that it would probably be better for all concerned if I got this book out of my system. Thanks, Marty, for your good judgment, critical readings, and friendship. The MacArthur Foundation, the Smith Richardson Foundation, and the U.S. Institute of Peace funded the collaborative project, and as it turns out, this book as well. I am very grateful to these accidental patrons.

I could not have written this book without the willingness of many of the participants to share with me their views and recollections. I depended on their insights for two, related reasons—the first obvious, the second less so. We are closer to having a reasonable documentary record of the decision-making process, but there remain critical holes that can be filled only by those who were situated in different parts of the UN. I wish I could write that I interviewed all of the key participants, but for many, particularly those who were in DPKO and are now in the Executive Office of the Secretary-General, Rwanda continues to be a subject they would rather not discuss. Still, many people were quite generous with their time, and they provided additional pieces of missing information, reflected critically on their views at the time of the genocide, and convincingly challenged some of the conventional readings on the subject.

There is a related but slightly more personal reason why I needed to ascertain the participants' views: I needed to minimize any possible hubris that the version of events as I learned them at the U.S. Mission represented the archimedean position. As a scholar I am wary of claims of "objectivity" and prefer Max Weber's insight that the best we can do is acknowledge and try to correct for the ever-present potential of our own subjectivity and experiences to inflect how we approach our objects of inquiry. I want to be very clear here, though. Although I temporarily served at the U.S. Mission, I do not believe that my view was ever U.S.-centric or that my written observations can be viewed in any way as intending to exculpate the United States. Instead, my concern was to recognize fully that my post at the U.S. Mission allowed me to see some features of the landscape quite clearly while obscuring others, and to correct for the partiality by gaining the insights of other policymakers located in different parts of the UN.

I was doubly fortunate. I was able to interview individuals who had been in the field, at headquarters, and in the council (and, as expected, discovered just how limited my view was). More significant, however, was that I received detailed advice on the manuscript from three "insiders" located in three different parts of the UN: the Security Council, the field, and the Secretariat. At the time Colin Keating was New Zealand's permanent representative to the UN, on the Security Council, and in the month of April the president of the Security Council. After sitting for a lengthy interview, he generously agreed to read the historical narrative. Brent Beardsley was General Dallaire's executive assistant and was by his side from the initial trip to New York in the summer of 1993 through late spring of 1994. I owe him much. We spent hours on the phone, at first for a formal interview and then for his line-by-line commentary on the manuscript. I also received wide-ranging comments from someone who was intimately involved in these events in the Secretariat. I am indebted to that person and respect the request for anonymity. I cannot for a moment claim to have constructed *the* view from New York, but my hope is that having incorporated many partial views I will have created something that is recognizable to each of the participants even as it strives to be greater than the sum of its parts.

Over the years I have exchanged views with numerous scholars and journalists who have also been pursuing the story of the Rwandan genocide. I think it is fair to say that most feel themselves to be part of a decentralized group project, individually collecting information and then freely sharing their findings and interpretations with each other. Among the many with whom I have exchanged views on the particulars of Rwanda, I want to thank Steve Bradshaw, Sian Cansfield, Alison Des Forges, Michael Hourigan, Daniel Krosalak, Alan Kuperman, Phil Lancaster, Linda Melvern, Carol Off, Mike Robinson, Michael Sheehan, Janice Stein, Astri Suhrke, and Nicholas Wheeler. Special thanks goes to Samantha Power, who provided detailed comments on the manuscript. I cannot express fully my appreciation to Howard Adelman. I met Howard when he was beginning the research for what would become one of the best of the inquiries on Rwanda. Over the years I have learned much from his scholarship on the subject and benefitted greatly from his views. When I was in the midst of the research, he invited me into his house and gave me free rein of his very impressive collection on the subject. And then he delivered twenty-two pages of comments on the manuscript. Although I know that we continue to disagree on some key matters, his commentary helped to sharpen my argument and to save me from various errors.

Many others contributed to this manuscript through their feedback on earlier articles and in the context of various presentations. The list is too long, however, to recite in its entirety. That said, a few individuals deserve special mention. Marion Smiley tutored me on critical issues in moral philosophy and steered me in profitable directions (and corrected the mistakes of the untrained). Don Downs and Marty Finnemore read parts of the manuscript and delivered, as expected, cogent advice. I gave the entire manuscript to Craig Murphy, Crawford Young, and Michael Doyle, expecting that they would have much to say. I was right, and the manuscript is the better for their efforts.

Roger Haydon deserves much more than his own line. I cannot imagine a better editor or intellectual collaborator. He has been involved in every step of the process, from its initial conception to its publication, displaying the admirable ability to play several roles simultaneously. He has been a terrific editor, proving quite capable of imposing unreasonable deadlines. He also provided expert commentary on the substance, gave shape to the structure and nuances of the argument, and tightened my wooden prose. I owe him much. I am grateful for his confidence in the project, his guidance of the manuscript, and his humor. Thanks also to Louise E. Robbins, who shepherded the manuscript through the final stage, and to Mary Babcock, who carefully copyedited the manuscript and improved it in many ways.

I dedicate this book to my daughters, Maya and Hannah. They are six and four, born after the Rwandan genocide and, blessedly, still too young to know that such events can exist. I was reminded of their blissful ignorance when they would occasionally ask me what I was doing in front of the computer. I would explain that I was writing a book, and they would invariably want to know what the book was about. At some future point they might recall that I lied. It is only a matter of time before they enter a world that includes genocide. For now, however, they possess the magical ability to transport me into a moral universe where such acts are unimaginable. I suspect that they will always have this miraculous effect on me.

Notes

Introduction

1. Primo Levi, "Beyond Judgment," *New York Review of Books*, December 17, 1987, p. 14, cited in Stanley Cohen, *States of Denial: Knowing about Atrocities and Suffering* (Malden, Mass.: Polity, 2001), p. 141.

2. See, for instance, Howard Adelman and Astri Suhrke, with Bruce Jones, *The International Response to Conflict and Genocide: Lessons from the Rwanda Experience* (Copenhagen: Joint Evaluation of Emergency Assistance to Rwanda, 1996).

3. United Nations, *Report of the Independent Inquiry into the Actions of the United Nations during the 1994 Genocide in Rwanda*, December 15, 1999, New York.

4. Boutros Boutros-Ghali, press conference, New York, May 25, 1994, SG/SM/5292.

5. Boutros Boutros-Ghali, *Unvanquished: A U.S.–U.N. Saga* (New York: Random House, 1999), p. 129.

6. For their statements, see Carol Off, *The Lion, the Fox, and the Eagle: A Story of Generals and Justice in Rwanda and Yugoslavia* (Toronto: Random House Canada, 2001), chap. 5.

7. The literature on the UN in Rwanda is large and growing every year. This literature can be organized according to whether it is interested primarily in explaining the genocide itself or in the involvement of the international community. Some contributions aspire to do both. For the contributions that focus largely on the dynamics that led to the genocide, see Mahmood Mamdani, *When Victims Become Killers: Colonialism, Nativism, and the Genocide in Rwanda* (Princeton, N.J.: Princeton University Press, 2001); Human Rights Watch, *Leave None to Tell the Story: Genocide in Rwanda* (New York: Human Rights Watch, 1999); Chris Taylor, *Sacrifice as Terror: The Rwandan Genocide of 1994* (New York: Berg, 1999); Gérard Prunier, *The Rwanda Crisis: History of a Genocide*, 2d ed. (New York: Columbia University Press, 1999); Rakiya Omaar and Alex de Waal, *Rwanda: Death, Despair, and Defiance* (London: African Rights, 1995); Alain Destexhe, *Rwanda and Genocide in the Twentieth Century* (New York: New York University Press, 1995); and Philip Gourevitch, *We Wish to Inform You That Tomorrow*

We Will Be Killed with Our Families (New York: Farrar, Straus, and Giroux, 1998). For the literature on the international community and the genocide, see Samantha Power, *A Problem from Hell: America and the Age of Genocide* (New York: Basic Books, forthcoming), and "Bystanders to Genocide," *Atlantic*, September 2, 2001, pp. 84–108; Off, *The Lion, the Fox, and the Eagle;* Arthur Jay Klinghoffer, *The International Dimension of Genocide in Rwanda* (New York: New York University Press, 1998); Bruce Jones, "Intervention without Borders: Humanitarian Intervention in Rwanda, 1990–94," *Millennium* 24, 2 (1995), pp. 225–49; Alan Kuperman, *The Limits of Humanitarian Intervention* (Washington, D.C.: Brookings, 2001); Boutros Boutros-Ghali, *The United Nations and Rwanda, 1993–1996* (New York: UN Press, 1996); Adelman et al., *International Response to Conflict and Genocide;* Philip Gourevitch, "Annals of Diplomacy: The Genocide Fax," *New Yorker*, May 11, 1998, pp. 42–46; David Rieff, "The Big Risk," *New York Review of Books*, October 31, 1996; Holly Burkhalter, "The Question of Genocide: The Clinton Administration and Rwanda," *World Policy Journal* 11, 4 (1994–95), pp. 44–55; United Nations, Department of Peacekeeping Operations, *Comprehensive Report on Lessons Learned from United Nations Assistance Mission for Rwanda (UNAMIR)*, 1996; United Nations, *Final Report of the International Commission of Inquiry (Rwanda)*, December 15, 1999; Belgium Senate, *Parliamentary Commission of Inquiry concerning Rwanda*, December 1997; Howard Adelman and Astri Suhrke, eds., *The Path of a Genocide: The Rwanda Crisis from Uganda to Zaire* (New Brunswick, N.J.: Transaction, 1999); Organization of African Unity, *Rwanda: The Preventable Genocide*, Report of the International Panel of Eminent Personalities to Investigate the 1994 Genocide in Rwanda and the Surrounding Events, Addis Ababa, Ethiopia, July 2000; Henry Kwami Anyidoho, *Guns over Kigali* (Accra, Ghana: Woeli Publishing Services, 1997).

8. Stuart Hampshire, *Morality and Conflict* (Cambridge, Mass.: Harvard University Press, 1983), p. 151.

9. On this latter point, see Alfred Schutz, *On the Phenomenology of Social Relations* (Chicago: University of Chicago Press, 1970).

10. This claim emanates from Weber's concept of theodicy. See his "Theodicy, Salvation, and Rebirth," in Max Weber, *Sociology of Religion*, trans. Ephraim Fischoff (Boston: Beacon, 1962), pp. 138–50. For the secularization of the concept, see Michael Herzfeld, *The Social Production of Indifference* (Chicago: University of Chicago Press, 1993); and Bryan Turner, *For Weber: Essays on the Sociology of Fate* (Boston: Routledge and Kegan Paul, 1981), chap. 5. In his famous essay "Politics as a Vocation," Weber extended the concept of theodicy from the religious to the secular realm in the context of his discussion of the ethics of responsibility. In H. H. Gerth and C. Wright Mills, *From Max Weber: Essays in Sociology* (New York: Oxford University Press, 1978), chap. 4.

11. Hannah Arendt, *Eichmann in Jerusalem: A Report on the Banality of Evil* (New York: Penguin, 1965). For a similar discussion of how the bureaucracy transfigures private morality, see Zygmunt Bauman, *Modernity and the Holocaust* (Ithaca, N.Y.: Cornell University Press, 1989), chaps. 6 and 7.

12. This summary comes from Larry May, *The Socially Responsible Self* (Chicago: University of Chicago Press, 1996), pp. 66–70.

13. David Rieff, "The Institution That Saw No Evil," *New Republic*, February 12, 1996, p. 20.

14. This is particularly true of the Organization of African Unity, *Rwanda: The Preventable Genocide*. However, even more sophisticated analyses can be premature in their conclusions. See William Schutz, "The Path Not Taken," *Foreign Affairs* 79, 2 (March/April 2000), pp. 180–81; Alison Des Forges, "Alas, We Knew," *Foreign Affairs*

79, 3 (May/June 2000), pp. 141–42; Philip Gourevitch, interview on "The Triumph of Evil," *Frontline* [television documentary], January 26, 1999. Transcript is available at www.pbs.org/wgbh/pages/frontline/shows/evil/interviews/gourevitch/html.

15. For a possible exception, see Alan Kuperman, "Rwanda in Retrospect," *Foreign Affairs* 79, 1 (January/February 2000), pp. 94–118.

16. Although moral philosophers do not always agree on the precise relationship between causal and moral responsibility, it is generally accepted that such a relationship exists in the main. See, for example, John Martin Fischer, ed., *Moral Responsibility* (Ithaca, N.Y.: Cornell University Press, 1986), and "Symposium on Moral Responsibility," *Ethics* 101, 2 (January 1991).

17. Moral philosophers have debated the issue of the causal effectiveness of omissions. For a general philosophical argument in support of this position, see Elazer Weinryb, "Omissions and Responsibility," *Philosophical Quarterly* 30 (1980), pp. 1–18. For the relationship between omissions and the Good Samaritan rule, see J. H. Scheid, "Affirmative Duty to Aid in Emergency Situations," *John Marshall Journal of Practice and Procedure* 3 (1969), pp. 1–16. For the general proposition on omissions and causality, see Dennis Thompson, *Political Ethics and Public Office* (Cambridge, Mass.: Harvard University Press, 1987), chap. 2; Judith Shklar, *Faces of Injustice* (New Haven, Conn.: Yale University Press, 1991); and Marion Smiley, *Moral Responsibility and the Boundaries of the Community* (Chicago: University of Chicago Press, 1992).

18. Much of this literature on humanitarian intervention has focused on its legitimacy, whether it might give the Great Powers a license to intervene against the weak when it suits their interests, and whether legitimating humanitarian intervention might destabilize the Westphalian international order. For a thorough overview, see Nicholas Wheeler, *Saving Strangers: Humanitarian International in International Society* (New York: Oxford University Press, 2000), chap. 1. This literature, however, has been surprisingly quiet on the question of the duty to aid, generally adopting a deontological approach and attempting to find measures that are neither excessively slippery nor antiseptically objective. In *Just and Unjust Wars*, 2d ed. (New York: Basic Books, 1992), Michael Walzer tackles this issue by asserting that the crimes committed must have reached a level that they shock the conscience of the international community.

19. Peter Singer, "Famine, Influence, and Morality," *Philosophy and Public Affairs* 2 (1972), pp. 229–43.

Chapter 1. It Was a Very Good Year

1. Boutros Boutros-Ghali, *Unvanquished*.

2. Farewell Statement of the Secretary-General to Staff of United Nations, Federal News Service, Friday, December 20, 1991, Major Leader Special Transcript, United Nations Press Release, Department of Public Relations, New York.

3. Boutros Boutros-Ghali, address to the National Press Club, Washington, D.C., May 13, 1992.

4. Stanley Meisler, "Kofi Annan: The Soft-Spoken Economist Who Runs U.N. Peacekeeping Forces," *Los Angeles Times*, June 19, 1994, p. M3.

5. Sashi Tharoor, "The Changing Face of Peacekeeping," in Barbara Benton, ed., *Soldiers for Peace* (New York: Facts on File, 1996), p. 220.

6. Lewis McKenzie, *Peacekeeper: The Road to Sarajevo* (Toronto: Douglas and McIntyre, 1993), p. 330.

7. "Changing Role of Peacekeeper Challenges UN," CNN, October 8, 1993, Lexis-Nexis.

8. "Clinton Reworks Limits in Somalia despite Pressure," Cox News Service, *Seattle Post-Intelligencer*, October 6, 1993, p. A1.

9. Statement by President Bill Clinton on Somalia, October 7, 1993, White House, Washington, D.C.

10. *Toronto Star*, October 10, 1993, p. F1.

11. One disgruntled American official reflected that the Americans had "acted like minnows in a pond—whenever a cloud passed over, they scurried for cover." Ibid.

12. James Bone, *New York Times*, October 12, 1993.

13. Julia Preston, "Vision of a More Aggressive U.N. Now Dims," *Washington Post*, January 5, 1994, p. A24.

14. Ibid.

15. See, for instance, Stephen Rosenfeld, *Washington Post*, October 1, 1993, p. A25.

16. For a good analysis of the dangers of enforcement, see Mats Berdal, *Whither UN Peacekeeping?* (London: International Institute of Strategic Studies, 1993); and Edward Mortimer, "Peace Role in Process," *Financial Times*, November 17, 1993, p. 14.

17. Barbara Crossette, "U.N. Chief Ponders Future of Peacekeepers," *New York Times*, March 3, 1995, p. A3; Meisler, "Kofi Annan."

18. Julia Preston, "U.N. Officials Scale Back Peacemaking Ambitions; Planned U.S. Withdrawal from Somalia Demonstrates Limitations," *Washington Post*, October 28, 1993, p. A40.

19. Meisler, "Kofi Annan."

20. Preston, "Vision of a More Aggressive UN."

21. Tharoor, "Changing Face of Peacekeeping," p. 216.

22. Paul Lewis, "Five Key Nations Urge Prudence in Setting Peacekeeping Goal," *New York Times*, October 1, 1993, p. A2. Also see James Bone, "Hurd Puts Limit on Peacekeeping," *London Times*, September 29, 1993.

23. United Nations, Security Council Presidential Statement, *Statement on the Conditions for the Deployment and Renewal of Peacekeeping Operations*, May 3, 1994, S/PRST/1994/22. This proposal was seen as a natural follow-up to previous resolutions, including the resolution of May 28, 1993 (S/25859).

24. Meisler, "Kofi Annan."

25. Barbara Crossette, "U.N. Falters in Post-Cold-War Peacekeeping, but Sees Role as Essential," *New York Times*, December 5, 1994, p. A12.

26. Preston, "U.N. Officials Scale Back Peacemaking Ambitions."

27. "Trotting to the Rescue," *Economist*, June 25, 1994, p. 22.

28. Preston, "Vision of a More Aggressive U.N."

29. Ibid.

30. Kofi Annan, "Peacekeeping, Military Intervention, and National Sovereignty in Internal Armed Conflict," in Jonathan Moore, ed., *Hard Choices: Moral Dilemmas in Humanitarian Intervention* (New York: Rowman and Littlefield, 1998), pp. 64–65.

31. United Nations, Security Council Resolution, *Renewal of the Mandate of the UNOSOM and the Process of National Reconciliation*, May 31, 1994, S/RES/923.

32. Boutros-Ghali, address to the National Press Club, Washington, D.C., May 13, 1992.

33. Boutros-Ghali, "International Peacekeeping in a Multipolar, Multiethnic World," address to the Center for Strategic and International Studies, Ninth Annual David Abshire Lecture, Washington, D.C., May 13, 1992.

Chapter 2. Rwanda through Rose-Colored Glasses

1. See, in particular, Mamdani, *When Victims Become Killers;* Human Rights Watch, *Leave None to Tell the Story;* Prunier, *Rwanda Crisis;* Destexhe, *Rwanda and Genocide in the Twentieth Century;* Catharine Newbury, *The Cohesion of Oppression: Clientship and Ethnicity in Rwanda, 1860–1960* (New York: Columbia University Press, 1989); and René Lemarchand, *Rwanda and Burundi* (New York: Praeger, 1970).

2. Prunier, *Rwanda Crisis,* p. 39.

3. Cited in ibid., p. 53.

4. Cited in Linda Melvern, *A People Betrayed: The Role of the West in Rwanda's Genocide* (New York: Zed Books, 2000), p. 17.

5. See Peter Uvin, *Aiding Genocide: The Development Enterprise in Rwanda* (West Hartford, Conn.: Kumarian, 1998).

6. Prunier, *Rwanda Crisis,* pp. 99–108.

7. Cited in Agnes Callamard, "French Policy in Rwanda," in Adelman and Suhrke, eds., *Path of a Genocide,* p. 169.

8. Colin Keating, interview with author, September 25, 2000.

9. Good summaries of this phase are provided by Human Rights Watch, *Leave None to Tell the Story;* Power, *Problem from Hell;* Off, *The Lion, the Fox, and the Eagle;* Prunier, *Rwanda Crisis;* Klinghoffer, *International Dimension of Genocide in Rwanda;* Jones, "Intervention without Borders"; Boutros-Ghali, *United Nations and Rwanda, 1993–1996;* Adelman et al., *International Response to Conflict and Genocide;* and Organization of African Unity, *Rwanda: The Preventable Genocide.*

10. Interim Report of the Secretary-General on Rwanda, May 20, 1993, S/25810, para. 23; see also addendum, June 2, 1993, S/25810/Add. 1.

11. Report of the Special Rapporteur on Extrajudicial, Summary, or Arbitrary Executions. Commission on Human Rights, E/CN.4/1994/7/Add. 1, para. 78.

12. Mike Trickey, "Envoy to the Killing Fields," *Ottawa Citizen,* May 19, 1994, p. A1. Dallaire would later write, "I, the least experienced UN member on this UN team, was appointed to lead this mission." Cited in Organization of African Unity, *Rwanda: The Preventable Genocide,* chap. 13, p. 3.

13. Organization of African Unity, *Rwanda: The Preventable Genocide,* chap. 13, p. 4; Roméo Dallaire, interview with author, December 5, 2000.

14. Dallaire, interview with author, December 5, 2000.

15. "International Observers Say Situation in Rwanda is Good," ITAR-TASS, September 3, 1993.

16. "UN Group Says Peace Prevailing in Rwanda," Agence France Press, September 2, 1993.

17. Brent Beardsley, interview with author, October 17, 2000.

18. Official from U.S. Mission to UN, interview with author, May 14, 2000.

19. Beardsley, interview with author, October 17, 2000.

20. *International Response to Conflict and Genocide,* chap. 3, p. 2.

21. Astri Suhrke, "Dilemmas of Protection: The Log of the KIBAT Battalion," in Adelman and Suhrke, eds., *Path of a Genocide,* p. 257.

22. Report of the Secretary-General on Rwanda, September 24, 1993, S/26488, para. 70.

23. Member of the U.S. Mission to the UN, interview with author, May 14, 2000.

24. Human Rights Watch, *Leave None to Tell the Story,* p. 131; staff from U.S. Mission to UN, interview with author, May 14, 2000.

25. Keating, interview with author, September 25, 2000.

26. Ibid.

27. Ibid.

28. Adelman et al., *International Response to Conflict and Genocide*, chap. 3, p. 2. Even France proposed that a force of one thousand might be able to do the job. United Nations, *Final Report of the International Commission of Inquiry.*

29. Agence France Press, October 5, 1993.

30. Ironically, UNAMIR's budget was approved on April 4, 1994, just two days before the beginning of the genocide.

Chapter 3. "If This Is an Easy Operation . . ."

1. Cited in Off, *The Lion, the Fox, and the Eagle*, p. 103.

2. United Nations, *Report of the Secretary-General on UNAMIR*, December 30, 1993, S/26927.

3. Stephen John Stedman, "Spoiler Problems in Peace Processes," *International Security* 22, 2 (Fall 1997), pp. 5–53.

4. Beardsley, interview with author, June 28, 2000.

5. Dallaire, interview with author, December 5, 2000.

6. Colonel Luc Marchal, interview on "Triumph of Evil," *Frontline* [television documentary]. Transcript is available at www.pbs.org/wgbh/pages/frontline/shows/evil/interviews/marchal.html.

7. Dallaire, interview with author, December 5, 2000.

8. Document in author's possession. See also web site for "Triumph of Evil," www.pbs.org/wgbh/pages/frontline/shows/evil/warning/cable.html.

9. Beardsley, interview with author, June 28, 2000.

10. Translation is, "Where there is a will there is a way. Let's go."

11. Document in author's possession. See also web site for "Triumph of Evil," www.pbs.org/wgbh/pages/frontline/shows/evil/warning/unresponse.html.

12. Iqbal Riza, interview on "Triumph of Evil." Transcript is available at www.pbs.org/wgbh/pages/frontline/shows/evil/interviews/riza.html.

13. Boutros-Ghali, *United Nations and Rwanda, 1993–1996*, p. 31.

14. Gourevitch, interview on "Triumph of Evil." Also see his "Annals of Diplomacy: The Genocide Fax."

15. Riza, interview on "Triumph of Evil."

16. Beardsley, interview with author, June 28, 2000.

17. Ibid.; also see Organization of African Unity, *Rwanda: The Preventable Genocide.*

18. On Baril's denial, see Human Rights Watch, *Leave None to Tell the Story*, p. 173.

19. Riza, interview on "Triumph of Evil."

20. United Nations, October 5, 1993, S/RES/872 (1993).

21. Riza, interview on "Triumph of Evil."

22. Dallaire, interview with author, December 5, 2000.

23. Ibid.

24. Document in author's possession.

25. Belgium Senate, *Parliamentary Commission of Inquiry concerning Rwanda*, December 1997.

26. Dallaire, interview with author, December 5, 2000.

27. Beardsley, interview with author, June 28, 2000.

28. Keating, however, contends that the council should have been involved. "The Security Council's Role in the Rwanda Crisis" presented at the Comprehensive Seminar on

Lessons Learned from the United Nations Assistance Mission for Rwanda, June 12, 1996, Merrill Lynch Conference Center, Plainsboro, N.J.

29. See Human Rights Watch, *Leave None to Tell the Story*, p. 172; and Turid Laegreid, "UN Peacekeeping in Rwanda," in Adelman and Suhrke, eds., *Path of Genocide*, p. 234.

30. Riza, interview on "Triumph of Evil."

31. Cited in Power, *Problem from Hell*, forthcoming.

32. Riza, interview on "Triumph of Evil"; italics added.

33. Boutros-Ghali, *United Nations and Rwanda, 1993–1996*, p. 32; italics added.

34. Document in author's possession.

35. Beardsley, interview with author, June 28, 2000.

36. Dallaire, interview with author, December 5, 2000.

37. Human Rights Watch, *Leave None to Tell the Story*, p. 176.

38. Prunier, *Rwanda Crisis*, p. 211.

39. Human Rights Watch, *Leave None to Tell the Story*, p. 176.

40. Tony Marley, interview on "Triumph of Evil." Transcript is available at www.pbs.org/wgbh/pages/frontline/shows/evil/interviews/marley.html.

41. See Power, "Bystanders to Genocide," p. 92.

42. Human Rights Watch, *Leave None to Tell the Story*, p. 176.

43. As cited in ibid., p. 161. Also see Laegreid, "UN Peacekeeping in Rwanda," p. 234; and Adelman et al., *International Response to Conflict and Genocide*, chap. 3, p. 5.

44. Human Rights Watch, *Leave None to Tell the Story*, pp. 176–77.

45. Document in author's possession.

46. Belgium Senate, *Parliamentary Commission of Inquiry*.

47. Adelman et al., *International Response to Conflict and Genocide*, chap. 3, p. 6.

48. Dallaire, interview with author, December 5, 2000.

49. Adelman et al., *International Response to Conflict and Genocide*, chap. 3, p. 6.

50. Cited from Off, *The Lion, the Fox, and the Eagle*, p. 111.

51. Dallaire, interview with author, December 5, 2000.

52. Document in author's possession.

53. United Nations, *Report of the Independent Inquiry*.

54. Ibid.

55. On November 23, Dallaire sent to headquarters a draft set of the rules of engagement (ROEs). Included in this draft was Paragraph 17, which permitted the mission to act, and even use force, in response to crimes against humanity. Specifically, it stated, "There may also be ethnically or politically motivated criminal acts committed during this mandate which will morally and legally require UNAMIR to use all available means to halt them. Examples are executions, attacks on displaced persons or refugees." The insertion of this ROE was something of a fluke that was only possible within the UN. When Dallaire's military attaché approached DPKO about what should be the ROE, he expected to be handed a standardized text. Instead he was told to draw up his own language, and that the Cambodian operation might be something of a model. So, the military attaché inserted these ROEs into the Rwandan operation. Luckily, this provided UNAMIR with the wiggle room it needed later on.

56. Human Rights Watch, *Leave None to Tell the Story*, p. 596; Suhrke, "Dilemmas of Protection," p. 255.

57. Adelman et al., *International Response to Conflict and Genocide*, chap. 3, p. 5.

58. Beardsley, interview with author, June 28, 2000.

59. Melvern, *A People Betrayed*, p. 107.

60. Roméo Dallaire, "The End of Innocence: Rwanda 1994," in Moore, ed., *Hard Choices*, p. 73. The independent inquiry also noted that "[t]he logistical problems run like a constant thread throughout the correspondence between the Force Commander and Headquarters." United Nations, *Report of the Independent Inquiry.*

61. United Nations, *Report of the Independent Inquiry.*

62. Ibid.

63. Ibid.

64. Ibid.

65. United Nations, *Second Progress Report of the Secretary-General on the United Nations Assistance Mission for Rwanda*, S/1994/360, para. 27.

66. Beardsley, interview with author, June 28, 2000.

67. In fact, UNAMIR also had requested an additional forty-eight military observers to help the situation in the south, but the secretary-general dropped that request from his report in anticipation of the council's objections.

Chapter 4. The Fog of Genocide

1. Dallaire, interview with author, December 5, 2000; Beardsley, interview with author, October 17, 2000.

2. United Nations, *Report of the Independent Inquiry*, p. 16.

3. Beardsley, interview with author, June 28, 2000.

4. United Nations, Security Council Presidential Statement, *Statement on the Conditions for the Deployment and Renewal of Peacekeeping Operations*, May 3, 1994, S/PRST/1994/22. This proposal was seen as a follow-up to previous resolutions, including that of May 28, 1993 (S/25859).

5. See Power, "Bystanders to Genocide," p. 102.

6. Ibrahim Gambari, interview with author, July 3, 2000.

7. Human Rights Watch, *Leave None to Tell the Story*, p. 600. Colonel Luc Marchal kept Brussels informed of the massacres on the ground and his strong preference to stay in Rwanda. Ibid., p. 620.

8. Ibid., p. 619.

9. Ibid., p. 620.

10. Beardsley, interview with author, June 28, 2000.

11. Gambari, interview with author, July 3, 2000.

12. Cited in Power, "Bystanders to Genocide," p. 98.

13. Keating, interview with author, September 25, 2000.

14. Keating, "The Security Council's Role in the Rwanda Crisis."

15. Dallaire, interview with author, December 5, 2000.

16. United Nations, April 20, 1994, S/1994/470.

17. Dallaire, interview with author, December 5, 2000.

18. Beardsley, interview with author, October 17, 2000.

19. Scott Feil, *Preventing Genocide: How the Early Use of Force Might Have Succeeded in Rwanda*. A Report to the Carnegie Commission on Preventing Deadly Conflict (New York: Carnegie Corporation of New York, 1998).

20. Human Rights Watch, *Leave None to Tell the Story*, p. 598.

21. Beardsley, interview with author, June 28, 2000.

22. Cited in Melvern, *A People Betrayed*, p. 153.

23. Riza, interview on "Triumph of Evil."

24. Ibid.

25. Ibid.; italics added.

26. Ibid.
27. Ibid.
28. As DPKO's Lessons Learned Unit concluded, "A fundamental misunderstanding of the nature of the conflict . . . contributed to false political assumptions and military assessments." United Nations, Department of Peacekeeping Operations, Lessons Learned Unit, *Comprehensive Report on Lessons Learned from UNAMIR*, October 1993–April 1996, December 1996, p. 3.
29. Document in author's possession.
30. Sylvana Fao, UN press briefing, November 27, 1996, cited in Bjorn Willum, "Legitimizing Inaction towards Genocide in Rwanda: A Matter of Misperception," *International Peacekeeping* 6, 3 (Autumn 1999), p. 13.
31. Document in author's possession.
32. Georgie Anne Geyer, "The World as Viewed from the U.N. Helm," *Washington Times*, April 3, 1994, p. B4.
33. Dallaire, interview with author, November 5, 2000; Beardsley, interview with author, August 15, 2001.
34. Cited in Melvern, *A People Betrayed*, p. 162.
35. Adelman et al., *International Response to Conflict and Genocide*, chap. 4, p. 2.
36. Suhrke, "Dilemmas of Protection," pp. 264, 269.
37. Human Rights Watch, *Leave None to Tell the Story*, p. 597.
38. Dallaire, interview with author, December 5, 2000.
39. Beardsley, interview with author, October 17, 2000.
40. Notes in author's possession.
41. Human Rights Watch, *Leave None to Tell the Story*, p. 621; Beardsley, interview with author, October 17, 2000; Melvern, *A People Betrayed*, p. 146.
42. Notes in author's possession.
43. Dallaire, interview with author, December 5, 2000. Also see Omaar and de Waal, *Rwanda: Death, Despair, and Defiance*, p. 688; Prunier, *Rwanda Crisis*, p. 275.
44. Prunier, *Rwanda Crisis*, pp. 234–35.
45. Human Rights Watch, *Leave None to Tell the Story*, p. 628.
46. Melvern, *A People Betrayed*, pp. 32–33.
47. This conclusion is implicitly supported by Power, *Problem from Hell*, and Human Rights Watch, *Leave None to Tell the Story*.
48. Laegreid, "UN Peacekeeping in Rwanda," p. 239.
49. Document in author's possession.
50. Melvern, *A People Betrayed*, p. 173.
51. Human Rights Watch, *Leave None to Tell the Story*, p. 595.
52. Similar conclusions are reached by Adelman et al., *International Response to Conflict and Genocide*, chap. 4, p. 1; and United Nations, *Report of the Independent Inquiry*.
53. Gambari, interview with author, July 3, 2000.
54. United Nations, April 20, 1994, S/1994/470.
55. "UN Troops Pray as They Scramble out of Rwanda," *Toronto Star*, April 21, 1994, p. A5.

Chapter 5. Diplomatic Games

1. Julia Preston, "'This Eerie Calm': The Rwanda Situation Confounds the Security Council," *Washington Post*, May 9, 1994, p. A8.
2. On the relationship between the council's vote and the acceleration of the genocide, see Human Rights Watch, *Leave None to Tell the Story*.

3. Letter from secretary-general to president of the Security Council, April 29, 1994, S/1994/518.

4. Dallaire, interview with author, December 5, 2000.

5. Melvern, *A People Betrayed*, pp. 177–78.

6. Ibid., p. 179.

7. Cited in ibid., pp. 179–80.

8. Author correspondence with Keating, August 15, 2001.

9. United Nations, April 30, 1994, S/PRST/21.

10. Melvern, *A People Betrayed*, p. 178.

11. Preston, "'This Eerie Calm,'" p. A8.

12. Mark Huband, "Ugandan Leader Urges Foreign Intervention," *Guardian*, May 6, 1994, p. 14.

13. Human Rights Watch, *Leave None to Tell the Story*, p. 640.

14. Larry Elliot, "UN's Rwanda Crisis: US and Russia Sink Plans to Send 5,500 Troops," *Guardian*, May 13, 1994, p. 14.

15. Paul Lewis, "U.S. Opposes Plan for UN Force in Rwanda," *New York Times*, May 12, 1994, p. A9.

16. Cited in Melvern, *A People Betrayed*, p. 178.

17. Paul Lewis, "UN Backs Troops for Rwanda but Terms Bar Any Action Soon," *New York Times*, May 17, 1994, p. A1; Douglas Jehl, "U.S. Showing a New Caution on UN Peacekeeping," *New York Times*, May 18, 1994, p. A1.

18. Hearing of the International Security, International Organizations, and Human Rights Subcommittee of the House Foreign Affairs Committee, May 17, 1994.

19. Power, *Problem from Hell*, forthcoming.

20. United Nations, Security Council Resolution, May 17, 1994, S/RES/918.

21. United Nations, *Report of the Secretary-General on the Situation in Rwanda*, May 31, 1994, S/1994/640.

22. Nor did many other countries exhibit a charitable impulse. Britain offered fifty trucks from their stock. In jest Dallaire quipped, "Do they work?" Much to his surprise, the British said that they would check. Then they withdrew the offer. Russia and China did not even offer broken trucks. Beardsley, interview with author, June 28, 2000. France is a completely different story.

23. United Nations, *Report of the United Nations High Commissioner for Human Rights on His Mission to Rwanda of 11–12 May 1994*, May 19, 1994, E/CN.4/SS-3/3.

24. Quotations in this and next paragraph from United Nations, *The Situation Concerning Rwanda, Report of the Secretary-General*, May 16, 1994, S/1994/565. S/PV.3377.

25. Boutros-Ghali, *United Nations and Rwanda, 1993–1996*, p. 50.

26. For French policy, see Prunier, *Rwanda Crisis*, chap. 8.

27. Dallaire was dead set against the proposed French intervention. Incredibly no one fully consulted with Dallaire before the UN decided to give the plan its seal of approval. When he found out, he informed the UN that France's presence would endanger UNAMIR troops. He also added that he would fight the French if they approached Kigali. When hearing the news that French troops would be coming to Rwanda, one Russian peacekeeper in UNAMIR exclaimed, "Have they gone crazy? At best we have to evacuate. At worst the rebels will take us all hostage." Because he feared for their safety, Dallaire ordered the evacuation of thirty-seven peacekeepers who were from African countries that were allied with France. This, in Dallaire's words, "devastated my whole capability." Dallaire, interview with author, December 5, 2000.

28. United Nations, Security Council Resolution, June 22, 1994, S/RES/929 (1994).

29. As the war ended, Dallaire proposed to the UN headquarters that he be allowed to go after and arrest the leaders of the genocide, as they were fleeing Rwanda for refugee camps. The proposal went over like a "lead fart," according to Dallaire, in part because officials at headquarters saw this as a violation of peacekeeping's principles. Off, *The Lion, the Fox, and the Eagle*, p. 81.

30. Beardsley, interview with author, June 28, 2000.
31. Cited in Prunier, *Rwanda Crisis*, p. 303.
32. Prunier, *Rwanda Crisis.*
33. Robert Block, "A Week in Goma," *Independent on Sunday*, July 31, 1994, p. 4; cited in Melvern, *A People Betrayed*, p. 218.

Chapter 6. The Hunt for Moral Responsibility

1. Cited in Shaharyar Khan, *The Shallow Graves of Rwanda* (London: I. B. Tauris, 2000), p. 133.
2. Remarks by the president, Kampala, Uganda, March 25, 1998, Office of the Press Secretary, Washington, D.C.
3. "Secretary-General Pledges Support of UN for Rwanda's Search for Peace and Progress," UN press release, May 6, 1998, SG/SM/6552 AFR/56.
4. "Secretary-General Reflects on 'Intervention' in the Thirty-Fifth Annual Ditchley Foundation Lecture," UN press release, June 26, 1998, SG/SM/6613.
5. United Nations, General Assembly, Report of the Secretary-General Pursuant to General Assembly Resolution 53/35. The Fall of Srebrenica, November 15, 1999, A/54/549, p. 111.
6. Boutros-Ghali, interview with author, November 6, 2000; also see Boutros-Ghali, *Unvanquished*, p. 132.
7. Boutros-Ghali, interview with author, November 6, 2000.
8. Ibid.
9. The secretary-general's report on Rwanda in late May 1994 contains a section entitled "The Massacres in Rwanda." At the end of the section the Secretariat wonders aloud whether it might have seen the massacres coming, and informs the Security Council that it should "be made aware of certain events, that, in retrospect, might have had implications regarding the massacres." After noting the inflammatory radio broadcasts and the importation of arms, the report states that "[o]n one occasion the Force Commander requested Headquarters for permission to use force to recover a cache of arms and was instructed to insist that the Gendarmerie conduct that operation under UNAMIR supervision." Of course, there was more than one occasion. But there is the possibility of another reinvention here. The fact that Boutros-Ghali links the Secretariat's refusal to permit UNAMIR to seize arms caches in the context of warning signs of the genocide suggests that he is referring to the January 11 cable because, of the many communications from Dallaire, this cable made the most direct link between the planned massacres and the arms caches. If so, this contradicts Boutros-Ghali's stated claim that he did not know of the January 11 cable until 1997. The more relevant implication is that he possibly possessed this information during April, if not before, and therefore, could have (and might have) deduced that Rwanda was no mere civil war. United Nations, *Report of the Secretary-General on the Situation in Rwanda.*
10. Dallaire, interview with author, December 3, 2000.
11. Confidential interview.
12. Riza, interview on "Triumph of Evil."
13. Dallaire, interview with author, December 3, 2000.

14. Keating, "Security Council's Role in the Rwanda Crisis."

15. Cited in Human Rights Watch, *Leave None to Tell the Story*, p. 142.

16. Belgium Senate, *Parliamentary Commission of Inquiry.*

17. Power, *Problem from Hell.*

18. In "In the Name of Humanity," *New York Review of Books*, April 27, 2000, Sir Brian Urquhart constructs a narrative that implicitly advances the excuse of duress.

19. Stephen Morse, "Excusing and the New Excuse Defenses: A Legal and Conceptual Review," in Michael Tonry, ed., *Crime and Justice: A Review of Research*, vol. 23 (Chicago: University of Chicago Press, 1998), p. 335.

20. Dennis Thompson, "Moral Responsibility of Public Officials: The Problem of Many Hands," *American Political Science Review* 74 (1980), p. 909.

21. Ibid.

22. Gambari offers a variant of the compulsion thesis in the context of the council's discussions, arguing that by mid-April the pressure to achieve consensus and vote for withdrawal was overwhelming. Gambari, interview with author, July 3, 2000.

23. Morse, "Excusing and the New Excuse Defenses," p. 364.

24. Quoted from Laengreid, "UN Peacekeeping in Rwanda," p. 239.

25. Keating, interview with author, October 18, 2000.

26. Cited in Human Rights Watch, *Leave None to Tell the Story*, p. 609.

27. See Feil, *Preventing Genocide.*

28. Smiley, *Moral Responsibility and the Boundaries of the Community*, p. 136.

29. Thompson, "Moral Responsibility of Public Officials," pp. 905–16. Also see Henry Shue, *Basic Rights: Subsistence, Affluence, and U.S. Foreign Policy*, 2d ed. (Princeton: Princeton University Press, 1996), afterword.

30. "Secretary-General Reflects on 'Intervention,'" UN press release.

31. Off, *The Lion, the Fox, and the Eagle*, p. 81.

32. Beardsley, interview with author, June 28, 2000; Prunier, *Rwanda Crisis*, chap. 8; Human Rights Watch, *Leave None to Tell the Story;* Human Rights Watch, *Rearming with Impunity*, HRW Arms Project, vol. 7, no. 4, May 1995.

33. William Pfaff, "An Active French Role in the 1994 Genocide in Rwanda," *International Herald Tribune*, January 17, 1998.

34. Anthony Lake, *Six Nightmares* (New York: Little, Brown, 2000), p. 93.

35. Keating, interview with author, October 17, 2000.

36. Dallaire, interview with author, December 3, 2000.

37. Mark Bovens, *The Quest for Responsibility: Accountability and Citizenship in Complex Organisations* (New York: Cambridge University Press, 1998), pp. 128–30.

38. Alex Duvall Smith, "Rwanda War Crimes Official Charged with Genocide," *Independent*, May 21, 2001, p. 12.

39. Elizabeth Spellman, *Fruits of Sorrow: Framing Our Attention to Suffering* (Boston: Beacon, 1997), p. 109.

40. Weber, "Politics as a Vocation," in Gerth and Mills, *From Max Weber*, p. 127; italics in the original.

Index

accountability, 179
Agenda for Peace
  definition of security, 27
  and peacekeeping rules, 46
Aideed, General Mohamed Farah, 33, 34, 36
Akasu, 53, 57, 100
Albright, Madeleine, 40, 43, 106, 137
  and opposition to UNAMIR II, 139, 141
Amin, Idi, 55
Annabi, Hedi, 79
Annan, Kofi, 28, 159, 179, 180
  and institutional ideology of impartiality, 158
  on moral division of labor, 170
  and peacekeeping rules, 46
  on responsibility, 154
  visit to Rwanda, 154
  See also UN Department of Peacekeeping Operations; UN Secretariat
Arendt, Hannah, 7, 8–9, 10
  and duress excuse, 165
  See also bureaucratic culture
Aristide, Jean-Bertrand, 39
Arusha Accords, 14, 17, 68, 113
  delay implementing, 14, 75, 76, 92–94
  negotiation of, 56, 57, 61–64
Ayala-Lasso, José, 145

Bagosora, Colonel Théoneste, 97, 171
Bangladesh, 104, 117
Baril, Maurice, 61, 78, 79, 85, 123, 142–43
Bauman, Zygmunt, 198
Beardsley, Brent, 79
Belgium, 56, 173
  and colonial mandate, 50–52
  Commission of Inquiry, 161
  death of soldiers, 98–99
  and ignorance excuse, 161
  and intervention, 121–22
  and January 11 cable, 88–89
  and withdrawal from Rwanda, 104, 117
Bicanumpaka, Jerome, 145–46
Booh-Booh, Jacques, 74, 87, 93, 129
  and categorization of April violence, 114–15
  on deteriorating security situation, 90, 91
Bosnia, 29, 102, 158
  and peacekeeping rules, 44
Boutros-Ghali, Boutros, 18, 28, 32, 43, 66, 147, 172, 179
  and April 20 report, 107
  and attitude toward U.S., 42
  and Belgian troop withdrawal, 104
  and categorization of violence, 94, 120
  on definition of security, 26–27

Boutros-Ghali, Boutros *(continued)*
    and duress excuse, 166
    and excuses, 20, 153, 156, 158–60,
        166
    and France, 121–22
    and ignorance excuse, 20, 156, 158–60
    on impact of Somalia on U.S., 38–39
    and January 11 cable, 81, 84, 89, 207
    and manipulation of information,
        118–21
    and moral responsibility, 15, 20,
        173–74
    and opposition to intervention, 14–15,
        119–24, 158–59
    and peacekeeping rules, 45, 91, 116
    and response to genocide, 3, 14–15,
        107–27, 133
    and response to pre-April violence, 91,
        92–93
    and Somali disarmament, 36
    and threat to suspend UNAMIR, 93
    and transitional government, 92
    on UN credibility, 47
    See also UN DPKO; UN Secretariat
broad-based transitional government
        (BBTG), 63, 66
    failure to establish, 76
    and relationship to violence, 92–93,
        113
bureaucracy, 59
    Arendt and, 8–9, 10
    rules of, 175
    Weber and, 7–8
    See also bureaucratic culture; peacekeep-
        ing rules; UN culture; UN Secre-
        tariat
bureaucratic culture, xi, 5, 8, 59–60, 112
    and categorization of genocide, 112–18
    and duty to aid, 175
    and humanitarianism, 181
    and ignorance excuse, 157–58
    See also peacekeeping rules; UN culture
Burundi, 17, 53
    violence in, 73, 75, 76
Bush, George H. W., 23, 24
    and PRD-13, 40–41

Cambodia, 29, 33
causal responsibility
    and moral responsibility, 17, 167–68
    and omissions, 17–18, 167–69

and UN, 167–69
    See also role responsibility; moral re-
        sponsibility
CDR (Committee for the Defense of the
        Republic), 54, 56–57, 75
China, 27, 101, 171
Christopher, Warren, 36, 106
Claes, Willie, 89, 104
Clinton, Bill, 2, 143
    and duress excuse, 164
    and Haiti, 40
    and ignorance excuse, 2, 156, 161–62
    impact of Somalia on, 37–39
    on moral institutions, 178
    and peacekeeping policy, 33, 41
    and peacekeeping rules, 45
    on responsibility, 178
    and visit to Rwanda, 153–54
    See also United States
Cold War, 12, 22–23, 25, 28
Collingwood, R. G., 5
Commission on Global Governance, 24
Commission on Human Rights, 145
Committee for the Defense of the Repub-
        lic. *See* CDR
Congress (U.S.)
    and Rwanda, 71
    and Somalia, 40–42
consent. *See* peacekeeping rules
Croatia, 31, 67
Cuéllar, Javier Pérez de, 28
    and UN credibility, 47
Czech Republic, 20, 100, 134, 146

Dallaire, General Roméo, 152, 167, 207
    and arrival in Kigali, 74
    biography of, 64–65
    and call for reinforcements, 2, 109, 110
    and categorization of genocide,
        109–10, 114–15, 133
    and concept of operations, 67, 90–91,
        110
    and evacuation of foreign nationals,
        100
    on ignorance excuse, 161
    and initial impressions of Rwanda, 65
    and January 11 cable, 14, 77–88
    and meeting with Bagosora, 97
    and moral responsibility, 174, 181
    on Operation Turquoise, 151, 206
    and reaction to April 6 crash, 98

and reports to UN, 109, 110, 118, 120
and rules of engagement, 203
See also UNAMIR
Democratic Republican Movement
(MDR), 54
Destexhe, Alain, 150
Djibouti, 135
Doctors Without Borders, 150
duress excuse, 19, 20, 162–66
and Arendt, 165
and Boutros-Ghali, 166
and Clinton, 164
and DPKO, 162–66
and Ibrahim Gambari, 208
and Secretariat, 20
and Security Council, 208
and United States, 164
See also excuses; ignorance excuse
duty to aid, 18–19, 169, 173–76, 199
and bureaucratic culture, 175
and moral responsibility, 18
and peacekeeping rules, 13, 18–19,
47–48, 175–77

Egypt, 27
Eichmann, Adolf, 8
Eichmann in Jerusalem, 8–9, 165
Eliason, Jan, 44
El Salvador, 29
excuses, 19–20, 155–66
definition of, 155
and Boutros-Ghali, 20, 153, 156,
158–60, 166
and bureaucratic culture, 158
and January 11 cable, 156
and moral responsibility, 155, 164
and Somalia, 163
and UN Secretariat, 21, 162–66
See also duress excuse; ignorance excuse; moral responsibility

France, 12, 56, 69, 101, 121, 173, 179
alliance with Rwanda, 56, 57
Anglo-Saxon conspiracy, 56, 148
and Boutros-Ghali, 121–22
and ignorance excuse, 161
and January 11 cable, 88
and moral responsibility, 171
and Operation Turquoise, 147–49,
151, 171
and response to genocide, 12, 171

Gambari, Ibrahim, 106, 126, 167
and duress excuse, 208
genocide, Security Council debate over,
130–36
Genocide Convention, 135, 169, 170
Germany, 50
Ghana, 117, 124, 143
Gharekhan, Chinmaya, 119
Goražde, 102, 107
Gorbachev, Mikhail, 23
Gourevitch, Philip, 81
Gramm, Phil, 37
Great Powers, 18, 170–73

Habyarimana, General Juvénal, 66, 79,
92, 93, 96, 97
and democratization, 54
and January 11 cable, 87, 88
and response to RPF, 55–57
and takeover in 1973, 52–53
Haiti, 29, 39–40, 43
"Hamitic hypothesis," 49–50
Hannay, Sir David, 135
Harlan County, U.S.S., 40
Hegel, G. W. F., 4
Hitler, Adolf, 21
Holocaust, 1, 8, 21, 169, 170
Howe, Admiral Jonathan, 33
humanitarian intervention, 199
humanitarianism, 4, 181
human rights, 24–25
Human Rights Watch, 115, 136
"Hutu Revolution," 52
Hutus, 49
social construction of, 50–52

ignorance excuse, 19, 156–62
and Belgium, 161
and Boutros-Ghali, 20, 153, 156,
158–60, 166
and Clinton, 2, 156, 161–62
Dallaire on, 161
and DPKO, 2, 156–59
and France, 161
and January 11 cable, 20, 156
and Iqbal Riza, 150
and Security Council, 156
and United Nations culture, 157–58
and United States, 20, 156, 161–62
See also duress excuse; excuses; moral
responsibility

impartiality. *See* peacekeeping rules
Inderfurth, Karl, 139
India, 27
Interahamwe, 78, 81, 97, 143
Inyenzi, 52

January 11 cable (1994), 14, 20, 77–88,
    156
    and Belgium, 88–89
    and Boutros-Ghali, 81, 84, 89, 207
    and DPKO, 79–88
    and excuses, 156
    and ignorance excuse, 20, 156
    and peacekeeping rules, 82–88
    Iqbal Riza on, 80, 81, 82, 85, 86
    and Somalia, 85
    and United States, 88–89
    justifications, 155

Kayibanda, Grégoire, 52, 53
Keating, Colin, 117, 146
    on desire to name genocide, 134
    and maintaining UNAMIR's presence,
        106
    on possibility of intervention, 167
    on secretary-general's professional duty,
        202
    on Security Council's ignorance of
        Rwanda, 58, 69, 70
    See also New Zealand
Kigali Weapons-Secure Area (KWSA), 67,
    70, 71, 74, 83–84
Kirkpatrick, Jeanne, 22
Kovanda, Karel, 134

Lake, Tony, 89, 140, 171–72
Levi, Primo, 1

Madame Agathe, 97–98
Mandela, Nelson, 169
Marchal, Colonel Luc, 74, 84, 167
March Report (1994), 93–95
McKenzie, Lewis, 31
MDR (Democratic Republican Move-
    ment), 54
media, 150
Mencken, H. L., 179
Mille Collines Radio, 54
Mitterand, François, 148
"Mogadishu line," 44, 71
moral distribution of risk, 168

moral division of labor, 169–70, 172
    Kofi Annan on, 170
    and Great Powers, 18
    and United Nations, 18
moral institutions, 177–78
moral responsibility, 199
    and accountability, 179
    Kofi Annan on, 154
    and Boutros-Ghali, 15, 20, 173–74
    and causal responsibility, 17, 167–68
    choosing between, 6, 176
    concept of, 16–17, 166–67
    as contract, 177
    and Czech Republic, 20
    and Dallaire, 174, 181
    definition of, 16–17, 166–67
    and DPKO, 20, 173–74
    and duty to aid, 18
    and excuses, 155, 164
    and France, 171
    and Great Powers, 18, 170–73
    and moral division of labor, 18, 169–73
    and New Zealand, 20
    and Nigeria, 20
    and omissions, 17–18, 167–69, 199
    and role responsibility, 167, 169–70
    and Secretariat, 16, 18, 20, 154–56,
        173–74
    and Security Council, 16, 18, 20,
        154–56
    and United States, 20, 171–72
    See also duress excuse; excuses; igno-
        rance excuse
moral universe, 5–6
Moynihan, Daniel Patrick, 22
MRND (National Revolutionary Move-
    ment for Development), 53, 56–57,
    87, 97
Museveni, Yoweri, 56, 135

Namibia, 29
National Revolutionary Movement for
    Development. *See* MRND
National Security Council (NSC), 89
Ndadye, Mechior, 73
Ndiaye, Waly Bacre, 63
neutrality. *See* peacekeeping rules
New Zealand, 100, 134, 149
    and moral responsibility, 20
    See also Keating, Colin
Nietzsche, Friedrich, 5, 9

Nigeria, 105, 135, 149
  and intervention, 100, 105
  and moral responsibility, 20
Nightline, 133
NSC (National Security Council), 89
Ntaryamira, Cyprien, 97
Nunn, Sam, 36

Obote, Milton, 55
omissions, 17–18, 199
  and causal responsibility, 167
  See also moral responsibility
omniresponsibility, 171
Operation Provide Relief, 35
Operation Turquoise, 147–52, 171

Parmehutu Party, 52
peacekeeping
  Clinton attitude toward, 33, 41
  and Congress, 40, 41
  and duty to aid, 47–48, 175–76
  and enforcement, 43
  expansion of, 28–33
  and failed states, 30
  restriction of, 72
  and UN culture, 10
  See also peacekeeping rules; UNAMIR;
    UN DPKO
peacekeeping rules, 10, 95, 101–3, 128,
    157
  and *Agenda for Peace*, 46
  Annan on, 46, 158
  and Bosnia, 44
  Boutros-Ghali on, 45, 91, 116
  and Burundi, 73
  debate over, 43–48
  DPKO on, 14, 43–45, 91, 117
  and duty to aid, 13, 18–19, 47–48,
    175–77
  enforcement, 43
  ideology of impartiality, 158
  and January 11 cable, 82–88
  and response to April violence, 116,
    117, 127–29, 173–77
  and Security Council, 45
  and Somalia, 44
  UNAMIR and, 82–85, 127–29
  and UN culture, 10, 157–58
  See also peacekeeping; UN DPKO; UN
    Security Council
Pedanou, Macaire, 59

Policy Review Directive-13 (PRD-13),
    40–41, 69
Presidential Decision Directive-25 (PDD-
    25), 41, 139
Presidential Guard, 97, 143
Prunier, Gérard, 56, 88

Reagan, Ronald, 22, 23
Resolution 704, 34
Resolution 767, 35
Resolution 794, 35
Resolution 846, 61
Resolution 872, 72
Resolution 918, 142
responsibility. *See* causal responsibility;
    moral responsibility; role responsibility
Riza, Iqbal, 79, 81–82, 100, 110, 111
  and bureaucratic culture, 112
  and categorization of violence, 113–14
  on ethnic conflict, 112
  on failure to transmit information to
    Security Council, 110–12
  and ignorance excuse, 160
  on January 11 cable, 80, 81, 82, 85, 86
  on solutions to violence, 113–14
  and visit to Rwanda, 142–43
role responsibility, 18–19, 169–75. *See
    also* duty to aid; moral division of
    labor
Rose, General Michael, 44
RPF (Rwandan Patriotic Front), 15, 60,
    66, 75, 113, 143, 149
  creation of, 55
  response to Operation Turquoise, 148
rules of engagement (ROEs), 43, 91,
    100, 117, 203
Russell, Lord Bertrand, 52
Russia, 101, 171
Rwanda
  categorization of violence in, 59–60,
    87, 94, 102–3, 109–10, 116,
    155–62
  and democratization, 54
  as "easy" operation, 14, 69
  and ethnic groups, 49–51
  evacuation of foreign nationals from,
    100
  Hamitic hypothesis, 49–50
  historical background, 49–57
  as member of Security Council, 77,
    145–47

Rwanda (*continued*)
  and refugee crisis, 149–51
  and relations with France, 56, 57
  See also Arusha Accords; Habyarimana,
    General Juvénal; RPF; UNAMIR

security
  and *Agenda for Peace*, 27
  definition of, 25–26
Siad Barre, Mohammed, 34
Sills, Joe, 39
Singer, Peter, 18
Smiley, Marion, 169
SNA (Somali National Alliance), 36
SNM (Somali National Movement), 34
Somalia, 13, 29, 33, 34–39, 68, 85, 116,
    117
  and duress excuse, 163
  and impact on Clinton, 37–39
  and impact on UN, 13, 39
  and peacekeeping rules, 44
  "shadow of," 13, 85
Soto, Alvaro de, 42, 46
South Africa, 150, 169
Soviet Union, 23
Srebrenica, 158

Tharoor, Sashi, 45
theodicy, 198
Thomas, W. I., 50
Tutsis, 49, 55
  social construction of, 50–52

Uganda, 55
UN. *See* United Nations
UNAMIR (United Nations Assistance
    Mission for Rwanda)
  authorization of, 68–73
  concept of operations, 70–71, 82–83
  initial deployment, 97
  January report on, 13–14, 74–77
  logistics situation, 92, 115–16, 168
  March 1994 renewal of, 14, 93–96
  peacekeeping rules, 82–85
  See also Dallaire, General Roméo;
    UNAMIR II; UN DPKO
UNAMIR II, 136–43
UN culture, xi, 5–7, 9–11
  and ideology of impartiality, 158
  and ignorance excuse, 157–58
  and peacekeeping rules 10, 157–58

  and Iqbal Riza, 112
  See also bureaucratic culture; peacekeep-
    ing rules
UN Department of Humanitarian Affairs,
    31, 44
UN DPKO (Department of Peacekeeping
    Operations)
  categorization of April violence,
    112–16
  and death of Belgian peacekeepers, 122
  and duress excuse, 162–66
  expansion of, 30–32
  and ignorance excuse, 3, 156–60
  and January 11 cable, 78–88
  and Lessons Learned Unit, 205
  and moral responsibility, 20, 173–74
  and peacekeeping rules, 14, 43–45, 91,
    116–17, 127–29, 175–79
  See also Annan, Kofi; Boutros-Ghali,
    Boutros; Riza, Iqbal; UNAMIR;
    UN Secretariat
UNITAF (United Task Force), 35
United Kingdom, 95, 171
United Nations (UN)
  and categorization of violence, 133–34
  and causal responsibility, 167–69
  charter of, 28
  and Cold War, 25, 27–29
  composition of, 11
  credibility of, 47
  and end of Cold War, 22, 26–28
  ignorance excuse, 162
  impact of Somalia on, 39
  initial impression of Rwanda, 57–60
  initial involvement in Rwanda, 60–70
  knowledge of genocide, xi–xii
  and moral division of labor, 169
  and moral overload, 18
  and moral responsibility, 16, 20
  moral responsibility for genocide,
    154–56
  and moral universe, 4–6
  role responsibility, 169–70, 172–74
  as scapegoat, 32, 39
  and security, 26–27
  subcultures in, 11
  threat to withdraw UNAMIR, 14, 93,
    95
  values of, 24–25
  See also UNAMIR; UN DPKO; UN
    Secretariat

United Nations Lessons Learned Unit,
205
United Nations Security Council Resolution 846, 61
United Nations Security Council Resolution 872, 72
United States, 12, 14, 107
  and APC incident, 143
  and authorization of UNAMIR, 71–72
  Boutros-Ghali's attitude toward, 42
  and broad-based transitional government, 93
  and duress excuse, 164
  and ignorance excuse, 20, 156, 161–62
  impact of Somalia on, 37–38
  and January 11 cable, 88–89
  and moral responsibility of, 20, 171–72
  and opposition to intervention, x, 2,
    11, 101, 105–6, 134–35, 138–42,
    171
  and Somalia, 35–40
  and threat to withdraw UNAMIR,
    95–96, 106
  and UNAMIR II, 138–41
  See also Clinton, Bill; Congress
United Task Force (UNITAF), 35
Universal Declaration of Human Rights,
169
UNOMUR (United Nations Observer
Mission Uganda-Rwanda), 61
UNOSOM (United Nations Operation in
Somalia), 34, 124
UNOSOM II, 35
UNPROFOR (United Nations Protection
Force), 31, 32, 44
UN Secretariat, 3, 14, 123, 167
  attitude toward U.S., 42
  and categorization of violence in
    Rwanda, 85–88, 109–10, 113–16
  composition of, 11
  and duress excuse, 20, 162–66
  and excuses, 20, 21, 156–60, 162–66
  and ignorance excuse, 20, 156–60
  and March report, 94
  and moral responsibility, 20, 173–74
  and opposition to intervention, 14–15,
    100–105, 127–29

and peacekeeping rules, 43–48,
  116–17, 127–29, 175–79
relationship to Security Council, 10
response to April violence, 108–24
See also Boutros-Ghali, Boutros; UN
  DPKO
UN Security Council, 172
  authorization of UNAMIR, 68–73
  and Burundi, 73
  categorization of violence in Rwanda,
    102–3, 130–32
  and Cold War, 22
  composition of, 11
  and debate on intervention, 14,
    99–107
  and debate over "genocide," 2–3, 14,
    132–39, 144
  and evacuation of foreign nationals,
    100
  function of meetings, 144
  and ignorance excuse, 156
  and March Report, 95
  relationship to Secretariat, 10
  and Operation Turquoise, 148–49
  and peacekeeping rules, 45, 99–107,
    127–29, 175–79
  threat to withdraw UNAMIR, 14, 93,
    95
  See also UN DPKO; UN Secretariat
"UN syndrome," 163–64
UN Transitional Authority in Cambodia,
  29
UN Trusteeship Council, 51, 52
Urquhart, Sir Brian, 23
Uwilingiyimana, Agathe, 97–98

Waldheim, Kurt, 22
Walker, Edward, 72
war crimes tribunal, 178
Weber, Max, 7–8, 9–11, 58, 116
  and "calling for politics," 181
  and theodicy, 198
  See also bureaucracy

Yugoslavia, 43

Zaire, 56